Queen Kaʻahumanu
of Hawaii

Queen Ka'ahumanu of Hawaii
A Biography

Thomas W. Goodhue

McFarland & Company, Inc., Publishers
Jefferson, North Carolina

LIBRARY OF CONGRESS CATALOGUING-IN-PUBLICATION DATA

Names: Goodhue, Thomas W., author.
Title: Queen Kaʻahumanu of Hawaii : a biography / Thomas W. Goodhue.
Description: Jefferson, North Carolina : McFarland & Company, Inc., Publishers, 2022 | Includes bibliographical references and index.
Identifiers: LCCN 2022009221 | ISBN 9781476684987 (print) ∞
ISBN 9781476645179 (ebook)
Subjects: LCSH: Kaahumanu, Queen, consort of Kamehameha I, King of the Hawaiian Islands, 1777–1832. | Queens—Hawaii—Biography. | Hawaii—History—To 1893. | Hawaii—Religion—19th century. | BISAC: BIOGRAPHY & AUTOBIOGRAPHY / Royalty | HISTORY / United States / State & Local / West (AK, CA, CO, HI, ID, MT, NV, UT, WY)
Classification: LCC DU627.1 .G56 2022 | DDC 996.90092 [B]—dc23/eng/20220405
LC record available at https://lccn.loc.gov/2022009221

BRITISH LIBRARY CATALOGUING DATA ARE AVAILABLE

ISBN (print) 978-1-4766-8498-7
ISBN (ebook) 978-1-4766-4517-9

© 2022 Thomas W. Goodhue. All rights reserved

No part of this book may be reproduced or transmitted in any form or by any means, electronic or mechanical, including photocopying or recording, or by any information storage and retrieval system, without permission in writing from the publisher.

Front cover image *Kaahumanu, Woman of the Sandwich Islands* by Ludwig Choris, 1816 (courtesy Honolulu Museum of Art, Gift of the Honolulu Art Society, 1944 [12158])

Printed in the United States of America

McFarland & Company, Inc., Publishers
Box 611, Jefferson, North Carolina 28640
www.mcfarlandpub.com

For the children of Hawai‘i
and New York,
who loved the tale of a queen
who broke the rules

Acknowledgments

It takes years and the help of many people to write a biography of an important but little-known historical figure. The children of Keolumana, Waimānalo, Kahalu'u, Riverside, Island Park, Bay Shore, and other communities loved my tale of two queens who broke social barriers. Eventually, it appeared as a record book in the *Women of Courage* series and in one of my story collections for Franciscan Media, which prompted further research into these remarkable women. My brother-in-law Robert Shull and Charlie Perdue and David Alff at McFarland helped me learn about Tagged Image File Format (TIFF) files, dots per inch (DPI), and other things I needed to know to track down illustrations for this volume. The Honolulu Museum of Art, where I spent many days admiring the arts of the Islands, graciously provided several illustrations and permission to reprint them, as did the Australian Museum, the Alexander Turnbull Library in New Zealand, the Smithsonian National Museum of Natural History, and the Boston Athenæum. And I owe a debt of gratitude to librarians and archivists everywhere. I owe a particular debt of gratitude to the archivists at the Hawaii Mission Houses Library, who have made available digitalized material from their vast trove of journals, letters, and publications by both Hawaiians and early missionaries. Mahalo nui loa (*thank you very much*). I am grateful, also, to the reference staff at the Amityville Public Library on Long Island, New York, for patiently taking innumerable interlibrary loan requests and borrowing materials from Worcester, Massachusetts, to Wahiawa, Hawai'i.

Table of Contents

Acknowledgments — vi
Preface — 1
Key People — 3

Chapter 1—Islands and Aliens — 7
Chapter 2—Royal Romance — 29
Chapter 3—Kaʻahumanu Breaks the Rules — 45
Chapter 4—Burning the Temples — 64
Chapter 5—The Coming of a New God — 73
Chapter 6—Reading, Writing and Religion — 91
Chapter 7—The New Kaʻahumanu — 109
Chapter 8—New Rules, New Riots — 132
Chapter 9—Law and Order, Church and State — 147
Chapter 10—Going Where the Mansions Are Ready — 167

Places to Visit — 174
Glossary — 179
Timeline — 181
Explore Further — 183
Chapter Notes — 185
Bibliography — 203
Index — 221

Preface

When I arrived in my first parish on Oʻahu, fresh out of seminary, I learned that I was expected to tell children a story each Sunday during worship. A few of my early attempts failed miserably, but the tale of how Kaʻahumanu and Keōpūolani overturned taboos separating men and women, boys and girls, soon became the best loved story I have ever told, not only in Hawaiʻi, but also in Manhattan, and on Long Island. The role of these two queens in upending the old rules after their husband Kamehameha the Great died remains controversial among native Hawaiians, some of whom see them as liberators of their people, while others believe that they betrayed their heritage. Kaʻahumanu outlived Keōpūolani, and many aspects of her eventful life are not well known, either in the Islands or elsewhere. The favorite of Kamehameha's many wives, she played a crucial role in uniting the Hawaiian Islands. She seized power after his death, preserving the unity of the archipelago. She ensured the perpetuation of the Kamehameha dynasty by kidnapping and marrying a high chief and his son. She gave American missionaries an icy welcome, eventually embraced this new faith, often exasperated its leaders, and struggled with another new concept: religious tolerance. She guided her nation through revolutionary change, helping this archipelago emerge as a major power in the Pacific. Her story illustrates the often-neglected history of female missionaries, African Americans, Central Europeans, Tahitians, Catholics, and Unitarians in the Hawaiian Kingdom. Her life casts new light, I believe, on how we view American history, immigration, sexuality, and pluralism today.

Hawaiians often had lengthy names, acquired additional ones during their lifetimes, and sometimes traded names with close friends. To avoid confusion, I will avoid the nicknames and varied spellings Euro-Americans bestowed on them and stick with the names that are most commonly used today. I will call Kaʻahumanu's first husband, Kalani Paiʻea Wohi o Kaleikini Kealiʻikui Kamehameha o ʻIolani i

Preface

Kaiwikapu kau'i Ka Liholiho Kūnuiākea, simply Kamehameha or Kamehameha the Great, for example, and his son Kalani Kalei'aimoku o Kaiwikapu o La'amea i Kauikawekiu Ahilapalapa Keali'i Kauinamoku o Kahekili Kalaninui i Mamao 'Iolani i Ka Liholiho, who ruled as Kamehameha II, simply Liholiho.

In this book, English translations follow Hawaiian quotations and are italicized. As is the custom these days in Hawai'i, Hawaiian words are not italicized, since they are not foreign in the Hawaiian Islands, where Hawaiian is one of the state's two official languages. I use italics for Hawaiian words and omit diacritical marks—the 'okina (') indicating a break in the word and the kahakō (ā ē ī ō ū) indicating a vowel is lengthened—only where an original source that I quote directly did so. This may be jarring to readers but should remind us that this is a tale of another time and place, where Americans are immigrants and English is a foreign language.

I have tried to tell the story of this remarkable woman from the perspective of those in the Islands rather than somewhere in Europe or North America. The history of this place has mostly been told from the point of view of foreign visitors rather than from that of those who welcomed them, tried to understand their ways, and all too often suffered at their hands. This is not easy to do when the earliest written sources come from Europeans and Americans, but even where we have only non-native accounts of events, it is possible to imagine how indigenous people may have understood them. These Islands have known both and shown much aloha to visitors and endured far too much exploitation by foreign powers. Reconciliation requires hearing other perspectives. I have tried to do so in writing this biography, and I ask readers to do the same.

I also have chosen to begin my tale, as Hawaiians often do their personal histories, with the creation of the archipelago and its discovery by Pacific Islanders, not with the arrival centuries later of Capt. James Cook. Cook can be called the "Great Navigator" of his time with some justice, but he ended up in this particular chain of islands only because Tupaia, a "wayfinder" from the Society Islands, suggested where to look. In this story, Cook is not the discoverer of the Hawaiian Islands, but rather someone who lands there, causes a ruckus, and gets himself killed needlessly.

Key People

Hawaiians

Kamehameha, later called Kamehameha the Great and Kamehameha I, conqueror of the Hawaiian Islands
Kalaniʻōpuʻu, ruler of Hawaiʻi, "the Big Island"
Kaʻahumanu, Favorite Wife of Kamehameha, later the co-ruler and Regent
Nāmāhāna ʻi Kaleleokalani, Kaʻahumanu's mother, widow of the king of Maui
Nāmāhāna Piʻia, Kaʻahumanu's sister, Kamehameha's wife, and governor of Oʻahu
Keʻeaumoku Pāpaʻiahiahi, Kaʻahumanu's father, advisor to Kamehameha
Keʻeaumoku ʻOpio, Kaʻahumanu's brother, governor of Maui
Keōpūolani, Sacred Wife of Kamehameha, mother of and Liholiho and Kauikeaouli
Kalākua, Kaʻahumanu's younger sister, another of Kamehameha's many wives
Hoapili, companion and ally of Kamehameha, governor of Maui, Kalākua's husband
Kalanimōkū, Kamehameha's war leader; prime minister under his cousin Kaʻahumanu, as well as Kamehameha, Liholiho, and Kauikeaouli
Liholiho (who ruled as Kamehameha II), son of Kamehameha the Great and Keōpūolani
Kamāmalu, Kamehameha's daughter, Liholiho's half sister and Favorite Wife
Boki, Kalanimōkū's brother, governor of Oʻahu, Kaʻahumanu's rival
Anthony D. Allen, former slave, mariner, and successful merchant in the Kingdom of Hawaiʻi
Kaumualiʻi, King of Kauaʻi; second husband of Kaʻahumanu

Key People

Keali'iohonui, son of Kaumuali'i; third husband of Ka'ahumanu
Kuakini, Ka'ahumanu's brother, governor of the Big Island and O'ahu
Kauikeaouli (who ruled as Kamehameha III), son of Kamehameha and Keōpūolani
Nāhi'ena'ena, daughter of Kamehameha and Keōpūolani, younger sister of Kauikeaouli
Liliha, Boki's wife and briefly the governor of O'ahu
Kīna'u, eldest daughter of Kamehameha, one of Liholiho's wives, Ka'ahumanu's niece, second Kuhina Nui, mother of Kamehameha IV and Kamehameha V

British

James Cook, British naval officer called the greatest explorer of his time
George Vancouver, British naval officer on Cook's voyage and leader of later explorations
John Young, English sailor, advisor to Kamehameha and governor of the Big Island
William Ellis, Methodist missionary sent to the Society and Hawaiian Islands by the London Missionary Society
William Buckle, captain of the whaling ship *Daniel IV*
George Anson, Lord Byron, commander of the *Blonde*, brother of the poet and politician George Gordon, Lord Byron
Richard Charlton, the first British Consul to the Kingdom of Hawai'i

Americans

Hiram Bingham (Binamu), leader of the First Company of Calvinist missionaries
Sybil Bingham (Binamuwahine), Hiram's wife and Ka'ahumanu's friend
Elisha and Maria Loomis, missionaries and the first printers between the Rockies and Asia
Nancy and Samuel Ruggles, missionary teachers on Kaua'i and at Hilo on the Big Island
Mercy and Samuel Whitney, missionaries on Kaua'i
Lucy and Asa Thurston, missionaries at Kailua on the Big Island

Key People

Lucia and Thomas Holman, missionaries on the Big Island
Harriet and Charles S. Stewart, Presbyterians in the Second Company who led the mission station in Lāhainā; he returned later as a U.S. naval chaplain
Clarissa and William Richards, members of the Second Company who served at Lāhainā
John Coffin Jones, Jr., first U.S. Consular Agent in Honolulu
Lt. John "Mad Jack" Percival, captain of the U.S.S. *Dolphin*
Capt. Thomas ap Catesby Jones, commander of the U.S.S. *Peacock*

Tahitians

Auna, a chief and former priest from Raiatea who had become a Christian deacon and chaplain
Taua, another Christian missionary

Germans

Georg Anton Schäffer, doctor and would-be ruler of the Hawaiian Islands
Otto von Kotzebue, Russian Navy officer sent to foil Schäffer's plot

Spanish

Don Francisco de Paula Marín, an innovative farmer who became Kamehameha's physician and advisor

French

Jean-Baptiste Rives, early settler and confidant of Liholiho
Alexis Bachelot and **Abraham Armand**, missionary priests

Irish

Patrick Short, missionary priest

He aliʻi naʻahe aloha....
No Kaʻahumanu he inoa.
(*A chief for me to love....*
Kaʻahumanu is your name.)
  "Kumulipo/E Pua Ana Ka Makani"
    Israel "Iz" Kamakawiwoʻole
    and the Makaha Sons of Niʻihau

Chapter 1

Islands and Aliens

Long before there were kings and queens, taboos and temples, wars and warriors, there was the kai, the sea, and the ʻāina, the land. As continents slowly drifted apart and the massive tectonic plates that make up the Earth's crust shifted, a crack opened in the floor of the Northern Pacific Ocean. Molten rock poured out from deep under the sea. This lava cooled as it hit the water, and an underwater volcano gradually rose thousands of feet toward the surface. Eventually, more than 70 million years ago, the peak of Meiji emerged from the sea as an island.

As continents and tectonic plates continued to separate, Meiji inched north. A million years later, a new volcano appeared above the "hot spot" in the ocean floor. Eventually, 107 volcanoes of the Emperor Seamounts and the Hawaiian Islands stretched north and west 3,600 miles from the island of Hawaiʻi almost to the Kamchatka Peninsula in Siberia. It is the longest archipelago on the planet.

The oldest islands formed by these volcanoes gradually eroded and sank back into the sea, leaving behind atolls and drowned coral reefs. Elsewhere, the newest and largest volcanoes soared thousands of feet into the sky. Kauaʻi and Niʻihau rose above the water 25 million years ago, then Oʻahu. Molokaʻi, Maui, Lānaʻi, and Kahoʻolawe came next. Haleakalā (*the House of the Sun*) on Maui, over 10,000 feet high, has the biggest volcanic crater on Earth, more than seven miles long and 2,700 feet deep. If Manhattan were dropped into its crater, New York's tallest skyscrapers would not clear the rim. Finally, there was Hawaiʻi, "the Big Island," largest in the Hawaiian chain and twice as large as all the others combined. One of its volcanic peaks, Mauna Kea, is the tallest in the Pacific at 13,796 feet. Another, Mauna Loa, reaches almost as high, to 13,680 feet above sea level. The first people to settle here said that Madame Pele, the volcano goddess, first made her home in Kauaʻi and Niʻihau, then moved on to Oʻahu, traveled next to Molokaʻi, Lānaʻi, Kahoʻolawe, and Maui, and then finally settled on the Big Island.[1]

Queen Kaʻahumanu of Hawaii

As the islands drifted slowly away from the mid-ocean hot spot, the older volcanoes first became dormant and then extinct. Polynesia has three active volcanoes, all of them on the Big Island. Kīlauea, Pele's current residence, is the most active volcano on earth, and Mauna Loa, the world's largest active volcano, still erupts every few decades. Just off the southeastern coast of the Big Island, a submarine seamount called Lōʻihi is forming today that will someday be the next island in the archipelago.

Years of rain and wind gradually broke down lava rock into soil, with older, northwestern islands such as Kauaʻi showing the most weathering and erosion. By about five million years ago, the land could support life. Birds, wind, and ocean currents carried seeds of plants, shrubs, and trees that took root and grew in the volcanic soil. Birds arrived and stayed, along with insects and a few small animals that drifted ashore on floating logs or coconuts from other islands.[2]

Without competitors or predators, these first plants and animals spread out across the Islands and adapted to the many tiny ecological niches they found. Ninety percent of the 1,200 species native to the Hawaiian Islands are found nowhere else. The first finches to arrive, for example, evolved into 50 distinct species of Hawaiian honeycreepers. More than 113 bird species evolved in the archipelago that existed no place else on Earth. The shallow, warm, bountiful waters around the islands nurtured the growth of diverse sea life.[3]

Eventually, the Islands became home to more than 700 species of fungi, 260 mosses, 170 ferns, 500 marine plants, 1,000 flowering plants, three reptile species, three mammal species, 57 types of corals, 685 types of fish, 1,000 types of land snails, 1,500 marine mollusks, 5,000 marine invertebrates, more than 6,000 insects and arthropods (crabs, shrimp, lobsters, and spiders), and thousands of other deepwater sea creatures. These are some of the most isolated islands on Earth—the nearest land mass, Alaska, is 2,000 miles to the north, and it is even further to the West Coast of North America and 4,500 miles to Japan and the Philippines. Plants and animals evolved on these volcanic islands, adapting to the local environment and cut off from the rest of the world. Ninety-seven percent of the native plants and most native birds were found nowhere else on Earth. Species also evolved to fill distinct niches. Ōhiʻa lehua could grow into a small bush on recent lava flows or a soaring tree nearly 100 feet tall on older volcanic soil.[4]

Much later, but still centuries ago, the first people arrived. They sailed double-hulled catamarans that were 50 to 75 feet long, with sails woven from pandanus (*screw pine*) leaves and flexible lashings braided

Chapter 1—Islands and Aliens

from coconut husk fibers. Their "wayfinders" navigated across more than 1,000 miles of open ocean to reach Hawai'i, an achievement unmatched elsewhere for centuries. This was not an accidental discovery, but rather a deliberate colonization, perhaps following the flight paths of migratory birds such as golden plovers. These were, in fact, some of the last places on Earth to be settled by humans.[5]

Why did they make such long voyages? Perhaps they were seeking valuable materials that were in short supply elsewhere. Maybe their population had grown so large on other islands that they were desperate to colonize new lands that had new resources. Or, possibly, their love of adventure was so great that it compelled them to explore. They may even have reached the coast of South America or Southern California.[6]

These explorers discovered an archipelago larger than almost any other they had ever found, with plenty of room to spread out. They brought with them useful plants and animals to create a new home: pigs, dogs, and chickens; coconuts, bamboo, sugar cane, breadfruit, ki (*ti*), yams, sweet potatoes, gourds, kalo (*taro*), rice, bananas, mountain apples, and kukui trees. Unintentionally, they also brought stowaway, such as skinks, geckos, and rats. With no rivals, poisonous animals, or deadly disease, both the people and the species they introduced flourished.[7]

They navigated back and forth between these Islands and their distant homelands without instruments, a feat achieved nowhere else on Earth. Then the long voyages stopped, and all contact between this archipelago and the outside world ceased. Three or four centuries later, Tahitians knew about many other lands, but not Hawai'i. Hawaiians chanted about their ancestral homelands, speaking of "lands far away" such as Kahiki (*Tahiti*), but eventually lost all knowledge of how to get there.[8]

Bits and pieces of foreign shipwrecks drifted ashore now and then, reminding them that they shared the sea with other peoples. Hawaiians ventured into the Pacific on fishing expeditions and visited Nihoa, west of Ni'ihau, and other islands, but found them uninhabited. A few people lived on Nihoa for a time but eventually abandoned it, since it lacked a dependable source of drinking water. Their explorations confirmed that they were living in isolation in the middle of a vast ocean.

They found relatively little land suited for agriculture but cultivated nearly every piece of fertile earth that they could. Using innovative farming techniques, they moved from a subsistence economy to one that generated food surpluses and supported a complex society.[9]

And there were rich fishing grounds. The upland forests provided birds and bats they hunted, edible fern, and pandanus that bore leaves, nuts, and fruit. They cleared forests near the shore and raised kalo, sugarcane chickens, dogs, and pigs for food. Poi, cooked from roots of kalo, whose starchy root was more nutritious than rice, was a staple of their diet. They planted breadfruit groves and fields of yams. They cultivated at least 50 varieties of bananas, though only men could eat them. They grew two varieties of kalo, one that flourished in low, wet soil that they watered with extensive irrigation ditches, and another that grew better on high, dry land.

Their population grew steadily and then soared during the 15th century. These descendants of the world's greatest sailors created the most complex, advanced civilization in the Pacific. The Hawaiian Islands became some of the most populous and densely settled of islands anywhere in the ocean.[10]

There was no metal in these islands, other than nails and other tiny bits of iron that sometimes washed ashore in driftwood, so Hawaiians built with wood and volcanic stone and covered their homes with grass to keep out the hot sun and heavy rains, binding leaves or boards with fibers they wove. They were skilled at fishing, knowing the habits, migrating seasons, and spawning times of local fish. They imposed rules strictly limiting how many fish could be caught to preserve this source of food for future generations. They built hundreds of stone fishponds, which greatly increased their food supply. The only people in Oceania to develop sophisticated fish farming, they had saltwater ponds, brackish ponds, freshwater ponds, and ponds that combined aquaculture and agriculture, raising kalo and freshwater fish together.[11]

They built sleek outrigger canoes ranging from the small wa'a kialoa that carried a single person to the wa'a kauluas, which could be more than 100 feet long. They felt at home in the water and called their homeland Nā Kai 'Ewalu (*the Eight Seas*), the waters surrounding their eight inhabited islands.[12]

They pounded the bark of paper mulberry trees into kapa (or tapa) cloth they used for everything from clothing to catamaran sails. They cooked in imus (*underground ovens*) lined with heated stones. For light, they burned the oily nuts of the kukui (*candlenut tree*). Hawaiian medical experts used more than 300 local plants to treat illness. Their astronomers recognized more than 120 stars—without telescopes. Their experts in botany and geology classified 43 types of trees and 57 varieties of rock.[13]

Chapter 1—Islands and Aliens

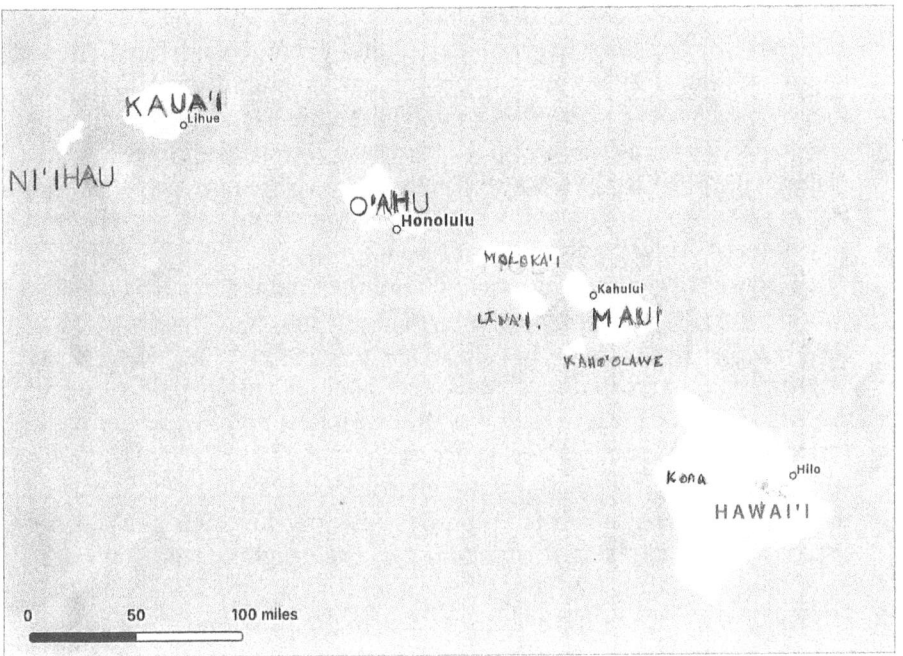

Nā Kai ʻEwalu (the Eight Seas/the Hawaiian Islands).

Children played kōnane (*checkers*), with colored pebbles moved on a board that was made by drilling holes in a flat stone. Children also enjoyed arm wrestling and wrestling in the ocean. They swam using only their arms, with their feet tied together. Older children and adults on the Big Island honored Pele with heʻe hōlua (*sledding*), down steep, lava-covered hillsides, following broad, smooth furrows lined with slippery grass. And above all else, there was heʻe nalu (*surfing*). Boys and girls, women and men rode the waves on surfboards carved from hardwood. People paddled short bellyboards elsewhere in the Pacific, as well as along the coast of West Africa, but nowhere did anyone exceed Hawaiians at surfing. Here, it was practiced by young and old, chiefs and commoners.[14]

Sometime around 1768, a girl was born on the eastern tip of the beautiful island of Maui. Her birthday is not known with any certainty, since there were no written records in those days, and among Hawaiians as was the case among Europeans, people often remembered different dates.[15]

Her mother, Nāmāhāna ʻi Kaleleokalani, was the widow of the king of Maui. Her father, Keʻeaumoku Pāpaʻiahiahi, was an advisor to Kamehameha (*One Set Apart* or *the Lonely One*), a name given to him because he was hidden after his birth to prevent a rival chief from killing him. Kamehameha was a nephew of a king on the Big Island, so this girl was born with ties to the rulers of both Maui and Hawaiʻi. Her uncle Kahekili had controlled all the islands from Maui to Niʻihau for a brief period. Her grandmother predicted that someday she would rule herself, "and all your relatives will bow in your presence."[16]

She was her parents' first child, and they named her Kaʻahumanu (*Cloak of Power*). No one in the world did better featherwork than the Hawaiians, sewing thousands of them together into a single cloak or long cape, harvested by skilled bird-catchers without killing a single bird. Such a cape was a symbol of the highest nobility, so her name reminded everyone of her royal ancestry.

Her mother gave birth on the fortress hill of Kaʻuiki that guarded the village of Hāna, site of many battles between the chiefs of Maui and those from the Big Island. Threatened by their high lineage, the ruling chief of Maui saw the marriage of her parents as an act of rebellion. They attacked while her father was away, forcing mother and child to seek refuge at Kaʻuiki, the last stronghold that the rulers of the Big Island held on Maui. While Kaʻahumanu was still a baby, her mother hid her in a cave near Kaʻuiki for several days, while a great battle raged around them.[17]

Only women were allowed to be present at birth, and her father was away fighting in one of the frequent dynastic wars anyway. Throughout most of her life, Kaʻahumanu was surrounded by intermittent combat. Women, children, and the elderly usually were not harmed, but battles still could be deadly for the warriors who fought with spears, swords, daggers, slings, and wooden clubs.

Combat usually was conducted in a way that minimized fatalities, and fighting was kapu (*prohibited*) several months of the year, and the nobles often agreed to single combat by champions rather than a battle between masses of warriors. Sometimes both parties said that they had been beaten, ending the war, saving face on both sides. Minimizing humiliation also reduced the chances of renewed conflict. Islanders valued courage but not foolish disregard for risk. In the face of overwhelming force, retreat was noble. An old ʻōlelo noʻeau (*proverb*) said:

> Aʻo i ke koa, e aʻo no i ka holo.
> (*When one learns to be a warrior, one also must learn to run.*)[18]

Chapter 1—Islands and Aliens

Soon, her father became commander of Kamehameha's army on the Big Island. Hawaiians had no standing armies and no professional soldiers other than a few who guarded kings, so it was his responsibility to hastily assemble a fighting force whenever war erupted. As if it was not terrifying enough to be surrounded by bloodshed, Ka'ahumanu nearly drowned as a child—twice. While she was still a baby, she rolled off the deck of a double-hulled canoe as she traveled with her parents off the coast of the Big Island. Fortunately, her parents quickly found her and fished her out of the ocean. When she was a toddler, she wandered away from her sleeping mother and into the surf. A huge wave suddenly knocked her down and pulled her out to sea, but a fast-thinking cousin swam out and rescued her.[19]

Ruling chiefs emerged in every district of every island, exercising control over—and responsibility for—their land and its people.[20] Initially, their society was marked by cooperation and relative equality. The chief was closely related to those he or she led. As hierarchies emerged, however, rulers claimed to be descended from gods. Kinship was replaced by divine kingship.[21]

By the time Ka'ahumanu was born, however, the Islands were dominated by a rigid hierarchy that included kings who ruled entire islands. At the bottom of Hawaiian society were a few kauā who were outcasts from birth and despised by everyone else—but whose descendants might become ruling chiefs. The vast majority were maka'āinana (*commoners, those who live on the land*) who served them. At least, unlike the serfs of feudal Europe, they were not bound to a single chief or place and were free to shift their loyalty to another chief. Of higher status were the kahunas, the experts or professionals, including kahuna pule (*priests, or experts in prayer*), teachers, and doctors. Above them all were the ali'i (*nobles*), the ali'i aimoku (*high chiefs*), and ali'i nui or mō'ī (*paramount chiefs* or *kings*).[22]

The largest islands usually were ruled by one or more mō'ī. Little Ni'ihau often was ruled by the king of Kaua'i, while Lāna'i and Kaho'olawe often were ruled by Maui's paramount chief. There were frequent attempts by chiefs to extend their territory. During Ka'ahumanu's childhood, war broke out on the Big Island and eventually spread to Maui, Moloka'i, Lāna'i, and O'ahu. Because all the great chiefs were closely related, these conflicts often were fought within families. Both Kalanikupūle and Pele'iholani on O'ahu were grandchildren of Kekaulike, who ruled Maui until about 1736. So were Kuakini, Boki, Kalanimōkū, and Ka'ahumanu on Maui. As was Kaumuali'i, who ruled Kaua'i and Ni'ihau.[23]

Queen Kaʻahumanu of Hawaii

Their religion included four supreme gods. Kāne represented sun, Kanaloa the sea, Lono the fruitful earth, and Kū was the war god. Beneath these akua (*gods*), there were thousands of lesser gods, including Pele, the volcano goddess, Hina, the goddess of the moon, and Laka, the god/goddess of the dance. During Kaʻahumanu's childhood, Ku became steadily more important, which fueled further warfare. For centuries, their worship involved only token sacrifices to the gods, but then priests said that the akua required human victims, and new luakini heiaus, temples for human sacrifice, were built. Military campaigns and rigid enforcement of the kapus provided plenty of candidates for these altars. Kū, whose full name was Kūkailimoku (*Kū who seizes the land*), consumed steadily more of the land's resources and the people of the ʻāina.

Religious ritual was woven into their daily lives. Everything they did had a particular ceremony, whether they were getting married, building a boat, planting kalo, or dancing a hula. Hawaiian religion gave immense power to aliʻi such as Kamehameha. Boys and girls, men and women, young and old all danced, often in honor of some god, but only men took part in public prayer in temples, and only male aliʻi could pray to the four highest deities, since the chiefs claimed them as ancestors. Nearly every family had its own kiʻi (*tiki*), a representation of an akua, carved out of wood, stone, or coral, sometimes with beads, claws, or feathers attached. Hawaiians did not think the statue was a god but instead believed it held the prayers offered to this particular deity and contained mana (*spiritual power*), as did the aliʻi themselves. Each day, Hawaiians set offerings of food and water before the statue and chanted prayers, seeking protection from the god or goddess it represented. Aliʻi claimed, in fact, to be able to control the akua through rituals they performed.[24]

Kaʻahumanu was born into a powerful family, but her life was controlled by an astonishingly complicated set of rules. The kapus did some good, preventing overfishing, for example, by limiting what could be caught, and reducing assaults among commoners. Taboos are found the world over, but they were extraordinarily complex in Polynesia—and became far more restrictive among Hawaiians. Makaʻāinana could not stand anywhere near aliʻi. Some clothing was kapu for everyone except the nobles. Girls and women could not eat coconut, pork, birds, certain fish, or nearly any bananas; they could eat very little other than kalo, some fruit, seaweed, some fish, and small dogs. If visitors came to their home, it was kapu for a girl and women to speak to them.[25]

With aliʻi claiming descent from gods, the taboos reinforced the

Chapter 1—Islands and Aliens

domination of the na lani (*the heavenly ones*). Hawaiians could approach the highest nobles only by prostrating themselves. The highest ranking chiefs often were carried in sedan chairs, since their footsteps could make any ground they touched kapu. Even lesser nobles had to prostrate themselves before higher ranking aliʻi. Since disrespecting a chief was punishable by death, many nobles sent a flag bearer ahead of them when they traveled, who called out a warning to commoners to prostrate themselves. As aliʻi aimoku such a Kamehameha conquered larger territories, they ruled new subjects who often had never seen their new chief before. Some traveled incognito in districts where they were not known, to avoid having to punish their new subjects for failing to prostrate themselves before a chief they did not know—and to observe what was taking place in the neighborhood.[26]

The penalties for violating a kapu could be severe, including summary execution, though the death penalty was not imposed very often. And those who violated the rules were pardoned automatically if they reached a place of refuge, as were those who had committed a crime or lost a battle. These puʻuhonua (*place of refuge*) sanctuaries were inviolable. After a few days, kahunas performed absolution ceremonies, and the refugees could return home safely. A proverb says,

> ʻAʻohe mea make i ka hewa;
> make no i ka mihi ʻole.
> (*No one has ever died for the mistakes he has made;
> only because he did not repent.*)[27]

In addition, the rules were relaxed each year during Makahiki, a celebration that could run up to four months from October to January. Crops were harvested, taxes collected, games and celebrations held, and fighting ceased. After Makahiki, the kapus that governed the relationships among the nobles, common people, and gods were restored.[28]

These kapus were based on the traditional Hawaiian religion, but half of the people were excluded from direct participation in religious ritual. Women and girls could not join in public prayer, they were told, because the gods preferred the company of men. Males were descended from gods; females from earth. Women could not eat with men, because every meal shared by men was seen as communion with the gods; the presence of women would pollute this sacrament.[29] Kaʻahumanu would spend her lifetime learning the rules, overturning them, and reshaping them.

Not that men had an easy experience, either. The average man had to prepare one meal for himself and another for his wife—cooking was men's work—running back and forth from one oven to another, and one eating hut to another. He also had to build and thatch two eating huts in the first place, as well a third hale (*house*) for them to sleep together.[30]

In January 1778, this intricate, restricted society was shattered. Out of the blue, after centuries of isolation, with no warning whatsoever, two huge, strange objects glided silently past Oʻahu. By the time people raced out toward them in canoes, they were gone. Next, ghostly lights were seen one night by fishermen off the coast of Kauaʻi, who raced to tell their chief. By morning, crowds gathered along the beach could see aliens on these floating islands, causing great panic. A canoe took a chief and a kahuna out to investigate these vessels with tree-shaped sails, which looked a little like a pair of giant temples gliding across the ocean. When the 91-foot *Discovery* and 110-foot *Resolution* sailed into Waimea Bay, it was more shocking than it probably would be to wake one morning and find an enormous flying saucer hovering over your home.

Who were these aliens? Did these aliens come to conquer? To harm them or help them? It was Makahiki, the season when Lono (*god of agriculture and rain*) was expected to return some year from exile on a floating island. Could these visitors be Lono, sailing on floating islands, with the towers of his temples flying his white banners? Were these ghosts? The 180 aliens were so pale that some thought they were dead, calling them "ha ole" (*without breath*) or "haoles."

It seemed inconceivable that these strange aliens had stumbled upon their islands by accident, but then, much about them was difficult to believe. For example, they traveled on floating islands, but few could swim. In contrast with the cleanliness of Islanders, they seldom bathed, either, giving their bodies a pungent smell. In addition, they wore heavy clothing that made them sweat all the more in the tropics. Many of them stuck small objects in their mouths and lit them, emitting an acrid odor. These creatures stank.

The behavior of these foreigners also was deeply disturbing. They invited people to come aboard, speaking words that sounded a bit like their own language. At first, people were afraid to climb onto these floating islands—as you might be if invited to board an unidentified flying object (UFO)—but then some brave Islanders greeted these strangers and gave them food, water, and fuel in exchange for tiny bits of iron and brass. These last items were precious gifts to the Islanders, who had almost no access to metal. How could anyone have so much iron that they used it rather than pegs or ropes to hold pieces of wood together?

Chapter 1—Islands and Aliens

Men of the Sandwich Islands in a Canoe by John Webber, 1781 (Wellcome Collection).

The haoles also offered them glass beads and indicated they were to be worn on earlobes, but these were rejected as useless. Hawaiians did not pierce their ears.[31]

Since these aliens accepted their hospitality, taking food, water, and the sexual favors of wahines (*women*), kanakas (*Pacific Islanders*) believed that they were owed something in return and helped themselves to whatever they found lying around that struck their fancy, particularly metal objects. Capt. James Cook, born halfway around the world, saw things differently. His lieutenant did what English law required. He executed the kanaka as a thief with a stick that belched fire.

Why were these strange haoles so upset by people using something they needed? If you saw a tool that nobody else was using and you could put it to good use, you used it. Why did these aliens kill kanakas for doing this? On Kaua'i, people concluded not that the man had been punished for theft, but rather for violating some unknown kapu. They remained uncertain whether this strange being was an ali'i or an akua.[32]

After visiting Kaua'i and Ni'ihau for 12 days and spotting the tiny uninhabited islands Lehua and Ka'ula, the aliens sailed away on February 2. Their swift departure stunned the Islanders almost as much their arrival had.

News of this encounter with aliens was passed rapidly across the archipelago to the Big Island, as well. Then, in November, the aliens returned. Their floating heiaus were spotted once more off the coast of Maui. Capt. James Cook named the archipelago "the Sandwich Islands" in honor of his sponsor, John Montagu, Great Britain's lazy and corrupt Lord of the Admiralty, the fourth Earl of Sandwich. Cook passed eastern Maui on November 26 and traded some goods for fresh food and water with Hawaiians who paddled out in canoes from Hāna. One chief who made a deep impression on the officers, Kamehameha, accompanied the British on a brief sail.[33]

James Cook by Nathaniel Dance-Holland, engraved by J. K. Sherwin, 1779 (Wellcome Collection).

Capt. Cook could not find a good place to land on Maui. There was not a natural harbor deep enough for the *Discovery* or *Resolution*, in fact, anywhere in the archipelago. He circled the Big Island for six weeks seeking shelter, which puzzled both Hawaiians and his own men. With his crew growing steadily more restive, he finally settled on Kealakekua Bay, which he entered on January 16, 1779. The bay was exposed to southwesterly storms and so shallow that he was forced to anchor his ships far from shore, but it would have to do.[34]

Not only did Cook arrive during the celebration of Lono's festival, the Makahiki, but he also anchored at Kealakekua Bay (*the Pathway of the Gods*). Here, Lono's image began and completed a circuit of the Big Island each year—and here, Lono was expected to return someday.[35] In addition, his ship looked a bit like the floating island on which the god was expected; its sails resembled Lono's white kapa banners, and it slowly circled the Big Island in a clockwise direction, just as Lono's image processed each Makahiki.

King Kalaniōʻpuʻu Bringing Presents to Captain Cook by John Webber, 1781 (Wikimedia Commons).

At least 800 canoes carrying 9,000 people raced out to greet them, a welcome never equaled anywhere in the Pacific by any Western voyager before or since. Many kanakas leapt into the sea to scramble aboard the ships, amazing the British—few of whom could swim. Kalaniʻōpuʻu, the elderly paramount chief of the Big Island, boarded the *Resolution*, along with his nephew and adopted son Kamehameha.

Queen Ka'ahumanu of Hawaii

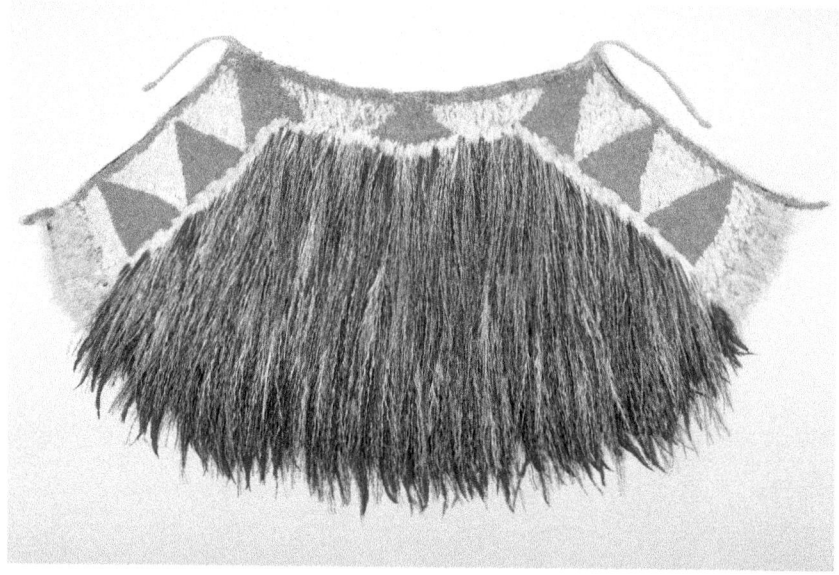

Feather and Fiber Cape presented to Captain Cook possibly by Kalani'ōpu'u (photograph by Abram Powell, H000104, courtesy Australian Museum).

The old ruler tried to initiate diplomatic relations with this foreign chief, presenting Cook with extraordinary gifts, a mahiole (*feather helmet*) and 'ahu 'ula (*feather cloak*) made from the feather of more than 20,000 small birds. But Kamehameha, with his immense size and shrewd, appraising eyes, made the greatest impression on the British and stayed overnight for a second meeting with the captain.[36]

Hawaiians saw Cook as an ali'i. This son of a lowly Yorkshire farm hand commanded hundreds of sailors and represented Beretania (*the Kingdom of Great Britain*) and the mightiest navy on the planet. Hawaiians welcomed this stranger with great honors, and women welcomed his crew with open arms. Nor did Hawaiian men hesitate to express sexual interest in some sailors, much to the consternation of the British. Did they also think Cook was a temporary embodiment of Lono, the cheerful god of agriculture, peace and prosperity, who was expected to return during Makahiki to seek a bride? Or did they simply see a chief who might be a useful ally? Even being the latter would make him someone who was descended from gods.[37]

David Samwell, a Welsh surgeon, wrote in his diary that their hosts were "so obliging and friendly that no quarrels could possibly arise...." Pleased with Kealakekua Bay, Cook thought this archipelago "in many

Chapter 1—Islands and Aliens

A Man of the Sandwich Islands Dancing by John Webber, 1781.

respects to be the most important that had hitherto been made by Europeans throughout the extent of the Pacific Ocean." He was supposed to have another year of exploration, but this turned out to be his last discovery—and his final journal entry.[38]

Cook had maintained strict discipline on board but when they went ashore, his sailors ran amuck. Not only did they tear apart a fence from Lono's temple at Kealakekua for firewood, which the priests graciously gave them permission to do, perhaps believing that Lono could do what he wanted with it, but they proceeded to break up wooden and stone images of gods in the presence of the priests and chiefs and burn them—a terrible sacrilege and a serious offense to their hosts. The kahunas gave Cook permission to pitch tents for his shore party in a sweet potato field near the heiau (*temple*) and issued a kapu protecting the shore party and ships from theft, but then the English housed sick sailors and buried their dead there, desecrating this sacred site. Capt. Cook's men tried to entice women there, even though bringing wahines within its confines was strictly kapu. One chief was so upset that when Cook tried to give them in compensation an iron hatchet—something Hawaiians craved—he angrily rejected it. John Ledyard, an American serving as a British marine, said, "It was the beginning of our subsequent misfortunes."[39]

Misreading their welcome, the Britons abused the hospitality they were shown. As an old proverb says,

> 'A'ohe hale i piha i ka hoihoi;
> ha'awa mai lawe aku no.
> (*No house has a perpetual welcome;
> it is given and it is taken away.*)[40]

Lono was supposed to leave at the end of Makahiki. By February 2, Kalani'ōpu'u was asking anxiously when his guests, who already had consumed nearly all the available food in the region, might be leaving. The king feared that Cook might want to spend the rest of the winter with him. The British were startled to learn that their hosts thought they had come to the Islands because there was famine in their home country, and that the purpose of their journey was to fill their bellies.[41]

There was great relief when the *Resolution* and *Discovery* sailed toward Maui two days later, after receiving generous farewell gifts. It was Kona season, however, when strong southwesterly winds and storms are common. By February 8, a gale had broken the mast of the *Resolution*, forcing Cook to return to Kealakekua Bay to make repairs.

Chapter 1—Islands and Aliens

This time, no one came to greet him. Lono was not expected to come back until the next Makahiki. What were these aliens doing?

The priests of Lono remained friendly, but both ali'i and maka'āinana were now quite reserved. On the surface, the relationship with their hosts remained cordial, but the sudden return of the English roused Hawaiian suspicions about the true intentions of these aliens. It also created a crisis for the Hawaiians, who felt obligated to feed 180 guests even though they now had barely enough food left throughout the region to feed themselves. How could Cook be a god, some wondered, if he were this vulnerable to the weather? And why did these strange aliens kill people who never took anything, even if they somehow, inexplicably, thought that exchanging food for iron constituted theft? Lono never would have committed such an injustice.[42]

Ominously, the only things their hosts wanted now from the British were knives, shaped like traditional Hawaiian daggers, which Cook's men fashioned from iron spikes he had requisitioned for this expedition to barter with those he encountered. Kamehameha himself exchanged a beautiful feather cloak with Capt. Charles Clerke, commander of *HMS Discovery*, for nine knives.[43]

Hawaiians also kept helping themselves to any other metal they could grab. When the Britons fired bird shot to drive them away, the ship's surgeon, John Law noted, they seemed "not to have any idea they were doing wrong." On February 13, someone took a pair of iron tongs, and the British responded brutally, inflicting 40 lashes on a suspect and hanging him from the rigging until the tongs were returned.[44]

Neither Cook nor anyone in his crew seems to have asked why the Islanders did not see themselves as doing wrong or why they felt entitled to appropriate items in exchange for the gifts they gave. These haoles from Beretania were puzzled by the way Hawaiians paid homage to their captain on land but then, once on board the *Resolution*, grabbed every bit of iron they could. They apparently never asked themselves why Hawaiians believed a visiting chief or god might owe them something.

Then, Cook sent a party in pursuit of a Hawaiian who took some metal tools from the *Discovery*. They quickly encountered a canoe that was actually returning the tools to the ship, but inexplicably seized the canoe as a sort of hostage until the "thief" could be punished. The innocent owner of the canoe, a chief named Palea who had befriended the English and whom the English knew was the king's young aikāne (*lover*), objected to them seizing his boat. A sailor responded by bashing him on the head with a paddle, knocking him out. Outraged, Hawaiians struck back, nearly killing Cook's young officer, George Vancouver. Only the intervention of a reawakened Palea saved the lives of the British crew.[45]

Then, some Hawaiians took a small boat from the *Discovery*'s cutter, vital to the expedition. In an attempt to get the cutter back, Cook took Kalani'ōpu'u as a hostage and blockaded the entrance to the bay. Then, Kalimu, a popular chief, was killed by British guns when he tried to run the blockade. On February 14, a large crowd of warriors attacked, seeking to avenge Kalimu and free their god-king from these aliens. In the melee, Cook and four of his marines were killed, the captain stabbed with a knife that his crew had sold them.[46]

In retaliation, Cook's men fired muskets and cannon into a crowd on the shore, killing dozens of Hawaiians, burned a temple, and destroyed entire villages. Kamehameha himself was wounded in the leg and learned the power of their "fire sticks"—not to mention their cannon—and their willingness to murder Hawaiians, two of whom they beheaded. Young Ka'ahumanu watched from the shore near Kealakekua as sailors burned her village, including the homes of priests who had aided the haoles, and killed a kahuna who had been particularly helpful in maintaining order during their visit. When Hawaiians sent a peace embassy, British sailors fired on them.[47]

And then these aliens sailed away. Hawaiians were left in shock, both by the death of god-like Cook and by the brutal revenge exacted by his men. Seven wahines sailed with them to O'ahu, insisting that they would gladly go all the way to England, wherever that was. They were put ashore, however, after repeatedly telling other Hawaiians about the death of the captain.[48]

Halfway around the world, Europeans and Americans eagerly read about these voyages in the Pacific. Capt. James Cook was called the Great Navigator—even though it was Tupaia from Raiatea in the Society Islands who navigated his ships across most of Polynesia and told him about an archipelago far to the north—and nations at war with Great Britain ordered their navies not to fire on him.[49]

Cook's visits made the ali'i eager to acquire haole weapons, which in turn unleashed ambitions to conquer and consolidate islands. Less than a year after Cook's visits, Kalani'ōpu'u destroyed every village on Lāna'i and slaughtered nearly every man, woman, and child on Kaho'olawe. When he died in 1782, fighting broke out immediately over how land should be redistributed. Kīwala'ō, Kamehameha's rival, captured Ka'ahumanu's father, Ke'eaumoku Pāpa'iahiahi, in a battle at Ke'ei on the Big Island, one that raged for eight days. Her kahu (*guardian*) ran

Chapter 1—Islands and Aliens

to the scene, carrying her in his arms. He found Kīwalaʻō standing over Keʻeaumoku, telling his warriors not to splatter the captive's blood on his clothes when they killed him. Her kahu fired off his slingshot. Struck in the head, Kīwalaʻō fell onto her father, who slit his enemy's throat with a shark-tooth dagger he wore, saving his own life and winning Kamehameha his first great victory—and control of the Big Island.[50]

Bogged down in warfare with her rebellious colonies in North America, Great Britain did not rush to claim the Islands. But the published accounts of Cook's voyages were eagerly devoured in Europe and North America. One edition of his journal sold out in three days. All of them focused on the death of Cook, largely ignoring the killing of Kalimu, but they stoked interest in the archipelago.

Europeans and Americans began to make their way to the Islands. After visiting Kauaʻi and Niʻihau, Cook's expedition had sailed to the Oregon coast and explored north to Alaska and the Bering Straits. This showed fur traders that they could make hefty profits by purchasing pelts from natives in the Pacific Northwest and selling them in China, with a stop in the Islands to resupply. Once Britain's war with France and the rebellious American colonies was out of the way, fur traders from Great Britain, Spain, Russia, and the United States rushed to exploit this new market. Soon, both Spain (which controlled California) and Britain planned to seize Nootka Sound, the center of the coastal fur trade, and the two empires nearly went to war.

Before long, nearly every European or American vessel that ventured into the North Pacific stopped in the Islands to reprovision and recuperate. In 1785, Capt. James Hanna from Beretania (*Britain*) stopped at the Islands while taking furs from Oregon to sell in China. In May 1786, Jean François de Galaup, Count de La Pérouse, a French admiral who helped American colonists defeat the British in the Revolutionary War, visited Maui with two frigates. Like Cook, La Pérouse refused to claim for his nation every island he stumbled upon: "I did not think it my right to take possession of it in the name of the King. The customs of Europeans in this respect are completely ridiculous." That same month, Nathaniel Portlock and George Dixon, who were with Cook when he died, visited the Islands in a British expedition on the *King George* and the *Queen Charlotte*, returned in November to spend the winter there and came back a third time in September 1787. The 220-ton *Columbia Rediviva*, commanded by Robert Gray, the first ship from Amelika (*America*) to sail around the world, stopped in Hawaiʻi during its 1788–1790 voyage. In 1791, Lt. Manuel Quimper came on

Spain's *Princesa Real* (*Princess Royal*). Étienne Marchand visited on the French fur-trade *Solide* expedition that same year, calling the Islands "a great caravanserai" for ships crossing between Asia and North America. After the official account of Cook's last voyage was published in 1794 with a chart of the Hawaiian Islands, even more haoles headed to the archipelago, finding it a convenient and relatively safe place to pick up fresh water, food, and other supplies—and enjoy the wahines.[51]

Visitors arrived with a bewildering variety of uniforms, customs, and languages. Hanna, an Englishman, sailed under a Portuguese flag to avoid conflicts with those who claimed a monopoly on British trade. Even more confusing, the first European resident of the Islands, John Mackay, an Irish doctor, arrived in 1787 on the British ship, the *Imperial Eagle*, which sailed under the Austrian flag. It also brought Frances Barkley, the captain's 22-year-old wife, the first European woman to visit the archipelago and one of the first women to circle the globe.

The vessel of one nation might even have a skipper from another country, such as the British captain who commanded Sweden's *Gustavus III*.[52] When two Russian sloops, the *Nadezhda* commanded by Lt.-Capt. Ivan Fyodorovich Krusenstern and the *Neva*, commanded by Lt. Yuri Fyodorovich Lisyansky, visited the Big Island, O'ahu, and Kaua'i in 1804, Krusenstern (or Kruzenshtern in Russian) was a German of Swedish ancestry who was born in Estonia, and Lisyansky (or Lisianski) was Ukrainian, but both served the Czar. How could anyone tell these haoles apart? Even before Cook's voyages, Hawaiians used the word *haole* to refer to anyone with a pale complexion, but it came to be used primarily for Europeans and Americans (whom indigenous peoples of North America would call *palefaces*) to mean something like "people from strange lands" or "strangers whose ways are different from ours."[53]

Adding to the confusion, haoles from one place often slandered other foreigners. Capt. James Colnett, commander of the British ship, *Argonaut*, told kanakas that the Spanish planned to enslave them—even though Spain never attempted to seize the Islands or establish a settlement there and offered sanctuary to those who escaped from slavery in the English colonies of North America. When Colnett unexpectedly met Manuel Quimper in the *Princesa Real* at Kailua Bay on the Big Island in 1791, the rival European ships nearly fired on one another.[54]

Thoroughly at home on the water and seeing the Pacific as an extension of their homeland, Islanders did their own exploring. Seen by haoles as "almost amphibians," they found ready employment wherever swimming, diving, or boating skills were needed. Many signed

Chapter 1—Islands and Aliens

on to work on foreign ships as sailors to see the world beyond their archipelago. Two Hawaiians sailed off to the United States with Robert Gray on the *Columbia Rediviva*, for example. One of them, Opai, became the first Hawaiian to circle the globe, returning home in 1791. Soon, kānaka maoli (*native Hawaiians*) were the majority of the crews on American fur-trading ships and were employed at trading posts across Oregon. Kamehameha sent 100 of them to help build Astoria on the Oregon coast and to work as far east as Idaho. Before long, an estimated one-fifth of young Hawaiian men had traveled abroad as sailors, whalers, diplomats, adventurers, and pilots. Kamehameha promised a daughter in marriage to a Tahitian prince, but the boy died before they could wed.[55] Kaumuali'i paid a small fortune to an American sea captain to take his 5-year-old son Humehume to New England for a Yankee education, so the boy could learn about the haole world.[56]

Haoles affected the Hawaiian Islands in myriad, unpredictable ways. Kanakas initially were reluctant to drink the intoxicating wine and spirits that Capt. Cook offered. They had made 'awa (*kava*), a mild narcotic, but never alcohol. Soon, many grew overly fond of rum and other new drinks, leading to wild intoxication. Cook left three goats on tiny Ni'ihau, two English boars, and some seeds from melon, pumpkins, and onions, all of which were welcome additions to the local diet. Soon, other alien plants and animals followed, both enriching the lives of Hawaiians and threatening native species. Goats in particular wreaked havoc on local ecosystems. European muskets and cannon also proved more lethal than clubs and spears. In 1790, the British-American surveyor and fur trader, Simon Metcalfe, unwittingly delivered guns, cannon, and a competent military advisor, John Young, into the hands of Kamehameha—who used Young's skills effectively in battle.[57]

Foreign sailors also brought sexually transmitted infections (STIs), which their physicians had no ability to treat effectively. Syphilis, gonorrhea, and other STIs were unknown to kānaka maoli, who had no resistance to these afflictions. Knowing his men were diseased, Capt. Cook had tried with little success to keep them away from women on Kaua'i and Ni'ihau. But Pacific Islanders saw sex as a form of hospitality. The king offered the captain his own daughter, who reported that these strange haoles groaned in pain when she dug her fingernails into them while making love. This suggested to her that they must not be gods after all. The trinkets that sailors gave Hawaiian women guaranteed that they would return to the ships. Early visitors such as Clerke were shocked at the confident, assertive way Hawaiian women of all ages sought sexual satisfaction from these aliens. By the time Cook returned, a year later, syphilis had spread all the way from Niʻihau to the Big Island, and he abandoned any attempt to restrain his sex-starved men. Hawaiians soon realized the source of this new plague. When the *Resolution* and the *Discovery* returned to Kauaʻi the following year, their welcome was far less cordial. On Oʻahu alone, 10,000 people died of syphilis and gonorrhea within two decades of Cook's visits.[58]

As if this were not bad enough, haole vessels also brought disease-carrying vermin. The *Discovery* and the *Resolution* were infested with cockroaches and rats; within a few years, the Old World rat had displaced its Pacific cousin. After centuries of isolation from the rest of the world, Hawaiians were a healthy people who had never experienced epidemics such as bubonic plague, cholera, malaria, typhoid, influenza, and tuberculosis that swept through other nations. Consequently, they never developed antibodies to fight them nor any knowledge about how to help the afflicted or prevent transmission. Unlike Euro-Americans, they were not exposed to mumps or measles in childhood, so they had no resistance to them in adulthood. In addition, foreign sailors frequently carried dysentery from Europe, along with yellow fever and hookworm from their travels in the tropics, and often were infested with lice and fleas. Nearly everyone got sick at the same time, overwhelming the medical kahunas and leaving few people to care for the ill. Even those who survived haole disease often were weak, malnourished, and overcome with grief for family and friends who died. And one epidemic followed another.[59]

Haoles also introduced new animals that devastated indigenous species. With the best of intentions but the worst consequences, Capt. James Cook left two goats on Niʻihau in February 1778. They multiplied rapidly and drove native plants and wildlife to extinction. The aliʻi recognized the risks posed by foreigners, but they found themselves almost powerless to prevent contact with them. In 1787, Frances Barkley, the young wife of the *Imperial Eagle*'s captain, hired "Winee," who had paddled out to the ship seeking employment and adventure, to accompany her to Nootka in the Pacific Northwest. Winee was the first wahine to sail abroad and the first to visit what is now Canada. That same year, two kānaka maoli sailed all the way to England. When the *Prince of Wales* and *Princesa Real* wintered in the islands in 1788–1789, aliʻi tried in vain to prohibit wahines from having sexual intercourse with sailors, with little success.[60]

Chapter 2

Royal Romance

Kamehameha found a crafty way to prevent aliʻi who swore loyalty to him from later rebelling against him. He "honored" the chiefs by including them in his court as he traveled, keeping an eye on them and preventing them from plotting against him, and he moved his court often. He also gave them access to land that was widely scattered, a piece of land in this valley and one on another island, to prevent them from consolidating power anywhere. All land belonged to him; everyone, noble or commoner, needed his permission to use any of it. This understanding of land tenure was expressed in a famous prophecy that Kamehameha would rise to power:

> To the chief belongs the island, the land.
> The chief holds the uplands and the ocean....
> All precious property, above and below.
> The chief holds all fixed property.[1]

His chief adversary, Kahekili, the aliʻi nui of Maui (and later of Lānaʻi, Molokaʻi, and Oʻahu), excelled Kamehameha in military tactics but treated rivals so harshly that he often could not hold territory he conquered. Rather than integrate the aliʻi of Oʻahu into his rule, for example, he slaughtered them and replaced them with his relatives from Maui, which left Maui vulnerable.[2]

Some things, the Lonely One realized, were more important than winning a battle. One of these things was love. For a long time, Kamehameha had admired young Kaʻahumanu's beauty and her intelligence. Two rival chiefs also sought her as a wife, but when she was 9 or 10 years old, her father promised Kamehameha that he could marry her someday. When she was older, her father sent her to live in her future husband's household in North Kohala until she was old enough to marry. For Hawaiians, such a union was a way of sealing an alliance between families, as it was among European royalty. By marrying her, Kamehameha aligned himself with the most powerful aliʻi of Maui, and may

Queen Ka'ahumanu of Hawaii

never have ruled without her sharing power with him. When Nathaniel Portlock returned to the Islands in 1786, he noted that Kamehameha, who had been a minor chief in 1778, was now a king whose power extended beyond the Big Island.[3]

While engaged to Kamehameha, Ka'ahumanu lived in a grass-covered hut that was set apart from the home of her future husband. Two female guardians kept a close watch on her—and kept her isolated from other people. She escaped this seclusion by learning to ride a surfboard. The waves were a place where men and women freely interacted, often naked or nearly so. In the surfing competitions during Makahiki, women often defeated men.[4]

Already a strong swimmer, her courage, daringness, and agility made Ka'ahumanu a graceful and skilled surfer, just as her mother had been. It took considerable strength to carry hardwood longboards, which often weighed 100 to 150 pounds. She even learned to ride the waves on some of the most challenging beaches, such as Maliu in the Kohala district of the Big Island.[5]

Her prowess in the water did little good, however, when a wave drove her into a canoe one day while she was surfing. Striking her head against the side of the canoe, she was knocked unconscious, then pulled under by the powerful undertow. The fishermen in the canoe were afraid to touch her, and a companion started wailing in grief, certain she was dead. She would have drowned had Kamehameha not seen the accident as he surfed a quarter of a mile away. He paddled his board furiously and pulled her, stunned and bleeding, to shore. However, not even this close call kept either of them out of the water. Both became proficient at riding the surf in an outrigger canoe, and she even learned "canoe leaping"—jumping out of a boat onto the crest of a wave and riding it to shore.[6]

No one knows when the couple finally married, but it may have been sometime in 1785. She was still a teenager, and he was perhaps 10 years older. We are no more certain of the year of his birth than we are of hers, but 1758 seems likely. It is even possible that Ka'ahumanu was younger than his first son, Kaoleioku, his child by his aunt Queen Kānekapōlei, the wife of Kalani'ōpu'u. Such a relationship was not unusual among the nobles. Neither was such a son.[7]

Most Hawaiians had only one mate, but ali'i took as many husbands, wives, or lovers as they wished. Kekupuohi, one of Kalani'ōpu'u's wives, is said to have had 40 husbands and lovers. When Kamehameha boarded Capt. Cook's *Resolution* in 1778, the surgeon David Samwell

Chapter 2—Royal Romance

was appalled by Kamehameha's open fondness for a young man who accompanied him, a relationship the chief was "not the least anxious to conceal." Many aliʻi had aikānes (*younger, intimate, same-sex companions*). One chief wanted Cook's lieutenant to stay in the Islands and become his aikāne, but the young officer declined. The travel logs of several early visitors mention Kamehameha's aikānes, and he was said to have been an aikāne of Kalaniʻōpuʻu.[8]

Today, a relationship between a middle-aged man and a teenage boy is punished as child abuse. Any sort of homosexuality was a hanging offense in the Royal Navy, as Cook reminded his crew when they sailed into Kealakekua Bay, but it carried no stigma among kanakas, who considered aikānes to be adults, not children. Samwell reported with amazement, "This, however strange it may appear, is fact, as we learnt from frequent Enquiries about this curious Custom, and it is an office that is esteemed honourable among them." Nor did being an aikāne mean that a man was either exclusively homosexual or māhū (*effeminate*). Legends celebrated the devotion of Lono's aikāne, the māhū who were famous priests and healers, and a hermaphrodite who became king of Maui. Most aikānes were young nobles, but some were commoners who rose to the rank of the aliʻi, along with their children, one of the few avenues of upward mobility in Hawaiʻi's otherwise rigid caste system.[9]

Nor is it clear which disturbed Britons more, the same-sex relationships they observed among Islanders or the openness about them. Homosexuality was hardly unknown among the British but usually was practiced in secret. Capt. John Meares was a notable exception, taking Kaʻiana, the handsome prince of Kauaʻi, with him to Canton in 1787 as his aikāne. What particularly upset John Ledyard, who sailed with Cook, was the fact that many aliʻi appeared to be more devoted to their aikānes than to their wives. Not that these men from Beretania necessarily loved their own wives all that much. Many of their marriages were arranged or forced, and it remained common, though not legal, for Englishmen to publicly sell wives and children whom they no longer wanted. He also was appalled at the way old Kalaniʻōpuʻu, who had at least five aikānes, delighted in having his young lovers publicly ejaculate onto his body.[10]

Kamehameha's name may have meant "The Lonely One," but he already had nearly a dozen wives when he married Kaʻahumanu, and he eventually took many more, perhaps 30 of them, including her sisters Kalākua and Nāmāhāna Piʻia.[11] This was not unusual; sisters often shared a husband, and brothers might share a wife, particularly among the ali'i. Every society prohibits marriage or sex between some close relations, but they differ when it comes to defining which unions are prohibited—and exceptions often are made for those who belong to the elite. In the Islands, as in ancient Egyptian and Incan empires, it was considered normal rather than incestuous for nobles to marry their siblings, maximizing their political and spiritual power.

Having multiple sexual partners simultaneously, regardless of whether or not one was married, was perfectly acceptable among Islanders; jealousy was not. As an old proverb says,

Portrait of Kaneena, a Chief of the Sandwich Islands by John Webber, between 1770 and 1800, engraved by A.W. Warren (Library of Congress).

> Aloha mai no, aloha aku;
> o ka huhū ka mea e ola 'ole ai.
> (*When love is given, love should be returned; anger is the thing that gives no life.*)[12]

The two most important of Kamehameha's many wives, Keōpūolani and Ka'ahumanu, cared for each other and raised at least two hānai (*adopted* or *foster*) daughters together. Parents often entrusted others to raise their children as hānai, not because their birth parents were inadequate and/or did not want the children, but rather because they wanted them to be a blessing to those who raised them. Keōpūolani was simultaneously wife, cousin, and niece of Kamehameha, and she had a second husband herself.[13]

Keōpūolani (*the gathering of the heavens*) was the highest ranking chief in the Islands, Ka Wahine Kapu, the Sacred Woman set apart from all other people. The child of high-ranking siblings, she was believed to be the reincarnation of the water goddess and thought to possess an enormous amount of mana (*spiritual power*). Yet she, like Ka'ahumanu, could play little role in religious ritual. Kamehameha took her as

Chapter 2—Royal Romance

a captive when she was still just a child, when he conquered Maui. She became his Sacred Wife when she was about 13 years old, but they did not have intercourse until she was old enough to bear children to inherit his throne and her high spiritual power. Even then, she did not live with him. Since nobility was based more on the mother than the father, any children they had together would rank higher than him.[14]

But Kaʻahumanu was his Favorite Wife. His other wives had his permission to take additional husbands or lovers. Keōpūolani first married Kalanimōkū, whom she loved far more than Kamehameha, and later Hoapili. But the king reserved Kaʻahumanu for himself. He assigned a man and a woman to guard her. If his queen had an affair and they did not warn him, he proclaimed, these attendants would be put to death. The same fate awaited any man who slept with Kaʻahumanu. Some decided she was worth the risk, including, it was said, one of the king's own sons.[15]

Kaʻahumanu lived in Kamehameha's compound, which consisted of 13 houses surrounded by a wall made from lava stone. Her sister, who was also married to him, and the daughter her sister had by Kamehameha's younger brother, shared the home with her, along with the men who cooked for them. She was not allowed in the largest house in compound but had a smaller home of her own. Between the big house and her home was a smaller hut where they had sexual intercourse—at least when he was not with one of his other 20 wives or many lovers. If she left the compound without him, she was accompanied by a guard who kept a close eye out for any flirtation.[16]

As is often the case with intense romance, the couple had plenty of quarrels. One ancient chant recalls Kamehameha's love for another woman. He keeps asking her to come to him so they can have intercourse; she keeps replying, "I am afraid of Kaʻahumanu." Often in their marital spats, kanakas sympathized with his Favorite Wife more than they did with their king. When there was a massive volcanic eruption in North Kona on the Big Island, some thought Pele was angry that he was neglecting Kaʻahumanu for her younger sister Kalākua, who was already married to Kamehameha's brother. An old proverb warned that Pele's rage devoured everything before her: "Akua lehe ʻoi." (*"She is a sharp-lipped goddess."*)[17]

Jealousy may have been shameful, but Kaʻahumanu was deeply wounded when Kamehameha took her younger sister as his Second-Favorite Wife, living exclusively with her for a time and having a child with her. Kaʻahumanu, who could not conceive, was so upset that she swam more than five miles through shark-infested waters, apparently wanting to die. She survived only because she finally took pity on a boy who followed her, hoping to prevent her suicide.[18]

Another time, overcome with suspicion, Ka'ahumanu swam 18 miles from Kailua to Hōnaunau to spy on her husband, whom she thought would be meeting a lover on the beach. Distances such as this may seem impossible to most people today, but an American sailor noted that not long after this, "the women of this country are uncommon swimmers and have been known to swim 15 to 20 miles" and a British captain recorded his amazement that wahines could dive off one side of his ship and swim under it to surface on the other side. After hiding her large frame uncomfortably behind a big rock for several unpleasant hours, Ka'ahumanu finally glimpsed Kamehameha and his companion. Chagrined to see who it was, Ka'ahumanu sat perfectly still, hoping not to be noticed. His companion, though, ran ahead, recognized her, and raced back to tell the king about the discovery—with happy barks; Kamehameha was walking his dog. Peering behind the rock, he found his embarrassed wife. Roaring with laughter, he took her into his arms.[19]

In 1789, Kamehameha formed an alliance with Ka'iana, the high prince of Kaua'i who had sailed to China and returned home with muskets. They invaded Maui together, making good use of Ka'iana's firearms and a cannon that the king had acquired elsewhere. His superior leadership was decisive in his victories, but the haole weapons certainly helped. Kamehameha bought additional guns, cannon, and ships from early European and American traders—as his rivals also tried to do—and used them particularly effectively. Even more important, though, and unlike his opponents, he was gifted at consolidating his successes on the battlefield and holding on to the islands he won. This led first to an expansion of warfare and eventually to its end.[20]

Wahines frequently fought next to men in battle. The mere presence of Keōpūolani, the most Sacred Woman in the Islands, was enough to strike fear in the hearts of Kamehameha's enemies. Ka'ahumanu, who had been trained for combat by her father and Kamehameha, often fought beside her husband. She was "known to give no quarter in battle. She was absolutely fearless...."[21]

In 1790, Kamehameha and his ally, the high chief of Hilo, were attacked by Keōua Kū'ahu'ula while Kamehameha was on Maui. The Lonely One hurried back to the Big Island. When Kīlauea erupted in December, wiping out most Keōua's army, many Hawaiians saw this as a sign that Pele favored the Lonely One. In 1791, Kamehameha invited

Chapter 2—Royal Romance

Keōua to the dedication of a temple to Kū (*the war god*), promising to receive him with kindness and honor. As soon as his rival's canoe landed, implicitly surrendering to Kamehameha, Kaʻahumanu's father assassinated him, an act of treachery that made Kamehameha the undisputed ruler of the entire Big Island and much of Maui. He then sent a messenger to Kahekili, asking the old chief if he wanted war or peace. Kahekili replied that Kamehameha could take the island more easily after his death. Kamehameha waited. Three years later, he ruled the Big Island, Maui, Molokaʻi, and Lānaʻi.[22]

Kaʻahumanu was closely related to many aliʻi on Maui, which helped her husband win territory and prevent rebellion in the areas he conquered. Not having children of her own, she was free to form alliances with almost anyone, something other female aliʻi could not do without thinking about the consequences for their sons and daughters.[23]

She was the only one of Kamehameha's many wives whom he invited to meet many of the first foreign visitors to the Islands, such as the British explorer George Vancouver. Vancouver met Kamehameha while he was an officer on Cook's expedition and then when he returned in 1793 as commander of his own vessel. He described her as:

> Six feet tall, straight and well formed without blemish, and comely ... her eyes like that of a dove, her nose narrow and straight, in admirable proportion to her cheeks; her arched eyebrows shaped to the breadth of her forehead; her hair dark, wavy and fine ... one of the finest women we have seen on any of the islands. It was pleasing to observe the kindness and fond attention, with which on all occasions they seemed to regard each other....[24]

Hawaiians, like the Britons of this era, thought thin women were unattractive. Tall and strong, Kaʻahumanu was considered one of the loveliest women in the Islands. The king said, "She is as beautiful as a lehua blossom. She rides the waves like a bird. She knows the heartbeat of the people. There is none like her in all the land."[25]

Both had many lovers—despite the risk that hers were taking. Plural marriage and extramarital affairs were accepted among the aliʻi, as was sex among fairly close relatives. And marriage among first cousins was permitted, particularly in the upper classes, in Europe and the United States for decades to come, forbidden by neither church nor law.[26] In his final years, Kamehameha even took a young wife simply "to keep his flesh warm." Kaʻahumanu, however, remained the great love of his life, as he was hers. She celebrated their romance by composing many meles—poems that are chanted and accompanied by hula dancers, often to the beat of a drum or hollow gourd.

Queen Kaʻahumanu of Hawaii

Once while visiting her parents on Maui, she missed him so much that she sent a messenger to the Big Island to sing him a mele that she had just composed: "Papale au ʻāina kuu aloha" (*The crown that covers all the land is my most beloved one*), using her pet name for him:

> Kona is beautiful and becalmed, as at dawn,
> Flooded by the cool air of the Kahau breeze
> That sprays the silvery sea beyond the lea.
> Beloved is he who lives by himself in Hoʻolulu,
> But twice perfect is he who loves his beloved!
> I am yours—waiting with aloha,
> Aloha for you. Kaʻahumanu.

As soon as Kamehameha heard this mele, it is said, he hurried to her.[27]

Kamehameha loved Kaʻahumanu's independence, and sometimes was incensed by it. When George Vancouver made his final visit to Hawaiʻi in January 1794, he learned that the king suspected his Favorite Wife of having an affair, and his jealous rage had driven her away. Vancouver could see that he deeply missed her and believed she might be innocent of the charge—at least this time: "I understood from the king's attendants that the infidelity of the queen was by no means certain." The captain also suspected that Kamehameha treated her unfairly, noticing, for example, that the king failed to distribute gifts equally, sharing them with the men and boys in his family but not with the women and girls. If they were not reconciled, Vancouver feared, Kaʻahumanu's father might lead a rebellion to overthrow the king. Vancouver was glad to help the estranged couple, but Kamehameha's pride made this marital diplomacy all the more difficult. He wanted her back without admitting any mistake on his part.[28]

Vancouver invited the Favorite Wife, whom his clerk found "charming," and her father to visit the *Discovery* and arranged for the king to wander in, as if by accident. "I caught his hand," the captain recorded, "and joining it with the queen's, their reconciliation was instantly completed." The monarchs embraced, crying with joy and relief, as did nearly everyone on board. Fearing that Kamehameha might beat his wife, Vancouver got the king to promise he would not hit her and then accompanied them home, "to the utter mortification of those who, by their scandalous reports and misrepresentations, had been the cause of the unfortunate separation."[29]

Sometimes, though, Vancouver's good intentions had disastrous results. He introduced cows, sheep, and geese to the Hawaiian Islands, along with orange trees, grapevines, and almond trees. The plants

Chapter 2—Royal Romance

enriched the diet of Islanders, but the cattle devastated local plants and birds.

Vancouver was shocked by the population decline since his first visit with Cook and refused to sell arms or ammunition to warring faction, convinced that the introduction of Western firearms had made Hawaiian battles far more deadly. Fatalities had been few in previous decades; now, thousands of warriors, or even tens of thousands, died in a single conflict, and the movement of massive armies unleashed hunger and disease on a new scale. Alarmed by the devastation wrought by warfare—not that Britain had avoided civil war in recent centuries—he tried, unsuccessfully, in 1793 to broker peace between the chiefs of Maui and the Big Island. In February 1794, he did, however, negotiate an alliance between Kamehameha and George III—a treaty he had no authority to negotiate—that was promptly approved by a Council of Chiefs.[30]

Vancouver discussed Christianity with Kamehameha and explained his objections to many of the taboos that governed the lives of Hawaiians. He may have promised to send missionaries to the islands, too, but the British government neither sent any mikanele (*missionaries*) nor ratified the agreement that Kamehameha and Vancouver made. Great Britain might have dominated the Islands and their strategic position in the Pacific had not its ongoing warfare with France drawn her Navy into battles in the Atlantic. After voyaging around the world in service to his country, he died forgotten—along with the treaty he had negotiated.[31]

Kamehameha placed Peter Anderson, an African American who had been forced into service by the Royal Navy, in charge of his cannons when he invaded Oʻahu, and he made two other haoles, John Young and Isaac Davis, his advisors. They and other foreigners he recruited helped him win decisive battles, using foreign cannons to terrify his adversaries. They also raised questions about the evils of war that Kaʻahumanu pondered.

In July 1794, Kaʻahumanu became head of the ruling Maui dynasty after the death of her uncle Kahekili, which further increased her status and power. Between 1798 and 1802, Kamehameha had a "Brick Palace" built for his Favorite Wife at Keawaʻiki Point in Lāhainā. It was designed and built with locally produced bricks by an escaped convict called Mela (*Miller*), whom the British had transported to the Botany Bay penal colony in Australia, and by a black immigrant called Keakaʻeleʻele (*Mr. Black Jack*), who found the Islands far less racially biased than anywhere in Europe or the United States. Two stories high, about 40 by 20 feet, with glazed windows, this building briefly served as the seat of government.

Queen Kaʻahumanu of Hawaii

The first European-style building in the Islands, it served as the center of the king's encampment of 1,000 people in 1802. Visiting sea captains and other dignitaries were often received here, though Kaʻahumanu preferred to actually live in a traditional grass-covered home nearby.[32]

In 1795, Kamehameha invaded Oʻahu with a huge fleet and an enormous army. His war canoes covered the beach more than five miles from Waikīkī to Waialae-Kahala. His forces confronted the aliʻi of Oʻahu at Punchbowl Crater and then in Nuʻuanu Valley. As many as 25,000 warriors fought a decisive battle, larger than any of the American Revolution. It was bigger, in fact, than any battle that would be fought in the United States for another seven decades, when the Union and Confederate armies met at Gettysburg.

Kamehameha gave his Favorite Wife puʻuhonua, the power to protect women and children and pardon defeated warriors, deserters, and taboo violators. She established places of refuge on her lands on Maui, Molokaʻi, and the Big Island, and she spared the lives of the aliʻi her husband captured on Oʻahu after the decisive Battle of Nuʻuanu. After conquering Oʻahu, he abolished the traditional refuge sites on Oʻahu and asked her to choose new ones, honoring her in a way that transferred power from priests to his wife and his government.[33]

Kamehameha rewarded his haole soldiers and advisors for their loyalty, one of many things that convinced his armorer Peter Anderson that the Sandwich Islands were relatively free of bigotry and a better place for him to live than the United States. When George Vancouver offered Isaac Davis and John Young free passage to England, they chose to stay, saying they "preferred their present way of life.... Here they lived happily, and in the greatest of plenty...." Even the makaʻāinana ate as well or better than the average English peasant and enjoyed far more leisure. Rural people in England, in fact, were being steadily disposed of Common Land. Through "enclosure" wealthy landowners took over fields and pasture that had long been shared by small-farm farmers, driving those who were not rich off the lands and into destitution. When John Boit, master of the *Union*, offered to take Young to Canton in 1795, Young declined, saying that this was "the only Country that he was ever in where he would be allowed so many privileges ... poverty was a stranger in this land of liberty, and slavery was a term they did not understand...." Before long, Kamehameha appointed Davis the High Chief (*governor*) of Oʻahu and Young the High Chief of the Big Island.[34]

Kamehameha could be ruthless when he thought it necessary, but he often showed mercy to those he vanquished, winning the loyalty of

Chapter 2—Royal Romance

his new subjects. He remembered how he had rushed ashore in 1783 during a military campaign along the Puna Coast of the Big Island and attacked some men who were fishing. One of them hit him so hard on the head with a wooden canoe paddle that it splintered. When the man was captured 12 years later, Kamehameha pardoned him rather than executing him, and admitted that he had been wrong to attack innocent bystanders. One of the first laws he proclaimed was Ke Kānāwai Māmala Hoe (*the Law of the Splintered Paddle*). Henceforth, any chief who raided unarmed people would be severely punished; the weak, the young, the aged, and travelers had to be protected:

> A e mālama hoʻi e ke kānaka nui a me ke kānaka iki;
> E hele kaʻelemakule, ka luahine, a me ka kamaliʻi,
> A moe i ke ala,
> ʻAʻohe mea nāna e hoʻopilikia,
> Hewa nā, make!
> (*Respect alike the rights of people great and humble;*
> *See to it that our aged, our women, and our children,*
> *Can lie down to sleep by the roadside,*
> *Without fear of harm.*
> *Disobey, and die!*)[35]

To secure peace in his once-war-torn realm, Kamehama encouraged high-ranking chiefs of one island to marry high-ranking aliʻi of another island and often helped arrange these matches himself. His commanders also won support by showing the sort of mercy that he displayed. In 1785, while his rival Kahekili was on Oʻahu, Kamehameha dispatched his brother Kalanimalokuloku to invade Maui. Unlike many soldiers before and since, his brother showed respect for the personal property of civilians, earning him a new name, Keliʻimaikaʻi (*the Good Chief*). The people of Maui repaid his kindness by protecting him during a narrow escape when Kahekili's forces repelled the invasion.[36]

Even after adding Oʻahu to his realm, Kamehameha, who was now called Ka Naʻi Aupuni (*the Conqueror of the Islands*), dreamt of further conquest. Could he do what no one had ever done before? Could he also rule the other two inhabited islands in the archipelago? In 1796, he assembled a vast fleet of 1,500 canoes to carry 10,000 warriors across the treacherous Kaʻieʻie Waho Channel to attack Kaumualiʻi, the new, inexperienced, adolescent ruler of Kauaʻi and Niʻihau. It is the widest passage between any neighboring islands in the chain, and partway across, a storm struck, sinking many boats, scattering others, and driving the rest back to Oʻahu. About 1,000 fighters landed on the southeastern beaches of Kaua'i but were quickly defeated by Kaumuali'i's forces. Between this calamity and the outbreak of rebellion in the Hilo district, Kamehameha was forced to abandon his invasion plans. Putting down the revolt on the Big Island would turn out to be the last battle he ever fought.[37]

In the summer of 1804, Kamehameha and his Favorite Wife moved to O'ahu, preparing once more to try to invade Kaua'i. He assembled an army of more than 7,000 Hawaiians and 50 European soldiers, many muskets, six mortars, eight heavy cannon, and 40 swivel guns. He also had built a large fleet of war canoes and had 21 armed schooners, the largest navy in the Pacific. Kaumuali'i, who could muster a force only a third as large, began praying intensely—and planning an escape to a remote Pacific island or China. He also asked Lt. Yuri Lisyansky, commander of the *Neva*, for armed assistance in fighting Kamehameha, but the Russian naval officer was unwilling to involve Czar Alexander I in a distant civil war.[38]

Just as the invasion was about to begin, an epidemic swept through O'ahu and other islands. As many as a 1,000 warriors died, and so many of his soldiers got sick that Kamehameha was forced to call off the attack. Not only was his army decimated, but he also lost his most experienced commanders.[39]

Kamehameha fell ill himself but recovered. Ka'ahumanu's beloved father, Ke'eaumoku Pāpa'iahiahi, was struck down, too, and soon died. Devastated, she mourned him with this kanikau (*chanted lament*):

> O ku'u mukuakane lani,
> Hoa aloha wale ia la
> He aloha ia la e
> Aloha aku au a pau ke aho,
> Uwe aku ho'i o ka hoa mai ke anu....
> (*My father and chief,*
> *My beloved companion,*
> *My loved one.*
> *I am breathless with grieving for you,*
> *I weep for my companion in the cold....*)

When her mother died, Ka'ahumanu sang this kanikau:

> He ku'u makuahine me ke aloha,
> 'Auwana wale iho ko au i Kuahea.
> O 'oe o ka wahine 'ai makani,
> 'Ai makani malana'i-e—
> E 'ai e 'ao ama o le aloha.

Chapter 2—Royal Romance

(Love to my mother who has gone,
Leaving me wandering on the mountainside.
You are the woman consumed by the wind,
consumed by the trade wind—
Consumed, consumed, consumed with love.)[40]

Ka'ahumanu's brother Ke'eaumoku 'Opio replaced their father Ke'eaumoku Pāpa'iahiahi as a member of the king's Privy Council, an ancient institution that Kamehameha had revived. This Council of Chiefs advised him, oversaw the allocation of land, and managed fishing, trade, and tax collection. It both helped him govern his realm peacefully and provided checks and balances on the power of the king as the head of state. Kamehameha also appointed a governor of each major island, allowing for some local rule of local affairs. Ka'ahumanu attended the meetings of this council and became her husband's primary advisor, just as her father had been.[41]

Though his subjects viewed him as a god, Kamehameha knew he would not live forever. His advisors told him that he could only keep his kingdom united after his death if he chose an heir who was in the ruling line of his ancestors. So, he named his young son Liholiho as his successor, establishing a dynasty that would last until the end of the century.[42]

The boy's mother, Keōpūolani, was so sacred that she could not raise her own child. She could not walk outdoors except at night, lest her shadow fall on anyone. All had to bow in her presence. Even Kamehameha could approach her bed only when he was naked and on his knees. George Vancouver observed a hula performed in her honor. Whenever her name was spoken, every dancer stripped to their waists in respect for the Wahine Kapu.[43]

No one was supposed to even see the boy during the day, a kapu that had never applied to his lower born father, Kamehameha. Violating this taboo could be punishable by death. These restrictions, needless to say, complicated child-rearing, so the king made his Favorite Wife, who was childless herself, the boy's kahu *(guardian)*. Perhaps he knew that, with lower spiritual status than a son he had by the most sacred woman in the Islands, he would never be able to discipline the child. Raising Liholiho would prove a daunting task for Ka'ahumanu, too. Kahunas trained him in the religious rites his father performed and kapus that he would have to observe even more scrupulously than lower born Kamehameha did. He ended up ill-prepared, however, to deal with the radical changes that were coursing through the kingdom.[44]

Kamehameha was loved by his people, Lilikalā Kame'eleihiwa

contends, "because he put an end to war and gave them peace...." He earned his title "the Great" by being an even better leader in peace than in war. Kekūhaupi'o, the famous warrior who had trained him, had predicted he would become a great ruler only if he cared for the welfare of his people more than his own pleasure:

O ke ali'i lilo i ka le'ale'a a malama 'ole i ke kānaka me ke kapu akua, 'a'ole ia he ali'i e ku ai i ka moke.
(*The chief who is overtaken with pleasure-seeking and cares not for the welfare of the people or the observation of the kapus of the gods is not an ali'i who will become a ruler.*)[45]

Having led a warrior state, Kamehameha now demilitarized Hawaiian society—just as Europe was moving toward mass conscription during the Napoleonic Wars, a conflict that would spread to North America and much of the world. By reducing the ability of potential rivals to threaten his rule, Kamehameha cemented the unification of his realm. Now, his people said with admiration, "the aged could journey and sleep by the way." He also brought important local akua (*gods*) into a national pantheon of gods who were connected to his royal court and his kingdom as a whole, rather than a single island, and he shaped new rituals for worshiping the national gods. He respected tradition but was open to new ideas and adapted to changing conditions.[46]

To provide free health care for all, the king established a school to train medical kahunas. Agriculture had been neglected during the epidemic and thwarted invasion of Kaua'i in 1804, so Kamehameha now encouraged his people to increase food production, moving 8,000 of his warriors to O'ahu and giving them land to farm. The Boston sea captain, Amasa Delano, who visited the Islands in 1801 and 1806 on his ship, the *Perseverance*, found Kamehameha to be "a man of very good natural abilities, of tender feelings, and aiming to be just, making a very good ruler."[47]

He urged his people to avoid both waste and hoarding and led them in rebuilding neglected and damaged fishponds, enlisting thousands of people to repair the walls of one ancient pond at Kiholo on the Big Island. He restricted fishing to conserve fish for future generations—something many nations fail to do today. He worked a kalo (taro) patch with his own hands, wading up to his waist in mud, breaking down the separation of ali'i and common people while also ritually reenacting his connection to both his illustrious ancestors (his roots) and the next generation (his new leaves). "Turn your spears into digging sticks,"

Chapter 2—Royal Romance

he proclaimed, and encouraged people to take plantings from his gardens to improve their crops. He developed extensive agricultural ditches to distribute water fairly among farmers. George Vancouver said the Hawaiian irrigation systems were the best he had seen anywhere, and ancient canals near Kohala on the Big Island still carry water today. His people said, "He is a farmer, a fisherman, a maker of cloth, a provider for the needy, and father to the fatherless."[48]

Trade with visiting ships steadily grew, and when the British merchant, John Turnbull, landed on Oʻahu in 1804, he found that salt was "… dearer than we expected. The increased price was occasioned, not only by the scarcity, but by the frequent intercourse the natives have with Europeans and Americans, from whom they have learned to affix the proper value to the production of their country…." The king, he noted, had become a skilled negotiator:

> He is not only a great warrior and politician, but a very astute trader, and a match for any European in driving a bargain. He is well acquainted with the different weights and measures and the value which all articles ought to bear in exchange with each other; and is ever ready to take the advantage of the necessities of those who apply to him or his people for supplies.[49]

Trade provided the means for Kamehameha and his Favorite Wife to build a huge compound on the beach at Waikīkī, surrounded by fences and stone walls. It was large enough to house more than 2,000 aliʻi, kahunas, warriors, artisans, attendants, and servants in 700 grass huts, with kalo fields next to them. Kamehameha's home was 80 feet long and 60 feet wide, with ʻiliahi (*sandalwood*) posts that were 12 feet high.[50]

Sandalwood was at the center of a fragile ecosystem. It had been used occasionally by Hawaiians, but they did not consider it to be a particularly useful timber, so they seldom harvested it. It was prized in Asia, however, where it was burned as incense and joss sticks during burial ceremonies and other religious rites. Brahmins in India also used its ashes in a paste they applied to their foreheads to mark their high caste. As sandalwood forests were exhausted in Fiji and the Solomon Islands, merchants sought it elsewhere. Boston fur traders seized upon this lucrative trade and began paying Islanders to harvest it on Kauaʻi in 1790 and 1791. Initially at least, the wood was so abundant that no one thought it needed to be conserved. Soon, this commerce would devastate the forests of the Islands.[51]

Kamehameha's leadership during times of peace was tested in 1806, when a severe drought afflicted his kingdom. Not every island was affected to the same degree, but Hawaiians suffered everywhere. One American living on normally damp Maui reported that no rain fell from October to the following April.[52] As crops withered and animals died, people needed both the order that the king imposed and everything that he had taught them about farming, irrigation, fishing, and avoiding waste of food.

This drought may have helped convince chiefs that further warfare would be disastrous for their people—and might allow foreign powers to pick off the islands one at a time. In 1810, Kamehameha proposed to Kaumuali'i that they attempt to resolve their conflict peacefully. After protracted negotiations, the two monarchs finally agreed to unite their realm Islands under Kamehameha while preserving some autonomy for Kaumuali'i. Upon the latter's death, Kaua'i and Ni'ihau would pass to Kamehameha or his successor.

Diplomacy succeeded where force had failed, unifying the archipelago. It was time to "E uha'i ka maka o ka ihe" (*break off the point of the spear*): to cease fighting and make peace.[53]

Chapter 3

Kaʻahumanu Breaks the Rules

Kamehameha tried to control the impact of haoles on Hawaiian life. He welcomed the skills of foreign visitors but limited how many of them could settle among his people. He was a gracious host and employer but seldom gave them land.

But contact with visiting sailors brought Hawaiians thrilling new experiences, including the chance to travel to distant lands. By 1791, Hawaiians were working on New England merchant ships that crossed the Pacific, creating webs of interconnection throughout Oceania. That year, the American sea captain, John Kendrick, had given Kaʻahumanu a set of checkers; soon, she was an expert player. Eventually, she became so proficient at the game that not a single officer of the American ship, *Beaver*, could beat her even once. She also began making huge kites out of kapa cloth. Some were 16 feet long and 7 feet wide, with so much lift that they had to be tied to a tree. Kamehameha, meanwhile, constructed a hōlua (*sledding*) slide at Kona for his son Kauikeaouli that was more than 3,000 feet long.[1]

Other new experiences were less pleasant. Fleas probably arrived with the first voyaging canoes, but far more aggressive "leaping fleas" came to the Islands on European and American ships and soon infested local homes, along with cockroaches, wasps, termites, fleas, and other ship-born pests. As much as 90 percent of the native population was killed by epidemics from Europe and the United States within the first 50 years of contact with haoles. Foreign diseases ravaged the native population, and Kaʻahumanu and others realized that their religion and its kapus did not protect them from these new plagues. Animals, plants, and microbes introduced by haoles also decimated indigenous fauna and flora, but this damage was not as readily apparent.[2]

Other imports proved equally troublesome. British sailors from the *Discovery* and *Resolution* brewed beer from the roots of ti plants

Queen Kaʻahumanu of Hawaii

on Oʻahu in 1779. In 1791, a visiting captain gave Kamehameha rum on board his sailing ship. Not long after this, Kalanimōkū became the first chief to buy rum from haoles. William Stevenson, an escaped convict from the Botany Bay penal colony of New South Wales (Australia), taught Hawaiians to distill fermented roots of the ki (*ti*) plant to produce potent ʻōkolehao, which resembles bourbon. Hawaiians occasionally consumed mildly intoxicating ʻawa (*kava*), to relax after heavy labor, and it was used medicinally for toothaches and other ailments and in some religious rituals, but ʻawa induced calmness and drowsiness; alcohol lowered inhibitions and often led to brawls. Kamehameha himself hosted drunken bashes and enjoyed watching the ensuing quarrels and fights among his guests. Soon, nearly all the chiefs were making ʻōkolehao and rum—and both Liholiho and Kaʻahumanu were drinking themselves into oblivion quite regularly. It was not unusual for an entire village to be drunk at the same time.[3]

John Turnbull, an officer on the British ship, *Margaret*, was dismayed at the alcohol abuse he saw in 1802 in the Hawaiian and Society Islands:

> I know no sufficient punishment that the wretch would merit who should import a cargo of spiritous liquors into the Sandwich or Society Islands; it would in every respect be tantamount to the willful administration of an equal quantity of poison.[4]

Archibald Campbell, a Scottish sailor who arrived in 1809 on an American ship and lived in Honolulu for a time with Kamehameha's family, observed,

> Some of these people are sober and industrious; but ... many of them are idle and dissolute, getting drunk whenever an opportunity presents itself. They have introduced distillation into the island; and the evil consequences, both to the natives and the whites, are incalculable. It is no uncommon sight to see a party of them broach a small cask of spirits and sit drinking for days till they see it out.[5]

When Kamehameha was absent for long periods of time performing religious rituals at his heiau, Kaʻahumanu often got drunk. Her drinking partners often were two women from the Aleutian Islands who had been picked up by sailors off the coast of Alaska and left in Hawaiʻi. Since many kapus did not apply to them and they were not part of the Hawaiian social structure, she could be free with them. Eventually, though, she recognized the harm that overindulgence was doing to her health. She even managed to persuade her brother Keʻeaumoku ʻOpio to curtail his drinking.[6]

Chapter 3—Kaʻahumanu Breaks the Rules

Getting sober did not end her marital problems, however. Dismayed by how much time her husband was spending in his heiau, where she and other women could not go, Kaʻahumanu seduced handsome, 19-year-old Kanihonui, a nephew and companion of the king, whom she and Kamehameha had raised together.[7] In 1809, nobles who learned of the affair strangled the young man and laid his body on a heiau at Lēʻahi (*Diamond Head*), overlooking Waikīkī. These aliʻi may have been acting on behalf of the king, who feared the young man might supplant him if he continued to have intercourse with Kaʻahumanu, but when he learned of the crime and its punishment, Kamehameha broke down in tears.

His Favorite Wife was so furious that she thought seriously about raising a rebellion, seizing power, and making her ward Liholiho the new king. Kamehameha doubled his personal guard and gathered warriors in preparation for war. Kaʻahumanu, surrounded by the chiefs loyal to her, wept inconsolably. Kalanimōkū, the king's war leader, asked young Liholiho, "What do you think? Shall we wrest the kingdom from your father, make you king, and put him to death[?]"

The boy bowed his head in contemplation and then answered, "I do not want my father to die."[8]

European imperial powers eyed the Islands greedily, and as early as 1808, Russians hoped to establish a colony there. When the Russian sloop *Neva* returned in 1809, this time commanded by another German, Lt. Leontil A. Hagemeister (also spelled Gagemeister), Kaumualiʻi asked if some of his crew might stay behind on Kauaʻi to deter Kamehameha from invading, but the Russians once again refused to intervene in an internal conflict. Their empire was the world's largest fur trader, though, supplying the markets of Western Europe and parts of America, and Russia had expanded its territory into Siberia, Alaska, and the West Coast of North America in search of pelts. These Russian-American companies' fur traders needed a dependable supply of fresh food, and Hagemeister proposed establishing a colony in the Islands to provision them. Kamehameha initially welcomed the idea of a small settlement on Molokaʻi, but then Hagemeister arrogantly bragged that Russia could easily seize any land that the king did not grant voluntarily. He thought two warships would suffice. Had Czar Alexander I tried this, he might have learned how difficult it is to mount a naval invasion of a nation that lacks deep harbors. Had he tried to bombard the Islands without landing troops, he might have been stunned to discover how skilled kanakas were at swarming larger vessels. The czar rejected Hagemeister's proposal, but Kamehameha, who had sought good relations with the Russian Empire, remained furious.[9]

Contact with foreigners also led Hawaiians to question their taboos. When Vancouver's lieutenant visited Ka'ahumanu's home, she casually invited him to eat with her, despite everything she had been taught. When one of Kamehameha's other wives gave birth to a child who was born with only one hand, some said this occurred because his mother had eaten fish that were kapu for women. As early as 1810, it was rumored, Ka'ahumanu tasted forbidden shark and pork while on board a haole ship.[10]

As trade increased, Hawaiians could not help but notice that haoles did many things that were forbidden—and seemed to suffer no ill consequences. Many Hawaiians indulged in foods and practices that were kapu on land while they were on board foreign sailing vessels. Captains could entertain kānaka maoli without the normal taboos, because "masters of ships were treated as chiefs, their ships being their chiefdoms. As chiefs, the captains could exercise the privileges of chiefs in leveling kapus on goods they introduced or on behaviors of Hawaiians on their ships."[11]

If the rules did not apply to foreigners or to Hawaiians on a haole vessel, how powerful could their akua (*gods*) be? Hawaiians who had worked as sailors on western vessels on trips to the United States, China, and other lands were beginning to return home. They regaled their families and neighbors with tales of how other peoples lived and worshiped, raising fresh questions about their own beliefs and practices. Even Kamehameha had been eager to discuss with Capt. Vancouver the differences between his faith and Christianity, though he said in the end, "These are my gods, they are gods with mana through which I gained control of the government and became supreme chief."[12]

As haoles and Hawaiians reached an understanding about what constituted a fair exchange and what was theft, foreign ships stopped regularly in the Islands for fresh food, supplies, and repairs as they sailed between the Pacific Northwest and China. Learning from Cook's mistakes, Kamehameha and Vancouver instituted strict rules governing the interaction of hosts and crews to prevent misconduct on either side, which encouraged merchants to do business here. Between 1785 and 1794, at least 35 ships from Beretania and at least 15 from Amelika visited Hawai'i, and many fur traders were spending the entire winter in the Islands.[13]

Initially, Hawaiians primarily sold provisions to visiting ships,

Chapter 3—Ka'ahumanu Breaks the Rules

but even this nascent market economy undermined "the intricate web [of] responsibility and privilege that had characterized the relationship between commoners and nobles...." Kamehameha began acquiring western ships both for warfare and trade. By the mid–1790s, Hawaiians were building their own western-style ships. By 1811, the crew of John Jacob Astor's ship, *Tonquin*, was able to buy hogs, goats, sheep, and poultry. Foreign livestock had flourished sufficiently in the Islands to supply his trading company on the Oregon coast. A dozen Islanders joined the *Tonquin*'s crew to work for Astor.[14]

The United States was expanding rapidly westward. The Lewis and Clark expedition into the newly purchased Louisiana Territory was designed, in part, to expand fur trading. Astor's American Fur Company soon developed direct trade routes from Oregon to China—something the British North West Company and Hudson's Bay Company could not do, since the Crown had granted the East India Company a monopoly on trade with the Orient. In 1811, three Boston sea captains who had been trading furs took Hawaiian sandalwood to China for sale. Before long, the Chinese called the Islands "Tan Heong Shan" (*the Fragrant Sandalwood Mountains*). Sandalwood soon became the kingdom's biggest export and China her largest trading partner, with Americans dominating this new commerce.[15]

Soon, there were 200 foreigners living in the Islands, both drifters and some permanent residents, who seldom paid much attention to the taboos. One early resident from the United States, John Whitman, observed, "In former times the slightest infringement of these [taboos] was punished with death." Now, he noticed, minor offenses often went unpunished.[16] Could the chiefs be wrong, many Hawaiians began to wonder, about the kapus?

Still, people feared the anger of kahunas. About this time, Whitman heard, a haole noticed a small keg and made inquiries about hiring a priest to pray to death whoever took it, never planning to do any such thing. The keg was returned immediately, and the man who took it apologized profusely.[17]

Restricted on land, women flocked to visiting sailing ships, eager to explore exotic delights, often reasoning that their kapus did not apply on foreign vessels—as Ka'ahumanu did when she visited Vancouver on his ship. When she ate with Thomas Manby, a senior petty officer in Vancouver's expedition, nothing untoward happened to her, so she began to doubt that the gods cared that much about these prohibitions. On occasion, Kamehameha managed to stop women from going aboard foreign vessels, but such bans were mostly ignored. Women gladly ate pork and shark with haoles, who often were sympathetic to their curiosity, seeing how kapus constricted the lives of the wahines. Whitman concluded that they were "treated as an inferior order of beings."[18]

Archibald Campbell reported,

> They often swim off to ships at night during the taboo, and I have known them to eat of the forbidden delicacies of pork and sharks' flesh. What would be the consequence of a discovery I know not, but I once saw the queen transgressing in this respect and was strictly enjoined to secrecy, as she said it was as much as her life was worth.[19]

Women saw some visitors as ali'i, as James Cook and his officers were viewed, so sharing a berth with them could establish a connection with a powerful chief. Foreign sailors of less lofty status were happy to pay for sex with foreign goods, which kanakas generally were glad to accept. John Nichol and John Howell, the latter an ordained clergyman in the Church of England, recalled that when they visited the Islands in 1787 with Portlock, "Almost every man on board took a native woman for a wife...."[20]

Islanders did not see these encounters as prostitution; for them, this was hospitality to guests, exploration of new cultures, and the reciprocal exchange of gifts. The chiefs tried to monopolize all commerce, but trading sexual favors with haoles gave wahines prestige and new possessions. It also exposed them to the haoles' sexually transmitted infections.[21]

Contact with haoles called into question many of the kapus, but there also was powerful pressure to preserve ancient prohibitions. The complicated rules that separated things that were kapu (*sacred and forbidden*) from those that were noa (*not sacred, and thus permitted*) had supported the rigid hierarchy of Hawaiian society for centuries, and ali'i had good reason to fear change. Chiefs, who claimed to have descended from gods, insisted that the akua would punish anyone who violated these rules.[22]

When a man ate a coconut during a time of the year in which this was forbidden, Kamehameha ordered his execution, despite John Young's pleas for mercy. Keōpūolani tried to spare the lives of those who violated her kapus, but when she became seriously ill in 1807, her medical kahuna said she was sick because someone had eaten forbidden coconuts. Three men were sacrificed on the heiau at Lē'ahi (*Diamond Head*) overlooking Waikīkī. Had she not shown signs of rapid recovery, at least seven more would have joined them on the altar. When two

Chapter 3—Ka'ahumanu Breaks the Rules

young girls of high rank, Kapi'olani and Keoau, ate forbidden bananas, their lives were spared, but their guardian was executed. When a girl, younger than 5 years old, ate a banana, kahunas gouged out one of her eyes. One tipsy woman walked into a room where her husband was eating; the gods did not kill her, but the chiefs did.[23]

When kahunas attempted to enforce the rules, however, people often looked the other way. An old chant tells of Pamaho'a, who loved her husband so much that, long after his death, she carried his bones with her wherever she went. Half-crazed, she committed the mortal offense of entering the royal residence of Kamehameha and Ka'ahumanu with these bones. The king sent two warriors to take her away and kill her, but they took pity on her and let the mad, grieving widow escape.[24]

To haoles, these rules and retributions seemed barbaric, even though hanging was imposed in England for more than 200 offenses, including petty theft. English children could be executed for picking a few pennies from someone's pocket—and the list of hangable property crimes had grown in recent decades. In the Islands, on the other hand, people asked priests to determine the guilt or innocence of those suspected of theft. Stolen property was almost always returned, and the offender was fined a few pigs.[25]

As the old prohibitions began to wane, Hawaiians exuberantly celebrated those times when inhibitions were lifted. Archibald Campbell noted that when Kamehameha's popular younger brother Keli'imaika'i, who was much loved for his compassion for commoners and mercy toward foes, died in the summer of 1809, people ran around naked, cut off their hair, knocked out their front teeth in their grief, and had sex wildly with anyone and everyone: "The public mourning that took place on this occasion was of so extraordinary a nature, that, had I not been an [eyewitness], I could not have given credit to it."[26]

With each passing year, there were more kapu violations, which made some ali'i extremely uneasy. In 1812, the priest-prophet Kapihe predicted:

> E hui ana na moku;
> E hiolo ana na kapu akua;
> Ei ho mai ana ko ka lani;
> E piiana ko ka honua.
> (*The Island kingdoms will be united;*
> *The kapu of the gods will be overthrown;*
> *The chiefs who are the children of the gods will be brought low;*
> *The commoners fashioned of earth will rise.*)

Queen Kaʻahumanu of Hawaii

This was widely interpreted as a prophesy that Kamehameha would unite the Hawaiian Islands, taboos would be overturned, and ruling chiefs would lose their sacred status. In particular, Kapihe seemed to foresee the end of the ʻaikapu (*food restrictions*) and revolutionary change in the religious life of the Islands.[27]

By the 1810s, there were enough sailors, castaways, fugitives, and other haoles living in Honolulu, most of whom paid little attention to sanitation or hygiene, to swell the town's population from half a dozen huts to several hundred—and to exhaust the town's meager water supplies, pollute its streams, and spread pathogens. With few exceptions, historian Gavan Daws observed, early European and American residents were beachcombers or sojourners who had no intention of staying long. Merchants, who arrived next, were no better. They "took what they wanted from Honolulu and returned very little."[28]

Seeing the toll that alcohol was taking, Kamehameha urged his people to quit drinking. When the crew of the British ship, *Raccoon*, arrived in May 1814, they were dismayed to find no grog available, since Hawaiians were not distilling sugarcane to produce rum. By December 15, 1815, however, an epic brawl had broken out among more than 1,000 drunken Hawaiians and haoles.[29]

It was clear to Islanders that their gods could not protect them from haole sickness. Hawaiians died in droves from diseases that had little effect on Europeans. Throughout the Pacific, people began to question both the old ways and the old gods. In 1815, King Pōmare II of Tahiti, the ancestral homeland of Hawaiians, held a great feast in which he publicly embraced Christianity and gave wooden statues of gods to British missionaries to burn. On Moʻorea, near Tahiti in the Society Islands, priests and chiefs destroyed sacrificial altars and god images in a demonstration of their allegiance to Pōmare.[30]

It was also difficult to prevent haoles from infecting the kingdom with their imperial rivalries. Having repulsed an invasion by Napoleon Bonaparte's multinational *Grand Armée* of 685,000 soldiers, Czar Alexander I of Russia now was expanding its territory into Southwestern Asia and Eastern Europe and establishing outposts from Alaska to Northern California through its government-owned Russian-American Company. The company sent the Bavarian physician and adventurer, Georg Anton Schäffer, to the Islands in November 1815, ostensibly as a naturalist but with secret orders to recover cargo from a shipwreck on Kauaʻi and negotiate a trade treaty with Kamehameha. Since Spain had closed her colonies in California and Mexico to foreign commerce,

Chapter 3—Ka'ahumanu Breaks the Rules

the Islands could be extremely helpful to Russian colonists in Alaska and the Northwest. When the king and his Favorite Wife fell ill, the German doctor treated him for heart trouble and her for yellow fever, and both recovered. In gratitude, she escorted him to Honolulu on the British ship, *Beverly*, and the royal couple and her brother Kuakini rewarded him with the use of a generous tract of land on O'ahu, including much of Waikīkī and L'ēahi (*Diamond Head*) to the Ko'olau mountain ridge. Kamehameha built a heiau in honor of this European medical kahuna.[31]

Czar Alexander I by Henry Meyer, 1814 (National Portrait Gallery, Smithsonian Institution; purchased through generous contributions to the Victor Proetz Memorial Fund).

John Young, now a key advisor to the king, was deeply suspicious of Schäffer's motives. Schäffer, for his part, wrongly thought that Young was a deserter, when in fact, Capt. Simon Metcalfe had abandoned him to his fate in the Islands. He further spread the outrageous lie that Young was a cannibal and killed Hawaiian babies to give their flesh to Kamehameha for fishing bait, not the wisest way to slur an adversary. Schäffer's rivals spread rumors that he was a Russian spy, which was close to the truth. By May 1816, he had concluded, incredibly, that most kanakas opposed Kamehameha's rule and were eager for Russia to seize the archipelago.[32]

Ka'ahumanu warned him not to build a stone structure, fly any foreign flag from his land, or harvest sandalwood. Schäffer proceeded to do all three. Planning to build a Russian fort on each island, he built a substantial one out of lava rock at Waimea on the south shore of Kaua'i and another fort at Hanalei on the north, plus one at Honolulu on O'ahu, without Kamehameha's permission. At the last of these, the Russians took stones from nearby Pakaka Heiau at the mouth on the harbor, the most sacred temple for an order of O'ahu priests, who naturally were irate. Then he mounted cannons and flew the Russian flag. In 1816, Kamehameha dispatched a large fleet of ships and war canoes under the command of Kalanimōkū

***Kaahumanu, Woman of the Sandwich Islands* by J. J. Williams after Ludwig Choris' 1816 portrait.**

to seize the uncompleted fort in Honolulu; Schäffer and some 80 men fled to Kaua'i.[33]

For several years, Kaumuali'i had chafed at his vassal status and had nearly gone to war with Kamehameha in 1813 and 1814. Schäffer pledged an armed ship and the support of Russia, which had just defeated Napoleon and was rapidly expanding its empire. Kaumuali'i placed his kingdom under the protection of Czar Alexander I. This was a treaty that Schäffer had no authority to make. Preoccupied with problems elsewhere, Alexander had no interest in annexing any part of the archipelago. The king, for his part, may have thought he was agreeing only to retain Schäffer's services as an advisor, making him an honorary ali'i, not transferring his lands to the Russian Empire. Kaumuali'i flew the Russian flag over his capital, gave Russian names to various sites in his realm, and asked Russians to teach their language to his son. Then he announced that he would no longer make tribute payments to Kamehameha or honor his promise to bequeath his realm to Kamehameha

Chapter 3—Ka'ahumanu Breaks the Rules

or his successor. Schäffer built a lava-stone fort at Waimea and two earth-berm forts to protect Hanalei Bay. He also bought ships to bolster Kaumuali'i's small navy. The king built a heiau in honor of Schäffer, sacrificing two kauā to dedicate it. Finally, in a secret treaty signed on July 1, the king and the adventurer plotted to overthrow Kamehameha and divide his kingdom. Their relationship became strained over the following months, but Kaumuali'i nonetheless signed a trade agreement granting exclusive sandalwood trading rights to Russia. Schäffer soon claimed that Kaumuali'i was now a Russian citizen and that Russia had every right to seize the Kingdom of Hawaii from Kamehameha, whom he believed to be the tsar's declared enemy.[34]

The Russian-American Company initially approved his new colony in the Sandwich Islands, as did the Ministry of Foreign Affairs in St. Petersburg, Russia, but was unwilling to risk its limited resources on Schäffer's more ambitious scheme of fomenting civil war and seizing islands. The company decided that Schäffer's meddling in Hawaiian politics had made him a liability and sent word that it would not honor any agreement he made. Capt. Otto von Kotzebue, a German serving in the Russian navy who had visited the Islands with Lt.-Capt. Ivan Krusenstern as a naval cadet, was now leading the brig, *Rurik*, on a Russian exploring expedition circumnavigating the globe. Alexander dispatched Kotzebue to the Sandwich Islands with a message for Kamehameha: Russia disavowed Schäffer's schemes. When Kotzebue arrived in November 1816, Kaumuali'i and his people rose up against Schäffer and marched him under guard onto an American merchant ship that was bound for China. Schäffer made his way to St. Petersburg, where he tried unsuccessfully to persuade the Imperial Court to risk further adventures in

Kamehameha the Great by Ludwig Choris, 1816, presented to the Boston Athenæum by John Coffin Jones, Jr., in 1818 (courtesy Boston Athenæum).

the Islands. Schäffer, ever the rogue, then sought fame and fortune in Brazil.³⁵

Kotzebue was impressed with Kamehameha's rule, finding his government "distinguished for justice, the instruction of his subjects, and the introduction of useful arts." Kamehameha was so grateful with the czar's decision that he provisioned Kotzebue's ship free of charge. Then he sent a boat to Waimea to collect his annual tribute from Kaumuali'i, who now claimed to be happy to make the payment.³⁶

Kamehameha was appalled that foreigners saw his kingdom as fruit ripe for the plucking. Kalanimōkū and John Young finished the blockhouse guarding Honolulu Harbor that Schäffer had started. He installed his military advisor, Capt. George Beckley, a one-time English privateer (*a state-sponsored pirate*), as its first commander. Under Beckley, the fort prevented further Russian incursions in the town, which now was the political, religious, cultural, and trading center of his realm.³⁷

Kamehameha also set out to make his kingdom a major naval and diplomatic force in the Pacific, and by mid-century, it would become one of the greatest powers in Oceania. More than merely defend himself from foreign powers, he longed to meet the leaders of other nations as an equal, and this meant finding something he could trade. Selling food and water to sailors brought in a little money, but foreigners were willing to pay much more, he discovered, for Hawai'i's sweet-smelling

Vue du Port Hanarourou (View of Honolulu Port) by Ludwig Choris, 1816 (*Voyage Pittoresque du Autour du Monde*, Paris, 1822).

Chapter 3—Ka'ahumanu Breaks the Rules

Port de Hanarourou (Port of Honolulu), by Ludwig Choris, 1816 (*Voyage Pittoresque du Autour du Monde*, Paris, 1822).

sandalwood. The final end of the Napoleonic Wars (called the War of 1812 in the United States), which had raged around the globe, opened the way for booming trade with China.[38]

Kamehameha commissioned a flag for his realm, one that combined the United Kingdom's Union Jack with eight horizontal stripes representing the eight major islands, in the colors of Amelika: red, white, and blue. The Lonely One may have grown up knowing nothing of nations beyond his archipelago, but he quickly grasped the importance of pursuing close and amicable ties with the countries that posed the greatest threat to his realm. He also bought a sailing ship, renamed it the *Ka'ahumanu*, and sent it to China with a load of sandalwood to sell. Soon, Kamehameha added six trading vessels to his fleet, some of which he sent to California as well as China. He learned that he could make even more money by copying the practice of other nations and charging visiting ships port fees and harbor pilot charges. As foreign goods poured into his kingdom for repayment in sandalwood, ali'i forced the common people to spend more and more time collecting the fragrant timber—and maka'āinana had too little time to farm and were going hungry. Before the merchants arrived, the Islands were self-sufficient, and the common people lived fairly comfortable lives without backbreaking work. Within a few decades, most had been reduced to poverty. They toiled to repay the debts of the ali'i and became increasingly dependent on imported goods themselves. Repenting of his earlier excesses, elderly Kamehameha prohibited cutting any young trees, so that those that

Queen Kaʻahumanu of Hawaii

were harvested could be replaced—and so that his people could spend time growing crops.[39]

Kamehameha tried to slowly give some responsibilities to his designated heir. Kotzebue noted in 1816,

> [T]his prince, as successor to the throne, had already begun to exercise the rights of his father, which consist in the fulfilling of the most important taboos. Tamaahmaah [Kamehameha] has ordered this from political motives, that no revolution may arise after his death; for as soon as the son fulfills the most important taboo, he is sacred, is associated with the priests, and nobody dare dispute the throne with him.[40]

Throughout Oceania, contact with foreigners led women to challenge taboos, particularly food restrictions. In the Hawaiian Islands, these kapus grew more and more irritating each year, particularly for the common people and for women. Even though she was a queen, Kaʻahumanu could not enter Kamehameha's personal heiau: "[I]t would have been death for any woman to approach its sacred precincts." Women, Kotzebue noted, ate on board his ship, but only if their husbands were not present. Kaʻahumanu would not enter her husband's eating house when Kotzebue visited in 1816, but she invited the captain into her home and ate watermelon with him, a violation of a food kapu for which her servant could have been executed.

But the old rules were still enforced, at least occasionally, and sometimes brutally. Louis (Ludwig) Choris, a German-Russian painter on Kotzebue's expedition, recorded the visit to her home, but apparently never showed this particular canvas to her husband or any kahuna.[41]

Adelbert von Chamisso, a French botanist in Kotzebue's expedition, noted,

> The old inhibiting laws of the taboo still hold undiminished sway. We ourselves saw the corpse of a woman floating around our ship who had been killed because in a drunken state she had entered her husband's [eating house]. However, the women, when they know they are unobserved do not hesitate to transgress the many prohibitions with which they are burdened.[42]

Once, when a kapu confined all commoners to their homes for the day, an old man saw someone overturn a canoe in rough surf and appear to be drowning. The old man raced out of his home to save the apparently sinking man. Servants of the kahunas seized the old man in an instant, hauled him to the nearest heiau, and sacrificed him.[43]

Hawaiians grew increasingly perplexed—and annoyed—that they

Chapter 3—Ka'ahumanu Breaks the Rules

Queen Kaahumanu with Her Attendant lithograph by Jean-Pierre Norblin de la Gourdaine after a painting by Ludwig Choris, 1816 (*Voyage Pittoresque du Autour du Monde*, Paris, 1822).

were expected to obey the kapus, but that haoles were not. Nor were the restrictions enforced equitably. Russians who visited in October 1818 were surprised to be told by a chief that they could drink in his sleeping hut, but he would have to step outside the hut—since eating and sleeping areas were supposed to be separated—in order to drink to their health: "As foreigners we were not obliged to follow this rule...." The more important the chief, the king's Portuguese physician told the Russians, the less scrupulously they obeyed the kapus.[44] Both kanakas and haoles were eager to let the good times roll, as the saying goes.

Many ali'i had their own reasons to abolish other kapus, since they had grown fond of alcohol but could not drink it without polluting their religious ceremonies. In 1818, Kamehameha and the Council of Chiefs proclaimed stringent restrictions on liquor in an attempt to curb excessive drinking by his own subjects, as well as by fur traders, sandalwood merchants, and other haoles. He found it difficult to the get them to comply, however, as would every government that followed.[45]

Late in 1818, three men were sacrificed at Kalakekua on the Big Island: one for donning clothing that commoners were forbidden to wear, a second for eating kapu food, and the third for leaving a house

Queen Kaʻahumanu of Hawaii

Danse des femmes dans les Îles Sandwich (Women Dancing in the Sandwich Islands) by Ludwig Choris, 1816 (*Voyage Pittoresque du Autour du Monde*, Paris, 1822).

that was kapu and entering one that was not, thus "contaminating" the second home. The gods did not strike them dead, but their chiefs did. Archibald Campbell wrote, "He was immediately seized and carried back to the [temple], where his eyes were put out. After remaining two days in this state, he was strangled and his body exposed before the principal idol." Haoles often thought Hawaiians were worshiping statues of their gods, but Davida Malo describes kiʻis (*tikis*) as images that represented the akua, not idols in which gods dwelt.[46]

As people grew more dissatisfied with the restrictions on their lives, they also began to question the religious beliefs that upheld the kapus. Kamehameha, for his part, piously observed the old ways, and tried to prepare his son for future rule by giving Liholiho the duty of sacrificing three men who had violated kapus. Kamehameha found it difficult to hold the line against change himself. Passing by a group of women who were praying as they prepared to eat forbidden bananas, and hearing them invoke blessings on their king, he spared their lives—but warned them not to try this again.[47]

Many aliʻi, particularly the women, now recognized that observing the kapus was failing to protect them from foreign disease. Kanakas

Chapter 3—Ka'ahumanu Breaks the Rules

Danse des hommes dans les Îles Sandwich (Men Dancing in the Sandwich Islands) by Ludwig Choris, 1816 (*Voyage Pittoresque du Autour du Monde*, Paris, 1822).

sometimes destroyed household gods that failed to produce success and war gods that did not deliver victory. Some, including Ka'ahumanu, now believed that all of the akua had failed them or even betrayed them. Others wondered if they, like so many people, had fallen to some haole sickness.[48]

By 1818, foreign ships were entering Honolulu Harbor at the rate of one per week. Kanakas remembered their ancestral ties with Tahiti and the Society Islands, which they celebrated in chants and poetry, prayers and songs, history and legends. Now, foreign sailing ships gave Hawaiians a chance to connect with their distant relatives—a thrilling experience for people cut off from one another for so long. In 1818, a Tahitian named Toketa who had converted to Christianity came to the Islands and lived in Kuakini's household in Kailua-Kona. Then, the news reached the Islands that King Pōmare II had overthrown the taboos in Tahiti. Disillusioned with his war god, Pōmare had been baptized by Christian missionaries from England. Some Hawaiians hoped that Liholiho would marry a princess from the now-Christian ruling family of the Society Islands. Overturning the kapus in his own realm might be a necessary step toward uniting the two dynasties and their long-separated peoples.[49]

Kamehameha upheld the kapus throughout his lifetime but urged his son to abandon them when he took the throne. In preparation for this transition, the king began turning over the day-to-day administration of his kingdom to Kaʻahumanu and Kalanimōkū. Having already lived at least 60 years—twice the life expectancy of Americans born in the middle of the 18th century—he had good reason to believe that his son would reign soon.[50]

It was not at all certain, however, that the son would be able to hold together his father's realm. Kamehameha's achievement in centralizing authority under a single, absolute monarch was itself a break with Hawaiian tradition. The chiefs most closely allied with him feared that when he died, rival, traditional aliʻi would revolt against his heir.[51]

Camille de Roquefeuil, who visited the Islands in January 1819 and met with the king three times, recalled,

> [T]he country is prepared for revolution when Kamehameha dies, and his son Liholiho, quite different from his father, does not appear to have inherited more than a little of his father's authority and abilities. People generally think he is not destined to rule over the islands that his father had conquered. They predicted that local animosities and ancient family ambitions would resurface after his death.

Roquefeuil thought Kaʻahumanu might prove to be the most formidable threat to Liholiho's rule and that the kapu system might be abolished soon, just as it had been in the Society Islands.[52]

In May 1819, as Kamehameha neared his end, his priests got an altar ready at Kailua-Kona on the Big Island to sacrifice pigs to the god, Kū, as was customary when a great chief was gravely ill. They also prepared to offer human sacrifice, as also was customary when a king died. Some children, in fact, were designated from birth to be killed when a particular noble died. Fearful that the priests would want even more victims, residents of Kona fled for their lives.[53]

Kamehameha ordered, however, that no one be killed, neither to prevent his death nor to mourn it. "The men are kapu for the king," he insisted. Weeping, wailing, and chopping off their hair were fine; human sacrifice was not.[54]

Throughout his life, Kamehameha had both worshiped the old gods and also undermined the traditional authority of higher ranking

Chapter 3—Ka'ahumanu Breaks the Rules

chiefs, replacing those of more illustrious birth with people like himself who showed leadership ability and the capacity to innovate. He remained faithful to the gods himself to the very end, but the Lonely One, his Favorite Wife, and his Sacred Wife all knew the old ways had to change.

Chapter 4

Burning the Temples

As her husband neared his end, Ka'ahumanu secretly prepared for his death. On May 2, even though she was sick herself, she rounded up all the muskets that belonged to the chiefs and locked them up in the royal arsenal. She also arranged to be alone with Kamehameha as he drew his final breath—and thus became the only witness to his final instructions. When he died, "The air rang with her wailing" and she cried her lament:

> Auwe! Auwe! Great Kamehameha is dead.
> Dead is the friend of my heart in storm and in stillness.[1]

Priests asked Liholiho how soon he would like to offer the human sacrifice that traditionally followed the death of a ruler. If he did it immediately, one victim would suffice; if he waited, as many as 15 might have to be slaughtered. He curtly replied, "No." Kamehameha did not want anyone to be killed to prolong his life, and his son would not begin his own reign by shedding blood.[2]

In grief, people knocked out teeth and lobbed off hunks of hair. Ka'ahumanu inflicted small cuts on herself to show that a part of her died with Kamehameha and tattooed the date of his death on her arm. She and other female ali'i also took part in another traditional mourning ritual. They had sexual intercourse widely and wildly for days. Higher ranking chiefs practiced 'ai noa (*free eating*) with men and women together. As people let their passions run wild, some assaulted enemies, looted homes, and started fires. During this frenzy of mourning, ali'i had little authority, and priests could not keep women out of the temples. It even was common for a few heiaus to be destroyed. Ke'eaumoku 'Opio, "crazy with rum" as he was mourning the death of Kamehameha, tore down the white kapa flags marking the area where priests were praying to purify the region. Some kahunas responded by blaming Ka'ahumanu for Kamehameha's death.[3]

Don Francisco de Paula Marín, the royal physician, who was

Chapter 4—Burning the Temples

Andalusian or Spanish and possibly of Moorish ancestry, wrote in his journal on May 8,

> This day the king ... died at 3 in the morning, aged 60 years and 6 months. Today they were weeping all day and cutting hair in different figures and the women ate pork and cocoa nuts.

The next day, he noted,

> This day all the women and men, even the royal family, went to commit fornication one with another.[4]

It was the new ruler's job to impose the old taboos again, to re-establish order, but the passing of the Lonely One set the stage for revolutionary change. Keōpūolani, the Wahine Kapu, took the first decisive action. The day after her husband's death, she ate coconuts, which women were forbidden to eat, and dined with men. "He who guarded the god is dead," she proclaimed, "and it is right that we should eat together freely."[5]

The entire Kona district of the Big Island was thought to be spiritually polluted by Kamehameha's death, so kahunas spirited Liholiho away, lest he be defiled, as they performed lengthy rituals to purify the area. Along with his five wives, courtiers, and priests, he went to Kawaihae, 30 miles away. This left Ka'ahumanu in charge while kahunas hid the bones of her husband in a secret cave. With Liholiho away, the Council of Chiefs decided that Ka'ahumanu should have the honor of announcing the king's last words for his son—or at least what she claimed Kamehameha's message had been. After Liholiho had been absent for 10 days, a messenger informed him that the defiled territory had been ritually cleansed and was ready to receive its new ruler. Taking his favorite wife, his half sister Kamāmalu, Liholiho set out for Kailua-Kona.[6]

Young Liholiho must have been stunned by the sight that greeted him when he returned to Kailua. Ka'ahumanu normally preferred to wear a feather lei (*garland*), but today she asserted her authority by boldly donning her Cloak of Power, a long feather cape that only an ali'i warrior was entitled to wear, reminding everyone that she was precisely that. She also carried a spear, a weapon similarly reserved for noble warriors, reminding him and other ali'i that she was both a warrior and a chief. Surrounded by a circle of ali'i, she proclaimed that Liholiho had become an akua, but that she would rule with this god. She said her husband had decreed on his deathbed that they should share power. Kamehameha had made her guardian of the kingdom, she insisted, just as she had been Liholiho's kahu, and had named her Kuhina Nui (*co-ruler*): "I tell you what your father directed me to do. Here are the ali'i, here are your father's men and here is your land. But you and I will rule the land together." She would be not the power behind the throne, but rather, the power beside the throne.⁷

As if this was not enough to send the young man's head spinning, she then told Liholiho that rather than reinstitute kapus, as a new monarch was expected to do, he should abolish them. His father had seized a kingdom on the Big Island by killing the heir to the throne. Ka'ahumanu took power without shedding a drop of blood, using Kamehameha's heir to control other chiefs and keep his realm intact. Kekuaokalani, whom his uncle Kamehameha had entrusted with the war god, Kū—an akua whose worship had declined in recent decades of peace—sulked but did not challenge her. Nor did anyone else. Could she have made up this deathbed transfer of power? If so, how did she get away with it?

The male ali'i might not have liked this elevation of a woman, but there was widespread respect for her lineage and leadership—even if it did not equal Liholiho's ancestry. Perhaps Ka'ahumanu purchased their loyalty by promising to share the profits from the sandalwood trade with them. One of her first official acts was to abolish the royal monopoly on harvesting these trees, which distributed wealth more widely but also led to excessive logging that destroyed delicate ecosystems.⁸

Perhaps some suspected Kamehameha really wanted her to rule. Though kapus restricted the lives of women, female ali'i had exercised authority for centuries, including two ancestors of Kamehameha who had ruled the Big Island. Each male akua has an equally powerful female counterpart, and a male high chief often had a female high chiefess. Women sometimes ruled alone, too. As early as 1375, a woman ruled O'ahu with her husband but passed sole rule to her daughter, a warrior who was succeeded by her own daughter. Another four women ruled the island during the 17th and 18th centuries, when the O'ahu Kingdom was at the peak of its power. And during Ka'ahumanu's childhood, Kamakahelei had ruled Kaua'i and Ni'ihau.⁹

Without Ka'ahumanu as co-ruler, in fact, Kamehameha's dynasty might have ended with his death. Liholiho had been instructed in the strict observance of religious ritual but had little experience with governing. Succession was not automatically hereditary among Hawaiians. Chiefs had to earn the right to rule, and Liholiho had done little to earn anyone's trust. Widely considered unfit to lead, he was a notorious drunkard. Marín noted for five days in a row that he was inebriated. One day, his physician was surprised to find, "The King is in his senses."¹⁰

Kuhina Nui is sometimes translated as "premier" or "prime minister"

Chapter 4—Burning the Temples

but there was no equivalent of this position in either American or European government. She, for example, not Liholiho, appointed her brother Kuakini as governor of the Big Island, a position he held for a quarter of a century. As Ralph Kuykendall observed, "prime minister" describes well the role that Kalanimōkū played during the reigns of Kamehameha, Liholiho, Ka'ahumanu, and Kauikeaouli. Kuhina Nui was something else again:

> Technically and ceremonially, the king was the highest officer in the state; in the routine administration of the government, the kuhina-nui was ordinarily more active than the king.[11]

When Capt. Louis de Freycinet brought the French corvette, *Uranie*, to the Islands in August 1819, Ka'ahumanu skillfully handled the delicate question of how to properly receive a French scientific expedition without angering their rivals, the British. In doing so, she impressed the captain with her understanding of the rivalry between distant European powers. He found her to be the most attractive woman in the royal court.[12]

Jacques Arago, the artist on the *Uranie*, initially thought she was "prodigiously fat," but sympathized with the way she and others were constrained by kapus:

> The condition of the women here is truly wretched.... Next to taro, the food which the Sandwich Islanders most prefer are bananas, hogs, and cocoa-nuts. Yet a woman convicted of having only once eaten of these is instantly put to death.

Arago heard much about how dearly the former monarch had loved her, in contrast with the way many other men treated their wives:

> The attachment of Tammeamah for his favorite Queen is a subject of great praise; how is it that his example has not found a single imitator?[13]

If the kapus were reimposed after a mourning period, her life would be severely constrained, even as co-ruler. Overturning them would free women from onerous restrictions, free the common people, and further empower her as Kuhina Nui. Two days after Liholiho returned to Kona, Ka'ahumanu presided at his consecration, assuming a role normally performed by the High Priest. If the king proved unworthy, she quoted her late husband as saying, she would rule alone. Then she told the young king, "Let us henceforth disregard the restraints of kapu."[14]

Ka'ahumanu shrewdly decided to attack the 'ai kapu (*eating taboos*) first, since these rules were deeply resented by many people, and they were not important to the kahunas who upheld traditional worship.[15] She invited Liholiho to her home and asked him to end the 'ai kapu. Then she ate a banana right in front of him. Something amazing happened: absolutely nothing. She did not get sick. She did not fall down dead. No gods swooped down to punish her. Stunned and frightened, Liholiho turned and walked away without saying a word.

Then Keōpūolani invited him to sit and eat with her—which was kapu, of course. Liholiho shook his head, horrified, and angrily refused. Afraid he might punish Ka'ahumanu, the Queen Mother called young Crown Prince Kauikeauoli to her and ate with him. Shocked, Liholiho fled in fear.

Word of what the two women had done swept across the Islands. One of his cousins quickly urged the new king to reimpose the old ways, which could have meant killing his mother, his brother, and his kahu. Another cousin, Kekuaokalani, demanded that Liholiho punish any wahine who defied the eating kapu. To demonstrate his loyalty to the ancient gods, Liholiho decided to dedicate a new temple, even though he was too drunk to perform the religious rituals at all well. Then he announced that he was reinstituting the taboos that had been suspended during his nation's time of mourning—but hesitated to actually impose them. Because high-born Liholiho observed a set of religious commands stricter than those of his father, restoring the kapus would burden his people even more heavily. The young king himself doubted that it was wise to do so, but many ali'i whom his father had defeated were itching for any excuse to rebel, no matter which decision he made.[16]

Across Hawai'i, though, women began to eat forbidden foods, first secretly and then openly, as they called for 'ai noa (*free eating*). In defiance of Liholiho's edict, Ka'ahumanu proclaimed that in Kailua, at least, women were free to eat whatever they wanted, with anyone they wished. Those who clung to the old ways were free to do so, she said, but not to impose them on others. If the king wanted to observe the old customs, "...it is well and we will not molest you," she promised. "But as for me and my people, we intend to be free from the kapus." Alarmed, priests tried to impose even more stringent restrictions and demanded unquestioning loyalty to the akua—and the kahunas. Ka'ahumanu deftly pointed out their arrogance in doing so, and resentment of both the kapus and the priests grew quickly.[17]

As the most sacred woman in the realm, Keōpūolani had the status and spiritual power to challenge the kapus. She feared her son's life would be in danger if he continued to honor the old ways, but abolishing

Chapter 4—Burning the Temples

the old taboos carried its own risks both for him and for the new Kuhina Nui.[18] Free eating, 'ai noa, might prove popular, but overturning the old ways could just as easily alarm people, and traditionalists such as Kekuaokalani might rebel. Nor was it certain that the monarchy could survive without either Kamehameha or the kapus. For months, Liholiho remained undecided as to which way he should go—and often drunk.

Hewahewa, Liholiho's personal priest, urged the young king to support his mother and his guardian. The Kahuna Nui (*High Priest*) confessed that he no longer believed in the kapus and the akua himself and offered shocking advice: "Let the old gods die."[19]

Finally, at the beginning of November 1819, a huge feast was organized in Kailua-Kona to celebrate the Makahiki season and welcome Liholiho as the new king. In a hale that measured the size of 100 feet by 30 feet, places were set for men on one side and women on the other. As usual, the best food was placed before the men. As people gathered, Keōpūolani publicly ate a banana and drank coconut milk, both of which were kapu. The young king faced a fateful choice: abolish the 'ai kapu, or execute his mother, his brother, and his kahu. Ka'ahumanu whispered to the new king, "If you have the courage of your father, this will be a great day for Hawai'i."[20]

For a few minutes, Liholiho sat perfectly still, as if unsure what to do. Finally, as the feast began, he got up silently from the men's table, walked several times around the crowd, and then sat down at the women's table, next to his mother. The crowd gasped. "The king must be drunk!" some whispered.

"Or else he's crazy!" someone suggested.

"No matter," others said, "the gods will strike him down."

Next, Liholiho ate some of the women's food and ordered kapu delicacies to be brought to the women. Seeing that he was still alive, some men got up and ate with their wives and daughters and mothers and sisters for the first time in their lives.

Some people were deeply disturbed by this shattering of the rules. A young servant named Ioane (*John*) Papa 'Ī'ī started crying. He begged the king to stop this 'āi noa before the gods became angry. This plea itself, ironically, went against the old rules. To speak this way to a ruler, who was considered a god, was punishable by death. The boy feared change, but his actions showed how dramatically things already had changed.[21]

Others greeted Liholiho's shocking actions with joy. They began to whisper, "The kapu is broken! 'Āi noa!" Then they said out loud,

"The kapu is broken! 'Ai noa!" They shouted, "The kapu is broken! 'Ai noa!"[22]

Liholiho, relieved that the gods had not struck him down, sang and danced with the performers. Celebrations erupted all over the Big Island. Pork, previously kapu for women, was sent from the feast across the island with instructions that men and women should share it.[23] Boys and girls ate freely together for the first time. Girls and women ate wonderful things they had never tasted before. They spoke with people whom they had never talked with before. People went places they had never gone before.

Many people, surprised to find themselves still alive, concluded the priests had been lying. The kahuna who had strangled Kapi'olani's guardian admitted that what he taught about the kapus was false: "Those were dark days, though we priests knew better all the time. It was power we sought over the minds of the people to influence and control them."[24]

After the feast, Hewahewa told the new king, "We have made a good beginning, but the gods and *heiaus* cannot survive the death of the kapu."

"Then let them perish with it!" Liholiho replied.[25]

He and Ka'ahumanu sent swift messengers throughout the realm ordering their subjects to overturn taboos and temples, destroying the religion of the Islands. On Kaua'i, Kaumuali'i proclaimed an end to kapus and ritual sacrifice in his realm, too. Hewahewa destroyed 100 wooden images of akua in a nearby heiau (*temple*) himself, put the torch to his own temple, and led Hawaiians in burning other heiaus. He confessed,

> I knew the wooden images of deities, carved by our own hands, could not supply our wants, but [we] worshipped them because it was the custom of our fathers. My thought has always been that there is only one great God, dwelling in the heavens.

Resigning as High Priest, Hewahewa announced that he would await the coming of a "new and greater God."[26]

Keōpūolani, for her part, thought that burning images of akua was wrong. "What evil have our gods done to us that they should be burned?" she asked.[27]

Most ali'i opposed the permanent abolition of the eating kapus, at least initially, fearing that defiance of the gods would weaken their own authority. Most of the common people, on the other hand, embraced 'ai noa, though many agreed that torching temples was going too far.[28]

The abolition of kapus was liberating, particularly for women and

Chapter 4—Burning the Temples

the common people, but also frightening. Breaking the kapus and allowing the destruction of the temples revealed the young king's courage, but also undermined his power. In the Society Islands, Pōmare II had managed to concentrate greater power in his own hands by abolishing the taboo system and replacing the old religion with Christianity, but Liholiho imposed no new religious order. He eliminated the power of the priests but did not assign himself any new position of religious leadership.

Kekuaokalani, who continued to observe traditional religious rites at Kealakekua, was now the head of the priesthood, as well as guardian of war god Kū's statue. He gathered warriors and set out to overthrow his cousin Liholiho and restore the old religion. Kekuaokalani raised his army even though this was the season of Makahiki, when warfare had been kapu.[29] The defender of that old-time religion had lost confidence in some of the ancient taboos himself.

Liholiho and Kaʻahumanu wanted to avoid bloodshed, but also needed to demonstrate their authority while there was still euphoria over ʻai noa. They sent emissaries to Kekuaokalani, offering him freedom to observe kapus if he would grant others the right to not do so.[30] Kekuaokalani refused. Keōpūolani, the Wahine Kapu, the highest ranking and most sacred woman in the realm according to the traditional religion, insisted on going to Kekuaokalani, but the traditionalists would not listen to her, either, even though the old ways obligated them to do so. When she discovered that Kekuaokalani was planning to kill her—and it would have been decidedly contrary to tradition to kill the Wahine Kapu—her son Liholiho decided the rebellion had to be crushed at once.

At the end of December, Kalanimōkū led warriors armed with haole rifles and cannon, who quickly drove the rebels toward the shore. There, they found a fleet of double canoes waiting to fire at them, one with a swivel-mounted cannon, commanded by Kaʻahumanu and her sister Kalākua, which terrified the rebels. Both Kekuaokalani and his wife Manono died in the battle. Without a quick victory, Liholiho and Kaʻahumanu might have lost a protracted war. There were other, minor uprisings in Hamakua and Waimea on the Big Island, but these were easily quelled after Kekuaokalani was defeated.[31]

Everyone expected Liholiho to slaughter the captured rebels, perhaps sacrificing them ritually on an altar. For centuries, aliʻi had claimed that such a ritual was needed to appease the gods. Instead, the new king and Kuhina Nui demonstrated once more that they were no longer afraid of offending the akua. Showing a degree of mercy never seen

Queen Kaʻahumanu of Hawaii

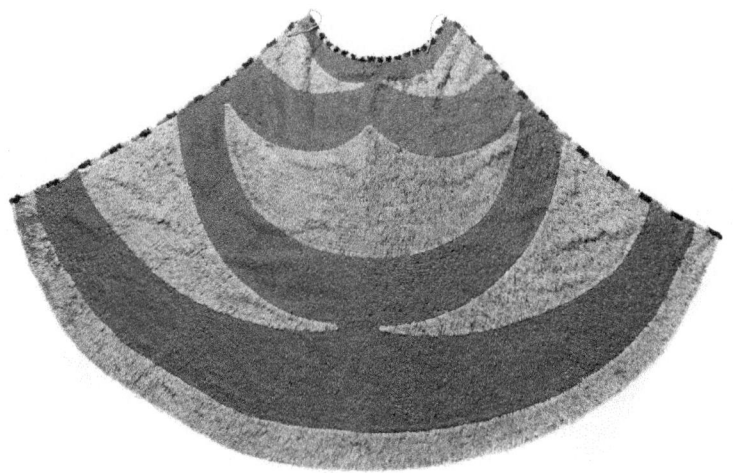

Kekuaokalani's Feather Cloak, said to have been taken by Liholiho and Kaʻahumanu from defeated rebels in 1819 (photograph by Donald E. Hurlbert, E76180, Department of Anthropology, National Museum of Natural History, Smithsonian Institution).

before, Kaʻahumanu exercised her power of puʻuhonua (*pardon*), sparing the lives of captured rebel leaders, and Liholiho then granted amnesty to all who had taken part in the rebellion.[32]

Only after the defeat of these rebels did the wholesale destruction of heiaus begin. Most images of the akua were tossed in the sea or burned, though a few were hidden and preserved. Most temples were destroyed, but some people continued to worship the old gods, particularly their regional or household deities, such as the volcano goddess, Pele, on the Big Island. Devotion to the old deities gradually was forced underground, though, and steadily declined.[33]

This new freedom was exhilarating, but also deeply frightening. The entire social order was shaken by the abolition of the kapus and the destruction of temples. Without prohibitions and rituals, an entire belief system collapsed overnight. For the first time in human history, an entire nation had no organized religion whatsoever. Troubled by the rapid change he had unleashed, the young king did another thing that helped prevent the disintegration of his realm. He traveled among his people, listening to their confusion about how they should live, now that akua, kapus, and kahunas no longer controlled their lives.[34]

Chapter 5

The Coming of a New God

Meanwhile in Amelika, a Hawaiian orphan named 'Ōpūkaha'ia had arrived in New Haven, Connecticut. As a child, he had seen his parents slaughtered in fighting between rival chiefs on the Big Island. His uncle was a kahuna who trained the boy to become a priest. Eager to see the world, though, in 1808, he joined the crew of the Yankee trading ship, *Triumph*. He visited China and the Seal Islands off the coast of North America, eventually made his way to New York, and then ended up in Connecticut. What most astounded him about life in Amelika was that women ate at the same table with men—and the gods did not harm them. In New Haven, some students at Yale befriended 'Ōpūkaha'ia. Called "Obookiah" by Americans, he became the first Hawaiian convert to Christianity, taking the name Henry in 1815 when he was baptized.[1]

Henry 'Ōpūkaha'ia pleaded with his new friends to send someone to his homeland to teach the religion he had just embraced. His fervent pleas eventually reached the American Board of Commissioners for Foreign Missions (ABCFM), a new, small, interdenominational organization made up primarily of Congregationalists and Presbyterians. Founded in 1810, it was the first American mission organization. Earlier, the followers of John Calvin had taught that God planned the salvation or damnation of each person. He believed that whether you ended up in heaven or hell was "predestined." The American Board represented a new variety of Calvinists: liberal evangelicals who believed each person had free will, the ability to make moral choices that shaped his or her life. Unlike some other Euro-Americans, they recognized the moral and spiritual agency of Native Americans, Pacific Islanders, Asians, Africans, and other "heathens" whom they hoped to convert to Christianity, preferably a Protestant form of Christianity. Some early visitors, such as the naval surgeon David Samwell, questioned whether the supposedly civilized Europeans were superior to Hawaiians, but the

American Board and its supporters believed it was their duty to "civilize heathens"—at a time when most Americans were enslaved or had been indentured servants. They enjoyed freedom of worship in America—the reason their ancestors had emigrated from England in the 17th century—but were happy to use the power of local rulers to eradicate polytheism (which they called paganism) in other lands.[2]

In the first 10 years of its existence, the American Board had already sent missionaries to India and Sri Lanka and Cherokees in Tennessee. ʻŌpūkahaʻia begged them to send him home with others who could help him teach his people his newfound faith. He and six other Islanders were among the first students at the Foreign Mission School in Cornwall, Connecticut, an experiment in training indigenous people as evangelists. The purpose of the school, its constitution declared, was to educate "heathen youths" to become "missionaries, physicians, surgeons, schoolmasters or interpreters, and to communicate to the heathen nations such knowledge in agriculture and the arts, as may prove the means of promoting Christianity and civilization." The Hawaiians were also effective fundraisers for the school, touring the Northeast seeking donations to support it.[3]

ʻŌpūkahaʻia was a particularly effective advocate for the missionary project. Many Euro-Americans thought the indigenous people of North America, Oceania, Africa, and elsewhere were "too ignorant to be taught." The Rev. Nathan Perkins, who accompanied ʻŌpūkahaʻia on fundraising visits to churches across Massachusetts, angrily denounced the bigotry of his fellow countrymen. Having enslaved and exploited people of color and deprived them of any opportunity for education, they "hastened to the conclusion that all the heathen are a race of idiots." Henry ʻŌpūkahaʻia was a living refutation of such racism.[4]

Like their Puritan ancestors, these evangelicals tended to be a bit dour, and they were deeply pious, talking incessantly about their faith whenever they were not busy praying to the Almighty. They scrupulously observed the Sabbath, which for them was Sunday rather than the Jewish Shabbat of Friday nightfall to Saturday nightfall. Like many liberal evangelicals, they also were socially and politically progressive and might even be fairly characterized as radical reformers. Unlike some earlier Calvinists who preached the "utter depravity" all human beings, they saw some goodness in all people. They saw individual conversion was necessary but not sufficient—Christians must work to bring God's rule to fruition on earth. They supported Islander self-rule, at least as long as local authorities did not interfere with their preaching.

Chapter 5—The Coming of a New God

They were committed to democracy and the abolition of slavery—and would be largely responsible for ending the slave trade and this "peculiar institution" in both the United States and British Empire. In a time of brutal jails, asylums, and workplaces, they urged humane treatment of workers, prisoners, and the mentally ill. A week before they reached the Hawaiian Islands, the members of the Pioneer Company agreed that they would hold everything they owned in common, practicing a sort of socialism or communitarianism. Before they left New England, Sybil Bingham donated all of her savings to the American Board, just as Daniel and Jerusha Chamberlain did with the proceeds from selling their farm. The missionaries also agreed they would decide their assignments to each mission station by vote, rather than choosing individually where they would live and work.[5]

To assist a future Sandwich Islands Mission, ʻŌpūkahaʻia had begun writing a Hawaiian spelling book, a grammar book, and a dictionary. He also had started translating the book of Genesis into Hawaiian, using the Hebrew text (which he already had learned to read) rather than English, since he found it to be more like his native language than English was. A friend of his in Connecticut recalled:

> His own fearlessness and zeal on this subject he exhibited about the same time to an aged minister, who asked him why he wished to return. He replied, "To preach the Gospel to my countrymen." He was asked what he would say to them about their wood gods. "Nothing." "But," said the clergyman, "suppose your countrymen should tell you that preaching Jesus Christ was blaspheming their gods, and should put you to death?" To this he replied with great emphasis, "If that be the will of God, I am ready, I am ready."

Henry ʻŌpūkahaʻia died of typhus before he could sail home, but the story of his conversion and death, which was published in 1818, strengthened the determination of the Commissioners to take Christianity to the Islands. It would be the first attempt by the American Board to evangelize the Pacific.[6]

On October 23, 1819, seven couples of the "First Company" (or "Pioneer Company") sailed out of Boston Harbor in the little brig, *Thaddeus*, 200 years after their Pilgrim ancestors set sail for the New World on a much larger ship, the *Mayflower*. They sailed for 157 days and 18,000 miles around Cape Horn, an arduous journey that included a missionary falling overboard and a horrifying encounter with a Portuguese slave ship. On March 23, 1820, the First Company signed a covenant, inspired by the Mayflower Compact: Everything they owned would be held in common. No one would undertake any business or engage in any gainful employment without the approval of the others, "and the profits in all cases shall be placed at the disposal of the mission." They would share, as Karl Marx later put it, "from each according to their ability, to each according to their need." Well into the 1830s, many missionaries strenuously opposed being paid individual salaries, saying that this would violate their principles. All should share alike, many missionaries believed.[7]

On board the *Thaddeus*, they greeted the new year by singing about the hoped-for day when they could say, "Owhyhee's Idols Are No More," adapting the words from a celebration of Pōmare's apostasy in Tahiti. After more than five months at sea, they finally spotted the peaks of Mauna Loa and Mauna Kea. Soon thereafter, the *Thaddeus* anchored at Kawaihae on the Big Island, bringing home four Hawaiian youths who sailed to Amelika and converted to Christianity. Thomas Hopu and John Honoli'i were particularly important in the early Sandwich Islands Mission, first as translators and later as teachers and evangelists. One of four young men, "Prince George" Humehume, was the son of Kaumuali'i, the king of Kaua'i.

Earlier, the American Board had delayed Humehume's return to Kaua'i, hoping to complete his training and conversion, but he never fully committed himself to Christianity. Perhaps, having traveled to Africa and Asia as a sailor and met faithful Buddhists, Hindus, and Muslims, it was more difficult for him to accept the doctrine of his teachers, because he knew that the akua and Christianity were not the only options. As the First Company prepared for to sail, the Board judged the three other kānaka maoli "far advanced in knowledge, and other qualifications." Humehume was intelligent—he impressed people in Cornwall with his ability to predict lunar eclipses—but spent money foolishly, was often irritable, and occasionally became drunk. They decided to send George home only because he was "impatient of delay."[8]

Having grown up far from home, Humehume could no longer speak or understand Hawaiian. He relearned his native language and culture from other youths at the Foreign Mission School. They treated him as a future paramount chief—and a god—while his teachers sought to humble him, and nearly expelled him. Then Humehume learned that his father had chosen his higher born half brother Keali'iohonui as heir. He would never become ali'i nui or akua. His conversations with the crew on the *Thaddeus* who were Deists—a philosophy that challenged much Christian doctrine in the 18th century—indicate that he increasingly questioned Calvinism.[9]

Chapter 5—The Coming of a New God

Humehume, Hopu, Kanui, and Honoliʻi were welcomed home and joyfully reunited with friends and relatives whom they had not seen in years. Aliʻi quickly appropriated the skills and knowledge that they had acquired abroad, using them as interpreters and teachers. This diverted them from the work of the Mission, but the American Board did not consider any of the kānaka maoli who returned on the *Thaddeus* to be a full member of the Pioneer Company anyway. The Rev. Herman Daggett, principal of the Foreign Mission School, referred to them as "helpers" or "the youths who are to accompany the mission" even though they were older than many "members" of the First Company. The rules also were different for them. The American Board expected missionaries to marry before leaving Boston, Massachusetts, for example, but insisted the Hawaiians remain single—and tried to keep dark-skinned students at the Foreign Mission School away from the young ladies in town. En route to the Islands, they were allotted less room on the crowded *Thaddeus*. Humehume was not even part of the First Company. He was, as Anne Spoehr put it, "a prince, a pauper, and a casualty of cultural change." The American Board had high hopes for the other three Hawaiians on the *Thaddeus* but underestimated how difficult it would be for them either to translate a language they had nearly forgotten or to return to a homeland that had changed almost beyond recognition while they were gone. Once home, Humehume proved to be a constant problem for his family, the Mission, Liholiho, and Kaʻahumanu.[10]

Having been at sea since October, the First Company had received no reports of the tumultuous changes in the Islands. When they landed on the Big Island, they were greeted with news they could hardly believe, an event "without parallel in the history of the world."[11] The kapus had been abolished and heiaus destroyed. They even received a warm welcome from Hewahewa, the last Kahuna Nui in the kingdom, who greeted Hiram Bingham as a brother priest, not an adversary. It was Divine providence, the Calvinists were certain, that they had reached the archipelago before any other religion could fill the vacuum created by the widespread loss of faith in the akua.[12]

Earlier Europeans and American visitors who claimed to be Christians often were poor representatives of their faith. Georg Anton Schäffer had tried to interest Kaumualiʻi in Christianity and to persuade him to abolish human sacrifice, but he had little success on either score. The previous November, a Catholic chaplain on the French warship, *L'Uranie*, had baptized Kalanimōkū and his brother Boki, the governor of Oʻahu. Kaʻahumanu witnessed the baptism, but it was not clear what either man understood about Christianity; they may have thought they were being invested with some special rank or office. Adele Marie Lemon, C.S.J., conceded, "Subsequent events prove that neither chief was too well instructed in the Catholic faith." French artist Jacques Arago quipped, that Kalanimōkū, "furnished with his passport to paradise, he went home to his seven wives, and to sacrifice to his idols."[13]

Ka'ahumanu was away on a fishing trip, so her brother and sister, Kalanimōkū and Kalākua, boarded the *Thaddeus* to greet the newcomers while the First Company waited for permission to land. A few missionaries then were permitted ashore to call on Keōpūolani. Thomas Hopu acted as translator, explaining as best he could the reason for their arrival and the nature of their faith, but the chiefs told one another, "This traveler is telling tall tales."[14]

Kalanimōkū and Kalākua brought gifts of fruit, poi, meat, and cheese to the missionaries, who gratefully received these gifts after five months of salted sea rations. Kalākua also brought some cloth and asked the mission women to make her a gown like theirs before they met with Liholiho. As Hiram Bingham reported:

> Kalakua, a widow of Kamehameha, having little sympathy with the Evangelical prophet, and shrewdly aiming to see what the white women could do for her temporal benefit, asked them to make a gown for her in fashion like their own. Putting her off till the Sabbath was over, apprising her that unnecessary labor was on that day prohibited to all by the great Jehovah whom we worshipped, they cheerfully plied scissors and needle the next day, and soon fitted out the rude giantess with a white cambric dress. Thus, feeble, voyage-worn, having been long without fresh provisions, and withering under a tropical sun as they crossed the equatorial regions the second time, they began before we cast anchor, to secure favor by kindness and demonstration of their ability and readiness to make themselves useful.[15]

Their hosts gave them many opportunities to make themselves useful. Kalākua's demands were soon followed by those of Ka'ahumanu, who sent fresh fish, coconuts, sweet potatoes, bananas, sugar cane, and bread fruit. Kalākua had every right to require this sort of work from any of her subjects, and Hawaiian etiquette required guests to reciprocate in some way for the gifts they received. The missionaries, particularly the men, were taken aback by these demands, tending to see the gifts they received not as expressions of kindness or compassion for bedraggled haoles, but rather as gratitude for the arrival of never-invited guests. Elisha Loomis thought, a bit presumptuously, that Ka'ahumanu's gifts conveyed "much satisfaction that we have come to bring them good things."[16]

Chapter 5—The Coming of a New God

The women of the First Company, however, quickly grasped that exchanges of labor for food could open doors to them to build relationships. While waiting on the *Thaddeus* for permission to land, Nancy Ruggles and Lucy Thurston organized the nation's first sewing circle, showing Hawaiian women how to make Western-style clothing. Shocked by the way Kalākua, Ka'ahumanu, and other wahines casually disrobed while paying social calls, they were glad to be able to encourage Hawaiians to cover more of their bodies.[17]

The women of the First Company quickly adapted their attire to the warm, humid climate of the Islands, creating the style that became popular in America and Europe as the "Mother Hubbard." This was a long, loose-fitting gown with long sleeves and a high neck, and a yoke rather than a tight waist. Usually made out of cotton rather than the wood that was traditional in New England, it was cool and freed them from the constrictions of corsets and preserved their modesty. Hawaiian women called it a holokū. Quickly adopted by female ali'i, the holokū evolved into a floor-length formal gown with a train.

Euro-American historians, Judy Rohrer notes, have often failed to see how important reciprocity is in Hawaiian society, including reciprocal relationship between commoners and chiefs. Delivering presents and demanding something in return was a traditional way to both demonstrate power and forge personal relationships. Ka'ahumanu and other ali'i women initiated a cycle of compulsory, reciprocal giving. Gifts had been exchanged with foreigners ever since Cook's first visit—even if haoles often viewed this as tribute offered to them and subsequent native theft. These clothing requests, however, required multiple fittings and took the American women into the homes of Hawaiians. Such gift exchanges forged lasting relationships that had a profound impact on both the Islands and the missionaries—even if the New Englanders did not seem to understand the power wielded by female ali'i.[18]

Mission work opened new roles to American woman at a time when they were barred from higher education, most occupations, and nearly all professions. Their success was remarkable, given that they had less opportunity to interact with Hawaiians than their husbands did. Drunken, rowdy kanakas and sailors on the streets made them feel afraid to leave their homes without an escort. Consequently, it took them longer to learn the Hawaiian language. The fact that they became fluent in the language, Jennifer Fish Kashay notes, demonstrates how intensely they yearned to evangelize Islanders—and befriend them. Mercy Whitney and Sybil Bingham made serious contributions to scholarship with their work, "The Hawaiian Language," which helped malihinis (*newcomers*) and guided mikanele (*missionary*) translators.[19]

The missionary enterprise required partnership between husbands and wives, not patriarchal domination. Maria and Elisha Loomis, for example, worked together equally as the mission's printers. And had it not been for the New England women, Liholiho and Ka'ahumanu might have ejected the First Company immediately. Hiram Bingham admitted, "The plan of taking females from this country to live or die among the barbarians of Hawaii appeared to many objectionable and forbidding." Thousands may have admired the mission, but "tens of thousands regarded it as foolish or fanatical, an uncalled for sacrifice of comfort, property, and life.... Nearly all the early missionaries from the United States, on resolving to devote themselves to the heathen, were strenuously opposed by their parents, relatives and friends."[20] But Lucia Holman thought they "would not have got permission to land had it not been for the females." She told her family, with some justice, "I believe the females of this Mission have done more, much more toward the prosperity of it thus far, than the men...."[21]

Though the American Board wanted Hawaiian women to conform to their own notions of proper gender roles, as part of their project to "civilize heathens," the Sandwich Islands Mission paradoxically opened up new opportunities for American and European women to do important, valued work. Their success overseas likewise opened up new roles back home for women in the church, from teaching to preaching, from nursing to social reformation.[22]

Fearing that bachelors might fall to the temptations of local wahines, the American Board accepted only married couples for the First Company. This meant that the mission included the first haole women to settle in the Islands and the first whom most kanakas had ever laid eyes upon. A few wives of sea captains had stopped briefly in the Islands, but they usually never left their ships. The Board's unwillingness to send unmarried evangelists led to a flurry of marriages that were hastily arranged by mutual friends. The American Board even kept an informal list of eligible young women who had expressed interest in mission work. Of the seven couples selected for the Pioneer Company, only Daniel and Jerusha Chamberlain were already married when they applied. Mercy Partridge accepted the Rev. Samuel Whitney's proposal two hours after meeting him. Lucy Goodale thought about Asa Thurston's proposal overnight before saying yes in response. The Binghams had each been engaged to someone else a few months earlier, and they met

Chapter 5—The Coming of a New God

only three weeks before their wedding, which was just six days before the *Thaddeus* hauled anchor. Samuel Morse, who was an established portrait painter before he began tinkering with telegraphs and codes, captured on canvas the handsome, naïve, young couple who would lead the Mission.[23]

Remarkably, these whirlwind courtships led to marriages that endured for decades. For penniless young men such as Samuel Ruggles, Asa Thurston, and Dr. Thomas Holman, joining the Sandwich Islands Mission was an opportunity to clear their debts with a grant from the Board, make a living, and see the world. For young women, it was an opportunity to do important work.

Reverend Hiram Bingham and Sybil Moseley Bingham by Samuel F. B. Morse, 1819 (Yale University Art Gallery).

Hawaiian fears that the New Englanders were bent on conquest were answered by a simple question, "Would a war-party bring women and children with them?" The Chamberlains, in fact, brought five children with them. Keōpūolani took a particular liking to the couple's young daughter and wanted to raise the girl as her hānai (*adopted or foster*) child, but they refused this honor. They allowed the girl to be taken ashore overnight for a visit, however, which helped convince the queens that these New Englanders, no matter how odd their behavior might have seemed, meant no harm.[24]

John Young, a devout member of the Church of England, had told Kamehameha and his court a little about Christianity before the First Company arrived. Some fur traders and sandalwood merchants had done the same, but their behavior often was little credit to their religion.

Queen Kaʻahumanu of Hawaii

Young joyfully welcomed the Calvinists to the Islands, seeing them as worthy representatives of his faith, but they were appalled to learn that he had married a native woman "without benefit of clergy," even if clergy were seldom seen in the Islands before the First Company arrived. Hawaiians received them with warmth and hospitality, delighted by the return home of the four long-gone kānaka maoli, but Young warned them it might take months for Liholiho, Kaʻahumanu, and other chiefs to decide whether to let them stay. When the *Thaddeus* sailed on to Kailua-Kona, the Pioneer Company was startled to find Liholiho, drunk, swimming in the surf, nearly naked.[25]

The king was concerned that Beretania might be greatly displeased to find missionaries from Amelika in the Sandwich Islands, concerned about the influence that Americans might have on the Hawaiian government. Sensing his apprehension, Hiram Bingham read him the instructions of the American Board to the First Company, ordering them to stay out of local politics. But many haoles enjoyed the Islands the way they found them and worried that the Calvinists might bring unwelcome changes. When the Pioneer Company landed, nearly every foreign resident subscribed to their "school fund for orphaned children." Before long, some claimed the missionaries "had usurped the government and monopolized the trade."[26]

The Sandwich Island Mission did neither of these but clearly intended to reshape Hawaiian society. The American Board told them,

> You are to aim at nothing short of covering these islands with fruitful fields and pleasant dwellings, and schools and churches; of raising up the whole people to an elevated state of Christian civilization; of bringing, or preparing the means of bringing, thousands and millions of the present and succeeding generations to the mansions of eternal blessedness ... and you are to abstain from all interference with local and political interests of the people and to inculcate the duties of justice, moderation, forbearance, truth and universal kindness. Do all in your power to make men of every class good, wise and happy.[27]

As Sarah Vowell points out, what may strike us today as a contradiction—reshape a nation but stay out of politics—looked to 19th-century New Englanders like religious liberty:

> Just as in the 1600s the Massachusetts Bay colonists would have rioted if ministers had been made magistrates, those same colonists thought it was appropriate for magistrates to consult the ministers and follow the ministers' advice. Church and state were separate in the 1820s—but quite cozy.[28]

Chapter 5—The Coming of a New God

When they met Liholiho, the young king listened politely but was not impressed. And with five wives, he was disturbed to hear, "If I receive and patronize these missionaries, I shall be allowed but one wife."[29]

Nor was the First Company much impressed with him, reporting in the *Missionary Herald*, the official journal of the American Board, "There is some reason to fear, that the government is not settled on the firmest basis, and that there is less of stability and sobriety in the present king than in his father." They liked Kalanimōkū, but this was largely because he was the only Hawaiian who boarded the *Thaddeus* in what they considered "full civilized dress."[30]

Without Kamehameha, akuas, and kapus, the realm was unsettled indeed. The young king's behavior was erratic, and chiefs who resented the unified monarchy were a continuing threat to the leadership of Liholiho, Ka'ahumanu, and Kalanimōkū. The Kuhina Nui and the prime minister may have formed an alliance with Kamehameha's heir in order to hold the reins of power, but that did not make him a dependable partner. They repeatedly called him back to Kailua Kona from other parts of the Big Island to limit his contact with potential rivals—and to keep an eye on him.[31]

When Liholiho told Bingham that he would have to ask the Kuhina Nui whether they could stay, the missionary could not imagine that a woman could wield such power and thought the king was deceitful. John Coffin Jones, Jr., who was appointed the first American Consular Agent to the kingdom, while continuing to represent the Boston company, Marshall & Wildes, soon made the same mistake, despite his earlier extended visit to the Islands. Both missionaries and Boston merchants were hindered by the rigid gender roles that they assumed were natural and immutable.[32]

Some ali'i, such as Keōpūolani and Kalanimōkū, warmly welcomed the First Company. Ka'ahumanu, who enjoyed playing cards and other pastimes that the missionaries deemed sinful, treated them with open contempt. After keeping them waiting for two weeks, she finally granted them an audience. Bingham described her as having a

> commanding eye, a deliberate enunciation, a dignified and measured step, an air of superiority, and a heathen queen-like hauteur; yet sometimes … stretched out prostrate on the same floor on which a large, black, pet hog was allowed, unmolested, to walk or lie and grunt.[33]

Bingham considered Ka'ahumanu, now in her fifties, "sprightly and beautiful for a Polynesian." As Hawaiians say, "Aia nō ka pua i luna" (*the flower is still on the tree*); she is older, but her beauty remains. The missionaries were appalled, however, when her return was greeted with a hula that included hundreds of dancing, shouting, clapping men and bare-breasted women in synchronized motion. The previous year, Adelbert von Chamisso thought hula dancers moved gracefully in a way that was superior to European ballet; Daniel Chamberlain exclaimed, "I scarcely ever saw anything look so Satanic."[34]

The open, unashamed, joyful sexuality, which mariners found so appealing, shocked the Calvinists. They were by no means opposed to sexual intercourse—six of the newlywed wives in the First Company became pregnant while on the crowded *Thaddeus*—but they were embarrassed by the Holmans' public display of affection. Like many Puritans of their era—and ours—they assumed that Christianity was synonymous with prudishness. They were appalled to learn that Islanders engaged in sexual intercourse freely in their teen years and routinely saw adults having sexual intercourse when they were far younger.[35]

Ka'ahumanu made it clear that neither she nor Liholiho wanted them to stay long. She told Bingham bluntly, "No longer do our people grovel before the gods. Because the gods oppress, enslave, and sadden, Hawaiians want no more of them. Americans must not bring this sort of thing back to the islands." French settler Jean-Baptiste Rives (1793–1833), Liholiho's tutor, translator, physician, and aikāne, who gave his twin daughters to Ka'ahumanu to raise, hoped that Catholics might evangelize the kingdom and urged Liholiho to not permit the Protestants to stay. John Young suggested putting the missionaries on probation: to let them stay for just one year, under limited conditions. They could teach reading and writing, if they wished, Young suggested, but not religion—and the American Board would not be permitted to send any additional mikanele during this probationary period. They were not, she insisted, "to bring oppression upon my people by making them slaves with another set of kapus." Bingham agreed, and she abruptly dismissed the Americans. She, after all, was busy governing the nation, enjoying life without gods and prohibitions, and raising several hānai children, including two daughters of her late husband's English officer, Capt. George Beckley. The Calvinists would see little of the Kuhina Nui during the following year.[36]

On Kaua'i, the Whitneys and the Ruggles received a warmer reception. Kaumuali'i, who had feared that he would never again see his eldest son, embraced Humehume silently for half an hour and said, "his heart was so joyful he could not talk much." Enormously grateful to

Chapter 5—The Coming of a New God

missionaries for returning him safe and sound, he sent a pair of charming wahines to sleep with Samuel Whitney and Samuel Ruggles, when they headed for bed. The two young men, who had traveled ahead of their wives, asked Humehume to explain to his faither and the two ladies that they were kāne kapu (*sacred men*) who could not accept such hospitality. Kaumuali'i was surprised. He had never met haoles this holy, telling the two mikanele, "you are strange white men." They asked permission to start a mission school, but the king suggested that they could become his business agents and he would make them ali'i. This, too, they politely declined, saying that they had come to teach, not to trade—and they would be glad to show Kaumuali'i how to read and write if they were permitted to begin classes. This immediately interested the king, who built a church near his home, on the grounds of a former temple—though this may have been less a display of piety than of his chiefly mana, creating a new, personal heiau to replace his old one.[37]

Soon, the Whitneys faced an uncomfortable request. When their daughter was born in October, the first child of the mission to be born in the Islands, Kaumuali'i wanted to raise her as a hānai child. Rebuffing this honor, the Whitneys found a way to appease a disappointed—and embarrassed—ali'i. They named her Maria Kapule, after Kaumuali'i's Favorite Wife. William and Clarissa Richards would give their daughter the middle name, Keōpuōlani, and the Binghams named theirs after Ka'ahumanu.[38]

The fact that the first mikanele came from Amelika had a profound impact on Hawai'i. In the normal course of things, Beretania might have dominated the kingdom. Nearly all of the first ships to visit were British, and "Britania ruled the waves." The young American Republic had barely reached the Pacific Northwest, and most of its population still lived along the eastern seaboard. The United Kingdom occupied what is now the state of Washington. Russia controlled Alaska and Northern California. The rest of California, Arizona, New Mexico, and Texas were part of newly independent Mexico. Alexander M'Konochie, a commander in the Royal Navy, had argued in 1816 that the United Kingdom should establish a colony on one of the Islands, but his government did not pursue his proposal. The London Missionary Society, made up of English Congregationalists, Anglicans (Episcopalians), Methodists, Presbyterians, and Baptists, already had missionaries in Tahiti and the Society Islands but rejected a proposal for a mission to the Sandwich Islands. Consequently, Americans rather than Britons got the chance to shape the kingdom.[39]

Queen Kaʻahumanu of Hawaii

The First Company sailed on a wave of resurgent nationalism in the United States. During the War of 1812, the United States had tried for a second time to invade and annex Canada—an effort so unpopular in New England that it almost shattered the young republic. In the wake of this failure, many Americans wanted to expand borders westward. Sending missionaries to Hawaiʻi was a way to spread both the Gospel and American influence.

The members of the First Company were well-educated but woefully inexperienced. The ordained clergy who led them, Asa Thurston and Hiram Bingham, had just graduated from seminary and had never worked as pastors, let alone as missionaries. Some others brought skills. One was a doctor, another a farmer, three were teachers, two were printers, and one was a mechanic. The physician, however, knew less about medicine than medical kahunas did, and the farmer knew nothing about growing crops in the tropics. Most were quite young for such a difficult undertaking. Elisha Loomis was only 20 years old.[40]

The evangelical revival of the Second Great Awakening in America both inspired Calvinists to believe that they were capable of personal transformation and led them to underestimate how difficult it would be to change either themselves or others. They had little idea how to explain their beliefs, for example, to those who did not speak their language—and Henry ʻŌpūkahaʻia had died before completing his Hawaiian dictionary, grammar book, or spelling book. Their only hope of success, they thought, was first to convert some chiefs.

Kānaka and mikanele did not begin to understand one another. Lucia Holman complained about being surrounded by "the noise and jabbering of the natives." When one of the New Englanders first attempted to speak in a small village near Honolulu, people fled in panic as he closed his eyes in prayer. When their own priests closed their eyes, kahunas often had sought to "pray them to death." When Hiram Bingham first preached (through a translator) in Kāneohe on the windward side of Oʻahu, his stern sermon made many listeners fear they were about to be sacrificed to a new akua.[41]

Nor did they understand each other's customs. Hawaiians greeted friends, guests, and even strangers with hugs and kisses. They usually welcomed haole visitors with warmth and affection—and often married those who stayed. These Calvinists seemed to want no physical contact with kanakas at all. And as Elizabeth Kapuʻuwailani Lindsey Buyers and Martha Noyes lament, "Nearly every one of our most deeply rooted traditions was looked upon as evil by these newly arrived Christian

Chapter 5—The Coming of a New God

missionaries." They would not even play card games that kanakas had learned from other visitors from Amelika. Why did these haole wahines not rebel against such kapus, the Kuhina Nui wondered, as she had?[42]

The Calvinists also discovered that devotion to the old gods had not vanished entirely when Hawaiians overturned their organized religion. The king may have publicly rejected temple rituals, but he remained fond of the hula. The hula pahu (*drum*) that embodied the motions of kahunas in heiaus no longer had the same meaning, and most dances were not particularly religious, but they still were performed before a statue of Laka. The dancers told the mikanele that no one took this god/goddess seriously anymore, but many still prayed to her/him all the same. Many Hawaiians also remained devoted to 'aumākua (*ancestral Deities*) and to some lesser gods such as Pele. These minor Deities and household protectors had never played a major role in the now-discarded temple rituals anyway.[43]

Hewahewa, the former High Priest, saw the Calvinists' Jehovah as the new god whose coming he had awaited. He envisioned native Hawaiians leading the nation in this new faith. But the American missionaries saw the often-intoxicated kahuna as an unreliable ally. They would not allow recent converts to hold decision-making power in the church and did not encourage kanaka clergy until years later. The old kahuna imagined an enculturated form of Christianity, led by kanakas, but the Sandwich Islands Mission sought to translate New England Protestant theology into the Hawaiian language, without Hawaiian culture and spirituality. As John Charlot has noted, elsewhere, Christianity learned much from cultures it encountered. Greek philosophy informed Christian theology, and the Roman Saturnalia evolved into the Christian celebration of Christmas. Here, however, Christian missionaries rejected everything connected to the old religion, which made it harder for Islanders to embrace this new faith. As Ralph Kuykendall observed,

> Unfortunately, none of the foreigners who came to Hawaii in the early period, or the missionaries who followed soon after, had any adequate understanding or appreciation of the native culture or considered it, any important part of it, worth preserving.[44]

Many early visitors liked what they saw when they arrived in the Sandwich Islands, however. James Cook saw "a handsome people and a beautiful land." In 1792, John Boit, a young American sailor on the *Columbia*, said that the inhabitants of "these beautiful isles ... appeared to me to be the happiest people in the world." The following year, Scottish surgeon and botanist Archibald Menzies was impressed by the terraced gardens he saw on Maui:

> Even the shelving cliffs of rock were planted with esculent roots, banked in and watered by aqueducts from the rivulet with as much art as if their level had been taken by the most ingenious engineer. We could not but indeed admire the laudable ingenuity of these people in cultivating their soil with so much economy. The indefatigable labor in making these little fields in so rugged a situation, the care and industry with which they were transplanted, watered and kept in order, surpassed anything of the kind we had ever seen before.

In 1796, Capt. Pierre François Péron had seen the Islands as "a new Eden" filled with handsome people. In 1814, William Black, captain of the British ship, *Raccoon,* said they were "the cleanest people I ever saw, both in their person and habitation" with houses that were "very neat and extremely clean."[45]

But when the First Company gazed upon the Big Island, they were horrified. And as naked swimmers approached the *Thaddeus* at Kawaihae, terror-stricken missionary women fled below decks. Sybil Bingham was shocked by "the sight of these poor degraded creatures, both literally and spiritually naked...." Lucia Holman lamented, a week after their arrival in these verdant islands, "The idea of spending my life on these barren rocks and among this heathen people, whose manners and habits are so rude and disgusting, appeared for a moment to almost overwhelm me." Hiram Bingham was even offended that Hawaiians did not wear hats:

> [T]he appearance of destitution, degradation, and barbarism among the chattering, and almost naked[,] savages, whose heads and feet, and much of their sunburnt swarthy skins[,] were bare, was appalling. Some of our number, with gushing tears, turned away from the spectacle. Others with firmer nerve continued their gaze, but were ready to exclaim, "Can these be human beings? ... Can they be civilized? Can they be Christianized?"[46]

These newly minted missionaries were perturbed that ali'i women who rode with them on the *Thaddeus* to Kailua-Kona did not eat on a regular schedule, but instead had their servants bring poi or fish whenever they felt like eating. "They eat when hunger suggests, without any regard to time or place...." Lucia Holman attributed this lack of routine to their lack of faith in her god. In an omen of things to come, Hiram Bingham had the temerity to upbraid nobles who played cards on Sunday en route on the *Thaddeus,* seeing this as desecrating the Sabbath. Smiling

Chapter 5—The Coming of a New God

graciously at this impudent young man, Kalākua replied that they were not bound by the kapus of the Christian god.[47]

Suspicious of all things Hawaiian, the Pioneer Company spent its scarce resources importing flour from the United States, which often arrived spoiled, while rejecting plentiful kalo. Poi, made from kalo, was highly nutritious and hypoallergenic, making it perfect for babies, as well as adults, but the New Englanders would have none of it. For them, the local produce was theologically suspect. Lucia Holman, wife of the mission doctor, complained that "the fruits and vegetables, everything that the Islands produce, tastes heathenish." She had every confidence, though, that "if the pleasant sunshine of the Gospel should beam upon this land, it would have no small tendency to sweeten its fruit." Gradually, the necessity of eating and the generous gifts of food they received led them to a Hawaiian diet built around fish, pork, chicken, bananas, kalo, poi, and sweet potatoes.[48]

Disturbed by kanakas' traditional attire—men wore a malo (*loincloth*) that left their buttocks exposed, while women wore a pā'ū (*skirt*) kapa cloth that covered the knees to waist but left their breasts exposed—the Calvinists hoped that providing ali'i women with new clothes might prove to be the first step toward inculcating Western habits, and eventually Christianity. Soon after Sybil Bingham started a school in her home in May 1820, just two months after arriving in the Islands, the king sent her material for five ruffled shirts, which he expected her to make for him within a few days. She both made the shirts and expanded the number of pupils whom she taught.[49]

Hawaiians enjoyed Western clothing as something novel and exotic, not as signs of civilization or conversion. Both royal women and commoners continued to wear the pā'ū. The missionaries encouraged more modest attire and objected to nude swimming, even though this was the custom in the coastal "watering places" of England and elsewhere at the time. King George himself frolicked in the waves at Weymouth *au naturelle*.[50]

Whether worn by ali'i on a lark, out of fashion, or as a sign of status, European and American clothing had an impact that the First Company saw and appreciated. "The adoption of our costume," Hiram Bingham noted with pride,

> greatly diminishes their swimming or sporting in the surf, since it is less convenient to wear it in the water than the native girdle.... The decline or discontinuance of the use of the surf-board, as civilization advances, may be accounted for by the increase of modesty, industry or religion, without

supposing, as some have affected to believe, that missionaries caused oppressive enactments against it.[51]

Foreign-style homes and goods also became fashionable. Ka'ahumanu was the first Hawaiian to have a wooden, two-story Western-style home built for her, and Liholiho had a similar one constructed for him. The imported goods sold by American, European, and Asian merchants may have appealed to ali'i, but Islanders showed little interest in anything that the mission had to offer. They were curious about Christian worship, which had been seen only on rare occasions. A naval chaplain might invite a few of them to observe services on board a visiting ship. Asa and Lucy Thurston started the Mokuaikaua congregation in Kona in 1820, and the Calvinists' outdoor worship drew crowds of curious gawkers, but so did missionaries doing laundry. Why did mikanele women do this sort of labor instead of having servants do it? And why did they do the cooking? This was work for kanes, not wahines. The hymns delighted Islanders, who had never heard these harmonies before, but they did not understand the rest of the service—nor were they impressed by it.

Even when their work seemed to be going well, the staid New Englanders were perplexed by unexpected challenges. When Ka'ahumanu gave the Hilo mission station a large, thatched building, the first worship service in it was disrupted by her large, heavily tusked pet boar.[52]

CHAPTER 6

Reading, Writing and Religion

The New Englanders may have intended to "civilize the heathens" but the latter often saw the Americans as primitive. Women, for example, clearly had less freedom in the United States than they did in the Islands. Kaʻahumanu and other aliʻi viewed the New Englanders not as enlightened teachers, but rather as amusing, ignorant, childlike creatures who did not have to be taken seriously.

What did impress Islanders, who had no written language other than petroglyphs, was the ability of these mikanele to read and write. The meles (*poems*) composed in the 17th or 18th centuries (or earlier) survived only because kanakas developed extraordinary memories. They did not even know at first what to call the books and letters that haoles used. *Palapala*, often shortened to just *pala*, originally meant patterns painted on kapa cloth or symbols carved on rocks, and it was the nearest word they could find for a completely new concept. Paper itself was unknown in precontact times, and the Islands did not naturally produce anything conducive to papermaking. Kanakas had seen haoles read, but the mikaneles were the first foreigners to make a serious attempt to express the sounds of the Hawaiian language in written letters and then to teach kanakas this new alphabet. Most haoles who arrived earlier had little interest in teaching Islanders to read any language whatsoever—or opposed anyone doing so.[1]

Translation always involves interpretation, and rendering a spoken language in written form is almost always an imprecise art. In creating an alphabet and in translating English into Hawaiian, the mikanele inevitably made choices that reflected their background. Being Calvinists, they coined the word *Kalawina* for *Protestant*, for example, leaving out the Anglicans, Methodists, and other non–Calvinist heirs of the Reformation. They also standardized spelling. Earlier, haoles often had called the Kuhina Nui *Kahoumanou* or *Cahoumanou* or *Tahoumanou*; now, it was more consistently rendered as *Kaahumanu*. They also influenced how Hawaiian words were pronounced. The king's name henceforth was usually pronounced the way they spelled it, *Liholiho*, rather than the way haoles had spelled and spoken it earlier, *Rihoriho*. And in creating a simplified Hawaiian alphabet, they included *k* but not *t*, thus favoring the Big Island's use of *kapa* for cloth over Kauaʻi's *tapa*.[2]

The New Englanders felt real warmth for kanakas. They still often seemed a bit aloof to the latter, but their work in the Islands was changing them as they sought to transform others. Sybil Bingham wrote about her students:

> I love them tenderly, and when endeavoring in a simple way to explain to them the word of God, have never failed to feel that the dearest spot among the dearest friends in my own beloved land was not as engaging as this.[3]

These Calvinists may have been stuffy, but their vision of society was fairly progressive. They wanted Hawaiians to learn to read and write their own language first, not English. They rejected the caste system and launched a crusade, now largely forgotten, to end the killing of babies. Young children were sometimes put to death when they were weeks, months, or even years old—just as many unwanted babies were left in the market square or church steps in England during this era, to be raised by the parish, if they survived at all. When the mikanele agreed to teach aliʻi before commoners, which violated their democratic principles and religious belief that everyone should learn to read and understand the Bible for themselves, they did so only temporarily, choosing their battles carefully. Liholiho had little interest in study himself but thought literacy was too valuable to be wasted on the common people. Kaʻahumanu, on the other hand, banned infanticide, savings thousands of lives. And eventually, the missionaries were allowed to teach commoners.[4]

On Kauaʻi, Kaumualiʻi and his wife immediately asked the mikanele to tutor him. Soon, students piled into Mercy Whitney's makeshift classroom, and the king and queen were so eager to learn the palapala that they studied their lessons while wading in the ocean. Before long, there were schools scattered across the archipelago, and the mikanele were sneaking Bible verses into their reading lessons. Their instruction, Hiram Bingham reported, included "reading, writing, morals, religion, arithmetic, geography, sacred song, and sacred history."[5]

One reason the missionaries taught in Hawaiian rather than English was to minimize the influence that sailors and merchants had on kanakas. As Bingham explained,

Chapter 6—Reading, Writing and Religion

the thought of making young men and women better able to comprehend and use that language, while subjected to the influence of frequent intercourse with an ungodly class of profane abusers of our noble English, was appalling.[6]

Chiefs flocked to schools run by "Long Necks," as they called the Calvinists, whose collars gave an appearance of elongated necks. Though some haoles opposed the Mission, others sent their Hawaiian wives and children for education. Before long, Kaumuali'i wrote Binamu "a few lines to you to thank you for the good book you was so kind as to send by my son. I think it is a good book, one that God gave us to read." The mission hoped piety would follow literacy, and soon, Kaumuali'i, Kuakini, Kalanimōkū, Kamāmalu, Boki, and other ali'i were writing to one another—but seldom attending worship. Kanakas who had worked to become literate while working abroad were exposed to diverse religious traditions and recognized that Christians had no monopoly on reading and writing. They could have the pala without the pule.[7]

Bingham recognized that the skill of Mission doctors could attract Hawaiians—and insisted that medical care be provided free of charge, just as medical kahunas had done under Kamehameha. Less than four

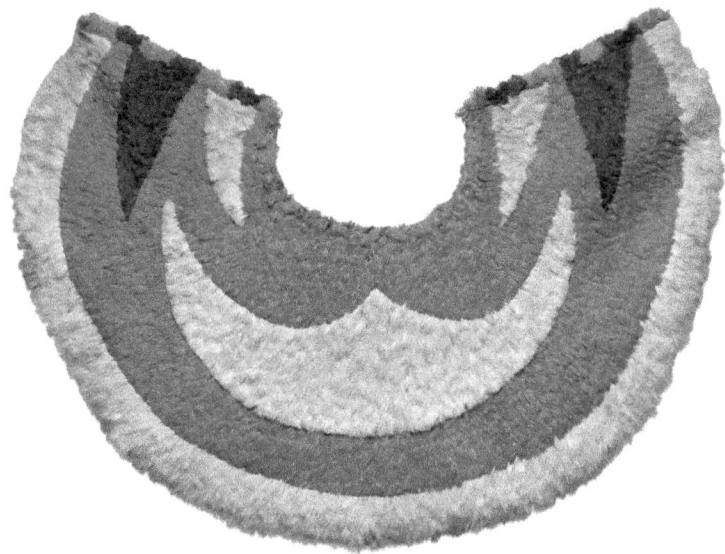

Feather Cape given by Ka'ahumanu to Lucia Holman in 1820 (Yale University Art Gallery, Gift of Harrison F. Bassett in memory of his wife Elizabeth Ives Bassett and her brother Arthur Noble Brown).

months after they arrived, Bingham sent Dr. Thomas Holman and his wife Lucia packing because Dr. Holman charged patients for his services. This, Bingham insisted, violated the values of the mission, though he also may have been jealous of the favor Liholiho and Kaʻahumanu showed them, such as the magnificent feather cape the Kuhina Nui presented to Lucia. The Holmans' departure was a cause of great concern among the remaining missionaries, who had few medical supplies and less medical knowledge. Samuel Whitney gave one infant a fatal overdose of laudanum, a mixture of opium and alcohol, thinking the child was much older. Not recognizing the skill of traditional healers, Lucy Thurston complained that after the Holmans were given the boot, "There was no physician in the kingdom."[8]

When it came to haole plagues, haole doctors knew more than kahunas, but Western medicine was still primitive. When Liholiho was quite sick, Hiram Bingham wanted to bleed him—a common practice in Amelika and Europe, a recommendation that his wife, his mother, and the Kuhina Nui wisely rejected. For decades to come, American doctors routinely treated burns by applying germ-infested cotton, which often led to serious infection. Hawaiians applied the sap of the aloe plant, which works far better.[9]

By the end their probation year, the mikanele had inspired Kaumualiʻi to ban the sensual hula on Sundays on Kauaʻi and Niʻihau—which he may have done primarily out of gratitude for them bringing his son back to him—but elsewhere, the mission had won barely enough acceptance from the aliʻi for them to remain a year longer. When Hiram Bingham asked Liholiho for permission to assemble the New England–style wooden-framed house in Honolulu that the American Board had just shipped, the king refused—until one of the mission women asked privately and more diplomatically than Bingham had. Still, Liholiho insisted, "When you go, take everything with you."[10]

Kaʻahumanu had little contact with the First Company before 1821, when Liholiho moved the seat of government to Honolulu. The Kuhina Nui, her sister Kalākua, and her brother Kalanimōkū visited the mission station in Honolulu, giving them supplies "still more liberally" than Liholiho had the previous week. And the Kuhina Nui asked the mikanele to beseech the Almighty to restrain Liholiho's alcohol consumption and gambling, which they were happy to do, no doubt at great length.[11]

Hiram Bingham finally began to realize how badly they had underestimated Kaʻahumanu's power, even though his wife Sybil had noted in her journal months earlier that she was "in a sense the head of the

Chapter 6—Reading, Writing and Religion

nation." He nonetheless approached the culture he wished to change with astonishing arrogance, freely and publicly criticizing its rulers. Some observers were amazed at the equanimity with which Liholiho received reproach from the Calvinists. In most of Europe, this would merit imprisonment or worse, but when the missionaries outraged the populace, the king defended them from attack. Liholiho was even planning to execute a Hawaiian who had assaulted them—until Asa Thurston begged him to spare the offender's life.[12]

As the First Company struggled to win its first converts, Kaumuali'i offered to take two of them on a trip he was planning to the Society and Georgian Islands in his newly purchased brig. Such an expedition could lead to more trade and closer relationships among scattered Pacific Islanders. It would also give the New Englanders at chance to consult with William Ellis, whose work in Tahiti for the London Missionary Society was flourishing while theirs floundered. Hiram Bingham and missionary teacher Samuel Ruggles won approval for this journey from Ka'ahumanu, who asked the mikanele to take a message to King Pōmare III in Tahiti, and also from Liholiho and Kalanimōkū. The two Calvinists headed to Kaua'i for the voyage.[13]

Traders in Honolulu, however, led by American Consular Agent Jones, dissuaded Kaumuali'i from making the trip, fearing that if he made this voyage, he might never repay his debts to them—and might come more thoroughly under the influence of missionaries. Claiming that "it would be injurious to bring speculators from the Society to the Sandwich Islands" and that such a voyage might offend the United States, Jones managed to block the expedition. The king and the mikanele capitulated to the merchants, but the incident left resentment on both sides. As Claire Laux noted, for the first missionaries, the influence of other Westerners was often far more difficult to overcome than that of paganism.[14] This conflict was probably inevitable. Like the First Company, most American merchants and sailors came from New England, the maritime center of the United States at the time, and many had been eager to escape the Puritans of their homeland. And there were far more traders and castaway sailors in the Islands than mikanele.

In July 1821, Liholiho sailed to Kaua'i for an unannounced, uninvited, and unprecedented state visit with Kaumuali'i, king of Kaua'i and Ni'ihau. Arriving without warriors, he was graciously welcomed. Both rulers publicly reaffirmed the peace treaty his father had made. Ka'ahumanu soon joined her coruler on Kaua'i and slept with Kaumuali'i, and they all made a leisurely tour of the island. Then, on September

16, Liholiho invited Kaumuali'i to board his luxurious yacht, *Ha'aheo o Hawai'i* (*Pride of Hawai'i*), for a farewell dinner and then suddenly sailed away, taking his host and his heir Keali'iohonui as prisoners.[15]

Liholiho and the Kuhina Nui may have abducted Kaumuali'i because they feared he would seek once more to sever his islands from the unified kingdom. On Oah'u, Liholiho announced that Kaumuali'i would remain king of Kaua'i and Ni'ihau and his allocation of land would remain unchanged, for the rest of his life, regardless of his current residence. Charmed by the handsome and gentlemanly king, Ka'ahumanu said she wanted to marry her prisoner, cementing his exile, a move that would give her considerable mana through him and would mean that she would share authority with the two most powerful men in the archipelago. To refuse might have cost him his life—and could have plunged the two kingdoms into war. Whether drawn to the Kuhina Nui or wanting to avoid bloodshed, he chose to marry her, doing so on October 9, 1821. Then she took—quite literally—his handsome, nearly 7-foot-tall, captive son as her second husband. Through abduction and two marriages, she achieved something that had eluded Kamehameha: bringing the entire archipelago into a single realm, one in which she exercised the greatest authority.[16]

Kaumuali'i may have suspected what she and Liholiho had planned, but the missionaries were stunned. They had not married for love themselves. Except for the Chamberlains, all had arranged marriages and hastily scheduled weddings, but the abduction of these two grooms horrified them. They saw Ka'ahumanu's marriage to Kaumuali'i, one of the first Hawaiians to embrace their faith, as potentially a step toward her conversion, even if it meant his own wife, who was now a devout Christian herself, would be abandoned. But they were almost as shocked to see a woman propose marriage in the Islands, which violated all the gender norms of New England, as they were to see her kidnap him. For a man to have more than one wife was bad enough, they thought, but at least the patriarchs in the Bible had done this. For a woman to take two husbands was perverse. And marrying both father and son was totally depraved.[17]

Only one member of the First Company, 26-year-old Mercy Whitney, who had built a relationship with King Kaumuali'i and Queen Kapule, seemed unsurprised by Ka'ahumanu's marriage to the king and his son. She also was the first missionary to recognize that Ka'ahumanu "has more influence in political affairs than any other person in the nation."[18]

After pulling off his bold annexation of Kaua'i and Ni'ihau,

Chapter 6—Reading, Writing and Religion

Liholiho became an increasingly erratic figurehead. John Coffin Jones, Jr., described him on October 5 as "only a boy, pleased with a rattle tickled with a straw. Rum is his god. Scarce have I seen him sober." The fact that 25-year-old Jones called the 24-year-old king "a boy" indicates the condescension he felt toward kanakas, which is not a good trait in a diplomat. Far away in Boston, the *Missionary Herald* reported that Ka'ahumanu was far more popular among her people than the king or any other ali'i.[19]

Then another disease opened a door for the missionaries. Sickness swept through Honolulu in the fall of 1821, and by December, Ka'ahumanu was "at death's door." Two doctors from the Russian Exploring Squadron treated her, leaving her with a lasting appreciation of its naval officers. In her illness, the Kuhina Nui welcomed visits by Hiram and Sybil Bingham and their prayers for her. "She was soon restored, and with her friends set a higher value on the religion which we were endeavoring to inculcate," Binamu noticed. She was also impressed that Commodore Michael Vascilieff, a conservative member of the Russian Orthodox Church, collected seven golden ducats and 86 Spanish dollars from his officers and crew, who were mostly Orthodox themselves, to support the Sandwich Islands Mission. "There was from this period a marked difference in her demeanor toward the missionaries." She even attended a tea party on December 16 that was hosted by Binamuwahine.[20]

She did not, however, embrace their beliefs. She continued to spend Sundays swimming and surfing, not listening to sermons or singing Psalms. Nor did she accept the Long Necks' notions of modesty. One day, she dropped by "Mission House" in Honolulu after a dip in the ocean and chatted casually with the mikanele, who were quite flustered by their visitor, because the Kuhina Nui was completely naked. As the new year began, Hiram Bingham lamented, "It is difficult to collect an audience on the Sabbath...." On January 20, he managed to gather 60 Hawaiians and 50 haoles for worship, including several ali'i, but Ka'ahumanu was not among them. Nor was the king who demurred, saying, "I am tipsy, and it is not right to go to church drunk...."[21]

Liholiho—and many merchants to whom he owed money—feared that if the common people studied the palapala, they would have no time to cut sandalwood, and he and other ali'i needed timber sales to pay for their extravagant purchases of imported goods. In fact, mission schools and lengthy Sunday worship services did conflict with traditional times for fishing and planting crops. Literacy, and the kanakas who returned after seeing the world, made it harder for haole merchants to cheat Hawaiians. J.C. Jones complained to his home office that the Calvinists were undermining his profits by teaching their students the true value of his wares. The Hawaiians who returned with the First Company told prospective buyers that frame houses, for example, sold for $300 in Boston, not the much higher price that Jones claimed. The following month, he reported with dismay:

> The natives are too much enlightened. They know well the value of every article. If they do not there are plenty of canting, hypocritical missionaries to inform them, even though unasked. Trade will never again flourish at these Islands until the emissaries from the Andover [Theological Seminary] mill are recalled. They are continually telling the King & Chiefs that the White traders are cheating and imposing on them....[22]

In January 1822, the First Company demonstrated another skill that astounded Hawaiians. With an old hand-powered press they had transported 18,000 miles, Elisha and Maria Loomis started making spelling sheets, written in a Hawaiian alphabet that the missionaries had just created. They were the first printers between the Rocky Mountains and Asia. Soon, they were publishing brief Scripture selections and reading exercises. Whenever a new publication came off the press, Hawaiians eagerly crowded around Mission House with pigs, goats, chickens, and bananas that they traded to buy reading material. Kuakini and Keʻeaumoku ʻŌpio, the governors of the Big Island and Maui, were excited by this achievement, which drew new students to the mission schools. Kaʻahumanu showed little interest at first in learning to read, but by February 1822, she, Kaumualiʻi, Kamāmalu, and young prince Kauikeaouli were all corresponding eagerly with members of the Pōmare ruling family in their ancestral home, Kahiki (*Tahiti*).[23]

But how would the missionaries educate their own children? Not only were they reluctant to feed poi to their sons and daughters, they also feared exposing them to Hawaiian culture. The Mission's schools only taught adults, and instruction was entirely in the Hawaiian language. A local boarding school might have provided acceptable isolation from kanakas, but none yet existed in the Islands; at least, none they judged to be adequate. They also feared exposing their offspring to Hawaiian sexuality, particularly the possibility of falling in love with or marrying kanaka classmates.

Before embarking with the First Company, the Chamberlains had sent their two older sons to the Foreign Mission School in Cornwall,

Chapter 6—Reading, Writing and Religion

where they studied with kanakas and learned some Hawaiian. Once in the Islands, both boys became fairly fluent in the language and provided valuable service to the mission as translators. The Rev. William Ellis, a British Methodist missionary in the Society Islands, warned the Chamberlains that they it would be impossible to "train them up for God" if they kept their children with them here, and recommended that Kaʻahumanu's hānai son David be allowed to speak only English when she sent him to live with a mikanele family.[24]

This reluctance to use Hawaiian at home made it more difficult to learn the Hawaiian language and win converts. The Board wanted the children to stay with their parents, but the Binghams, like most of the other early missionaries, decided to send their 7-year-old daughter back to the United States to live with relatives, taking a chance that they might never see her again.[25]

Meanwhile, other haoles poured into the Islands. Foreigners could still become residents of the kingdom only with the permission of the king, but they arrived in such droves that the chiefs found it almost impossible to control them. They kept coming, even though the sandalwood trade that brought many of them here was waning. The wholesale destruction of forests had stripped the best timber and glutted the market in Canton, driving down prices.[26]

As the sandalwood trade declined, however, whaling ships suddenly filled Hawaiian harbors. Two American whaling ships, the *Equator*, sailing out of Nantucket under Capt. Elisha Folger, and the *Balaena* from New Bedford, commanded by Capt. Edmund Gardner, had harpooned and killed a whale near Kealakekua Bay on the Big Island in the fall of 1819. Reaching Honolulu, they had found that it was indeed "a protected harbor," as its name means. This burgeoning industry constituted the most extensive commercial exploitation of wild mammals in human history, and these great creatures had already been hunted to a point of scarcity in the Atlantic. When Capt. Jonathan Winship spotted great schools of sperm whales off Japan, hunters hastened to the Northern Pacific. With Japan closed to all foreigners for centuries, Honolulu was the nearest port open to American whalers, and an ideal place to stop while hunting in Japanese or Arctic waters. The next year, more than 20 whaling ships came to Hawaiʻi looking for fresh fruit and vegetables, meat, and fish—and women.

In 1822, 60 whaleships per year stopped at Honolulu or Lāhainā for supplies and repairs, often spending weeks or months in port. A hundred stopped in the Islands in 1824. In 1829, 170 did. Mostly based in

Queen Kaʻahumanu of Hawaii

New England, they spent two or three months in the Islands each spring and fall, sending as many as 12,000 sailors ashore at a time for drinking alcohol, gambling, and seeking encounters with prostitutes. Soon, Lāhainā was the whaling capital of the world. For nearly half a century, the North Pacific supplied oil for lamps and lubricants for industry throughout much of the developed world.[27] As foreign disease ravaged the nation, more and more young Hawaiians signed on to the crews of whalers and trading ships. They saw the wide world, but many never returned.

Most haoles saw this labor as too dangerous for them and considered the working conditions to be intolerable, but many Pacific Islanders and Native Americans thought it was worth taking risks to earn both financial reward and respect. At sea, kanakas worked alongside haoles, African Americans, Native Americans, Tahitians, Māoris, Asians, and Latinos with remarkably little friction.[28]

A shipyard was launched in Honolulu to build boats for this lively trade; soon, other yards were rigging sails and repairing the hulls of large sailing ships. Before long, chandlers in Hawaiʻi sold everything needed to equip a floating whale-oil refinery, and waterfront saloons overflowed during the spring and fall whaling seasons. By the early 1820s, prostitutes from as far away as Boston and Europe were entertaining seamen in Honolulu and Lāhainā. On some ships, nearly half the crew deserted when they reached the Islands. Most ended up living on the beaches of Oʻahu. And when the captain of the American whaleship, *Globe*, hired deserters in the Islands, they mutinied and murdered their officers.[29]

As American consular agent, John Coffin Jones, Jr., was charged with assisting—and sometimes rounding up—Yankee seamen. With little guidance from the State Department—less than one letter a year, which rarely contained useful information—and serving without pay, he faced a nearly impossible task:

> I have at one time had sixty Americans confined in irons at the fort; and hardly a day has passed that I have not been compelled to visit one or more of the ships to quell a mutiny, or compel by force whole crews to their duty, who had united to work no longer. I should say, too, that there were over one hundred deserters now on shore from the American ships this season, regular outlaws, ready to embark in any adventure.[30]

The crew typically shared in the profits of each completed journey, but while one voyage might be quite lucrative, the next might be disastrous. It is little wonder that so many sailors sacrificed their pay and their share

Chapter 6—Reading, Writing and Religion

of the ship's profits to jump ship. Whaling was dirty, dangerous work. Crews were away from home for at least two years and sometimes as long as five. When their prey was spotted by a lookout high above the deck in the crow's nest, sailors rowed out to the leviathans to harpoon them with barbed spears, which were attached by a line to the rowboat. The huge mammals then might either try to smash the rowboat or drag it across the sea for miles, diving to try to free itself—or at least drown its tormenters. Whalers sardonically called this a Nantucket Sleigh Ride. Along the wharves of New England, it was often said, "One trip on a [whaleship] is one too many." A naval historian quipped, "Short of defending the Alamo, there were few jobs in the 1800s worse than crewing on a whaler."[31]

Sailors and traders often referred to their homelands as "Christian nations" but behaved in ways the missionaries condemned. Who were real Christians? The merchants? The whalers? The Long Necks? Nathaniel Winship, for example, a sea captain from Boston, who settled in the Islands in 1811, had seven Hawaiian wives. Adding to the confusion of

Dangers of the Whale Fishery, **artist unknown, from W. Scoresby,** *An Account of the Arctic Regions with a History and Description of the Northern Whale-fishery*, **1820 (Wikimedia Commons).**

Islanders, both the First Company and the first whalers were Americans, and both came from New England. A few sailors visited Calvinist worship services, but other haoles took girls from Sybil Bingham's first female school "openly and forcibly" as their mistresses. One pious sea captain told Lucy Thurston, "the debasing influence of the many foreigners that touched here was an insuperable obstacle to the conversion of this people."[32]

The First Company did not foresee this conflict. Soon after they had settled, Lucy Thurston was ecstatic about the arrival of a sailing ship from America, gushing: "God bless mariners. They are the links that [serve] to connect us to the fatherland." Before long, though, mariners were among their fiercest adversaries. As MacKinnon Simpson has observed,

> It is ironic that all the problems the missionaries anticipated finding in the Islands—tribal warfare, resistance (or perhaps attacks) by *kahunas* (priests) of the ancient religion, or even outright refusal to allow them to land—simply failed to materialize. And one problem they had not anticipated—the unruly, rambunctious whalers—had come around the horn from New England, just as they had.[33]

The Calvinists had the only ordained clergy in the Islands, but other malihinis (*newcomers*) were members of other denominations. Many of the Native Americans from New England and Long Island who signed on to whaleships, for example, were Christians who had joined the Baptists, the Methodists, and members of other churches. Some, such as the Rev. Solomon Briant, were pastors before going to sea. Such believers were likely to practice their faith a bit differently than the Congregationalists and Presbyterians.[34]

Haoles kept opening taverns, particularly on O'ahu where Governor Boki welcomed them. Soon, there were 17 bars in the little port town of Honolulu. In an attempt to control the bad behavior of both sailors and kanakas, Ka'ahumanu prohibited public drunkenness and the sale of brandy. This reduced public inebriation initially, but within days, Don Francisco noted, "King is drunk again." Before long, he found it easier to record the days when Liholiho was sober. The monarch spent a great deal of time drinking alcohol with sailors or sleeping off binges on the beach of Waikīkī, curled up with his pet pig. At least once, Liholiho nearly drank himself to death. Hiram Bingham found him in his beach house paralyzed, shaking with convulsions, bleeding from his mouth, and completely deranged.[35]

The Sandwich Islands Mission did not oppose drinking alcohol

Chapter 6—Reading, Writing and Religion

in moderation, at least not at first. The Rev. Asa Thurston grew up in a home that was filled with singing, dancing, and an occasional glass of "cheer." Sybil Bingham noted in her diary with appreciation that Anthony D. Allen, formerly enslaved but now a successful merchant, welcomed them into his home with "decanters and glasses with wine and brandy to refresh us" and ended their dinner "with wine and melons." Elisha Loomis expressed dismay at the behavior of drunken sailors one day in his journal, but two days later, celebrated his own success with brewing beer. The mission kept detailed records of purchases for their common stock, which show that the Binghams drank rum, wine, and brandy in roughly the same quantities that most Americans did in the 1820s—more than most people do today, but far less than the average foreign resident of Honolulu did at the time. The temperance movement flourished in New England long before the missionaries embraced it.[36]

The Calvinists were dismayed, however, to see foreigners selling rum to those who already drank to excess. They also were upset to see aliʻi, often in their cups, racking up huge debts to merchants with extravagant purchases of jewels, silks, and other foreign luxuries. The ban on cutting young sandalwood trees that Kamehameha had imposed was lifted after his death. Liholiho and other chiefs sold more and more of this rare timber to pay for their spending sprees, and the quality and price of Hawaiian sandalwood fell. Reckless logging did irreparable harm to fragile ecosystems, and chiefs often started forest fires to locate the scented trees, leading to massive soil erosion. Aliʻi forced commoners into backbreaking labor without pay to harvest it, leaving them with little time to tend their crops, and food prices soared. Clearly, the Sandwich Islands Mission was losing its battle with sin.[37]

By March 1822, alcohol had nearly killed the young monarch: "He had been seized suddenly with an alarming fit ... and shaken with convulsion and difficult respiration, and followed by profuse perspiration." Liholiho's mother and his *kahu* sat beside the king in tears, believing he was about to die. Liholiho continued his descent into alcoholism, even after the news arrived that booze had killed King Pōmare II in Tahiti.

When Asa Thurston finally preached against "the evils of intemperance" in 1822, Honolulu merchants were so offended that they turned their backs on the preacher and walked out of the church. John Coffin Jones, Jr., the son of a prominent Boston businessman, Federalist politician, and Unitarian layman, began his own Unitarian services on Sundays in response to Thurston's sermon. Many traders in this era had ties to the Unitarian Church, a new, liberal, market-oriented denomination that was in the process of separating from the Congregationalists. Jones conducted worship at Major Warren's Hotel on Hotel Street, between Fort Street and Nuʻuanu Avenue, familiar territory for merchants—and a convenient place to get a drink.[38]

Feeling besieged by their fellow Americans, the Calvinists were overjoyed at the end of March when George Bennet and the Rev. Daniel Tyerman, who were sponsored by the interdenominational London Missionary Society (LMS), joined William Ellis in stopping in the Hawaiian Islands for a five-month visit. Their nations had been at war only seven years earlier, but the English warmly and publicly embraced the American missionaries—and corrected some of the gossip that other Englishmen were spreading about them. For decades, the LMS mission had been transcribing Tahitian—which, like Hawaiian, had existed only as an oral language—into written form and had already published the Gospel according to Luke in Tahitian. Ellis, a British Methodist, had been working in the Society Islands for four years and spoke Tahitian fluently. It was similar enough to Hawaiian that Ellis was able to preach on April 17, his first Sunday on Oʻahu, and be understood, at least imperfectly, without an interpreter. Even Liholiho paid attention this time.[39]

Ellis appreciated the indigenous culture more than the Calvinists did, providing a detailed, nonjudgmental account, for example, of a hula he observed. Some Hawaiian dances, he noted, "exhibited nothing offensive to modest propriety," even if the chanted songs of others were offered in honor of both the old gods and great chiefs. Tyerman admitted that "it must be allowed that superstitious observances yet in vogue in our own land...." In many parts of England, in fact, there was still widespread belief in witchcraft. Ellis preached against "idolatrous dances" but felt no need to destroy images of the old gods. At the top of the Nuʻuanu Pali mountain pass and nearly every other steep or dangerous path he climbed, he found statues of akua, circled with garlands of fragrant flowers and beautiful kapa cloth. He did not criticize his Hawaiian companions who paid homage to them.[40]

The Islands were far more peaceful than the English clergymen expected, but they were marred by alcohol abuse and haole misconduct. When another Englishman, Gilbert Mathison, met the king, he found: "The royal beast lay sprawling on the ground in a state of total drunkenness and insensibility." Mathison heard that most kanakas would not embrace the new religion until they had heard:

Chapter 6—Reading, Writing and Religion

the King's express declaration in its favor.... The chief obstacle to its progress is perhaps the enmity and un[C]hristian conduct of the European and American residents, who are most of them directly or indirectly opposed to the cause of religion....[41]

The visiting LMS evangelists included seven Tahitian converts who now worked as teachers. Hawaiians forged relationships with these distant kin, learning about Christianity directly from other Pacific Islanders, fulfilling part of Hewahewa's vision of an indigenized church. Kaʻahumanu immediately invited Auna (c.1790–1835) and his wife to live in her home. Auna, a chief and priest from Raiatea who had become a Christian deacon and chaplain, convinced Liholiho that many of the charges that other haoles had leveled against the mission were false.[42]

Keōpūolani invited Taua, another Tahitian missionary, to join her household to continue her instruction in Christianity. She and Kaʻahumanu persuaded the Tahitians to extend their stay, rather than continuing on to the Marquesas Islands as they originally had planned. Keōpūolani also urged Ellis to return with his family, which he did the following year, building a house in Honolulu near those of Kaʻahumanu, Kamehameha's daughter Kīnaʻu, Kalanimōkū, Boki, and other aliʻi. Ellis and the Tahitian mikanele soon won wider support for their American colleagues.[43]

Kaʻahumanu, though, still showed little interest in the preaching of either Methodists or Calvinists. Mathison attended worship in Honolulu in 1822 and noticed, "Not many of the white residents were present, and but few of the natives." Kaʻahumanu had promised to attend, he heard, but decided on a whim to surf at Waikīkī instead. When William Ellis asked if she would like "to know and serve the true God," she replied that she could not embrace a new religion until the king did so first, even though she did, in fact, sometimes act without waiting for his approval. At least Ellis was able to draw a large crowd of native listeners, a week after Bingham had attracted few. Sybil was hurt that the Kuhina Nui still did not attend worship, even though it was now offered in Hawaiian. Kaʻahumanu, for her part, was indignant when the missionary women refused her gift of expensive satin dresses like those she wore herself. Their protests that they could never wear anything so luxurious made no sense to a monarch.[44]

The missionaries' disapproval of Hawaiian dancing was a further impediment to their success. The hula was used primarily for entertainment and celebration; it played little role in Hawaiian religion, and the abolition of the kapus and destruction of heiaus in 1819 had not affected it at all. Performers still bowed to Laka, the androgynous god/goddess of the dance, though, and the Calvinists also were shocked by the hula's nudity, mingling of sexes, and unabashed sexuality—particularly the hula maʻi (*procreation dances*) whose chants celebrated the genitals. Bingham urged Boki to prohibit the hula on Oʻahu, but the governor saw no reason that dancing and learning could not go together. Boki insisted: "It is well to have both the hula and the pala." Bingham then tried, unsuccessfully, to persuade Kaʻahumanu to ban the dance.[45]

Nor did the missionaries have much luck with trying to persuade aliʻi to give up polygamous and polyandrous marriages. Chiefs often had multiple wives, and as Ellis noted in disgust,

> among the reigning family, brothers and sisters marry. This custom, so revolting to every idea of moral propriety, that the mind is shocked at the thought of its existence, appears to have been long in use....[46]

From May through July 1822, Kaʻahumanu took both of her husbands on a tour of Molokaʻi, Maui, and the Big Island to demonstrate her authority and encourage her subjects to study the palapala. Traveling in royal style, she brought at least 800 people in her entourage. Knowing that some people secretly hoped for a return of the old religion, she demolished several heiaus, collected images of the akua that had been hidden, and publicly destroyed these statues. She was not ready to embrace a new religion herself, but in a single day, she burned 102 wooden statues of the old gods. Soon, 300 people were often participating in Sunday worship in Honolulu.[47]

The LMS missionaries shared the abolitionist convictions of the New Englanders. On the Fourth of July, American residents of Honolulu gathered to celebrate the holiday, and Hiram Bingham recited a poem that George Bennet had composed for the occasion. A decade before slavery was abolished in the British Empire, and four decades before Emancipation in the United States, Bennet wrote:

> Yet must it be told, that the sons of the brave,
> The founders of freedom, persist to enslave
> The sweet sons of Africa? Alas! it is so!
> And shall it continue? It shall not, O, no!
> Arise, Columbia! shake off the disgrace;
> In Liberty's home, let not bondage have place!
> Tell the cruel, the heartless, the holders of slaves,
> Desecration they cast on their forefather's graves.[48]

The Sandwich Islands Mission hoped to reshape the kingdom but had little success in reforming the king. He still was drunk much of the

Chapter 6—Reading, Writing and Religion

time and resisted pleas to sober up. Though he had helped to dismantle traditional beliefs, he clung to some old notions—including divine kingship, multiple wives, and his aikāne Kanaina. When Hiram Bingham criticized him for getting drunk and claimed that such conduct displeased the Almighty, Liholiho roared back, "I am God myself.... Get out of my house!"[49]

Another time, in a less belligerent mood, he told Binamu, "I cannot repent now. In five years I will turn and forsake sin. I have given my word to the Lord that I will repent in five years." He never quit.[50]

To some observers, however, the progress made in his realm within a few years was remarkable. Gilbert Mathison was amazed by the absence of warfare and this fact:

> Murder and robberies accompanied by violence are absolutely unknown.... Nor is the King surrounded, as in former times, by a crowd of armed attendants.... This must be considered a new state of things, indicative of actual improvement and material changes in the temper, and spirit, and condition of the people and the policy and liberality of the government.[51]

Liholiho's Favorite Wife, Kamāmalu, was drawn to the new religion and studied with the missionaries but did not convert, respecting her husband's suspicions of the Calvinists. Liholiho urged his subjects to attend the mikanele schools and occasionally attended their worship services himself, but showed no interest in joining their church. When Ka'ahumanu visited one chapel, she offended the preacher by being carried into the sanctuary on a chair and placed on the raised platform, facing the congregation, just as he did. The clergyman took this as an insult, unable to imagine that this was how royalty might be received in their own realm—or for that matter, how they were treated in European cathedrals. Overlooking his rudeness, she asked how Christians were supposed to behave in worship.[52]

The Kuhina Nui studied the palapala and asked the Sandwich Islands Mission to provide books for newly literate students to read. The missionaries rejoiced, thinking that they might finally be making some headway. When Ka'ahumanu and Kaumuali'i sailed in August to Kaua'i with a retinue of 1,200 people to collect sandalwood, they inaugurated a school at Waimea that immediately filled with 300 students. She wrote from Waimea to Kamāmalu on O'ahu, showing both affection and humor:

> Tell the posse of Long-necks to send some more books down here. I want 800 Hawaiian books to be sent hither. We are much pleased to learn the

palapala. By and by perhaps we shall be akamai [*wise*]. Give my love to Mr. and Mrs. Bingham and the whole company of Long necks.

She promised no allegiance to the church—but at least stopped throwing plates at Kaumuali'i when he knelt to pray.[53]

Ka'ahumanu and Kaumuali'i then sailed further than either ever had gone before, to the newly rediscovered island of Nihoa, known from ancient chants and stories and celebrated in a mele composed by one of her ancestors. A total of 120 miles west of Ni'ihau, tiny Nihoa had been visited by fishing expeditions from Kaua'i and Ni'ihau but was abandoned centuries earlier. Unoccupied, it was almost forgotten by Islanders and completely unknown to haole sailors. The Regent proudly annexed it to the Kingdom of Hawai'i, rather than attaching it to the realm that her husband supposedly ruled. Kaumuali'i acquiesced.[54]

CHAPTER 7

The New Kaʻahumanu

In January 1823, missionaries and monarchs were united in grief. Both Hiram and Sybil Bingham's newborn son, their first child, and Liholiho's sister died within days of each other. Kaʻahumanu and other chiefs attended Christian funeral services for both of them, which they found extraordinarily different from traditional Hawaiian death rites. As the Binghams mourned and stern New Englanders expressed emotion publicly, Islanders saw them in a new, far more sympathetic light. Kaʻahumanu's attitude toward these foreigners softened, and she asked them to pray for the royal daughter, "that the soul of the child might go to heaven."[1]

William Ellis and his wife Mary returned to the Islands on February 5, 1823. For English Methodists to join an American Calvinist mission was a radical idea, but the London Missionary Society agreed the couple should work in Hawaii as long as their help was needed. Liholiho now expressed approval of the mikanele, saying that they had brought "the word of the Great God of Heaven.... We are learning how to read and write." Kaʻahumanu at the very least no longer was predisposed to believe evil of them.[2]

On April 27, the First Company was overjoyed to receive the Second Company. This time, the American Board of Commissioners for Foreign Missions sent not only three ordained clergymen and two other licensed preachers—enough to launch new congregations in Hilo and Lāhainā—but also a doctor, a business manager, and three more Hawaiians who had studied at the Foreign Mission School in Cornwall. This group also included Betsey Stockton, once-enslaved Betsey Stockton, the first single woman missionary sent to the Islands, who quickly learned Hawaiian and became a skilled nurse and school superintendent. Her presence demonstrated that the missionaries could bridge racial divisions—at a time when slavery remained legal in most of the United States. Kaʻahumanu greeted them far differently than she had the

First Company: "Our hearts are glad you have come, very glad. We are glad you have come on a kapu day, and have been with us in worship."[3]

Some members of the Second Company, such as the Rev. William Richards and the Mission's new Superintendent of Secular Affairs or business agent, Levi Chamberlain, were transformed by the missionary experience, developed a deep appreciation for the compassion and generosity of those whom they sought to convert. Most, however, arrived with the attitudes that afflicted the First Company. The Rev. Charles Stewart, for example, resented that few people whom he met spoke English. He also was appalled that their homes were infested with bugs—not realizing that it was haoles such as him who had brought such pests as the aggressive leaping flea there. He saw "dreadful abominations daily taking place around us, drunkenness and adultery, gambling and theft, deceit, treachery, and death…." He even doubted that Islanders were fully human:

> A first sight of these wretched creatures was almost overwhelming. Their naked figures, and wild expression of countenance, their black hair streaming in the wind as they hurried the canoe over the water with all the eager action and muscular power of savages, their rapid and unintelligible exclamations, and whole exhibition of uncivilized character gave to them the appearance of being half-man and half-beast, and irresistibly pressed on the thoughts the query, "Can they be men—can they be women?—do they not form a link in creation, connecting man with the brute?"[4]

Stewart's reference to a "link in creation" is revealing in another way. In the 1820s and well beyond, most Euro-American scientists believed in a Great Chain of Being, one in which each species formed a link in the chain related to the one before it but which had not evolved into a new species. The great Swiss paleontologist, Georges Cuvier, critiqued this notion of a single Chain of Being, but it was embraced by even such brilliant pioneer geologists such as Charles Lyell, Henry Thomas De la Beche, William Buckland, and William Daniel Conybeare. It later become Charles Darwin's "sacred cause" to explain common human origins. Charles Stewart and many other haoles saw Pacific Islanders as a separate, inferior species, while Kaʻahumanu and other kanakas recognized haoles as fellow human beings, odd though their customs might be.[5]

Charles Stewart judged Kaʻahumanu to be haughty, a comment that nobles would have found remarkable, coming from a commoner such as him:

Chapter 7—The New Ka'ahumanu

She appears to be between forty and fifty years of age; is large and portly, still bears marks of the beauty for which she has been celebrated, but has an expression of greater hauteur than any other islander I have yet seen.[6]

The Calvinists might have had greater success if they had recognized that Hawaiians still believed Ka'ahumanu possessed immense spiritual power. She had rejected some of the old ways—but had not surrendered her mana.

The new arrivals did not receive a particularly warm welcome from Islanders, but Keōpūolani announced in May that she was moving permanently to Lāhainā and asked that a mikanele be assigned to live nearby and instruct her. The First and Second Companies decided by ballot that Charles and Harriet Stewart would lead the new mission station, assisted by William and Clarissa Richards, who also were new arrivals. Charles Stewart initially was frightened when surrounded by Hawaiians, feeling "exposed to trials and dangers," which is not the best way to begin proselytizing anyone. Months later, he still objected to their homes, saying, "Native dwellings are objectionable in many respects," rather than seeing how skillfully they fit the local climate and available building materials.[7]

Nor did Stewart begin to understand how they saw the world. Like Hiram Bingham, he was offended that Hawaiians allowed their pets indoors and did not grasp their sense of humor, such as the Kuhina Nui adopting a pig, once kapu for women, and naming it after herself, or giving a high chief the nickname *Boki* after a dog owned by a haole. Kanakas called lava "Pele's excrement."[8]

Islanders and mikanele also had sharply differing views of morality. The former—and many haoles—saw gambling not as a vice, but rather as an innocent pastime. A merchant as pious as Stephen Reynolds attended worship every weekly, sometimes three times on Sundays, and also enjoyed games of chance. Many people, both Hawaiians and foreigners, resented the missionaries' condemnation of their favorite recreational activities. In response, Charles Stewart quickly learned, merchants blamed the Calvinists for everything from port charges (which Kamehameha had levied years before the First Company arrived) to the high cost of goods in Honolulu.[9]

Even tolerant missionaries such as William Ellis expressed frustration that Islanders often seemed more interested in hula than in their preaching. While touring the Big Island in July, he encountered a large crowd that had gathered at Kailua to see a dance performance. He noted in his journal, with some dismay, "We were anxious to address

Queen Kaʻahumanu of Hawaii

the multitude on the subject of religion before they should disperse; but so intent were they on their amusement that they could not have been diverted from it." He later persuaded Governor Kuakini to cut short a dance performance so Ellis could talk about Christianity, but the missionary was embarrassed when the governor asked why the behavior of haoles who knew the Bible did not conform to its teachings.[10]

One high-ranking chief objected to Keōpūolani building homes and a house of worship for the missionaries and begged her to send them away, saying, "Their instructions are not good. They bind us too close. They will not permit us to drink rum, or do as we formerly did." But within months, the Tahitians whom she had invited to live with her had taught her more about Christianity than the New Englanders had in three years. The Wahine Kapu founded Waiola Church, the first congregation on Maui. Convinced that she should have only one husband, she gave up Kalanimōkū and kept Hoapili, Kamehameha's longtime ally (and perhaps also his aikāne) and now governor of Maui. Thus, the Queen Mother, the Wahine Kapu, became a follower of Iesu Kristo (*Jesus Christ*).[11]

On August 21, 1823, Kaʻahumanu, Kaumualiʻi, Kalanimōkū, and dozens of other chiefs arrived in Lāhainā to be with Keōpūolani in her final illness. As death approached, Kaʻahumanu and other aliʻi urged the missionaries to baptize her without delay. She pleaded:

> I do very much wish to have water sprinkled on me in the name of God before I die. I have already given myself to Jesus Christ, I am his. I love him, and I much wish to be like his people, and to be baptized in the good name before I die.[12]

The Revs. Richards and Stewart did not yet speak Hawaiian and were unwilling to administer the sacrament without an interpreter. Calvinists were reluctant to baptize anyone until convinced that her conversion was genuine, and they required proof of conformity to their own version of Christianity. Anthony Allen, for example, had worked for Kamehameha the Great, drilled the first well on Oʻahu, established the first hospital in the realm (a convalescent hospital for sailors), and was a great friend of the Sandwich Islands Mission. But Hiram Bingham refused to baptize his children, since he had taken two local wives, when he arrived in the Islands, as had many haoles—one merchant took 10 of them. Only one of Allen's wives was still alive, yet Bingham still objected to their relationship, because they had never been married by a clergyman, even though there were none to be found before 1820. The

Chapter 7—The New Ka'ahumanu

missionaries had baptized no one, in fact, except for Kaumuali'i's son Humehume, and this had hardly turned out well. He spent most of his time with haole castaways and deserters, got drunk often, and had set fire to the home of a sea captain who refused to give him gin.[13]

By now, however, William Ellis spoke Hawaiian fluently. As a Methodist, Ellis was not bound by Calvinist rules, and the Americans could hardly question the legitimacy of a sacrament performed by a far more experienced and successful missionary. Through Tahitian teachers and a visiting Methodist, Christianity finally became a religion that Hawaiians could embrace. Ellis baptized Keōpūolani an hour before her death.[14]

There were fears that chaos would erupt, as often had occurred upon the death of royalty in the past. Many on Maui asked the mikanele to guard them in the Lāhainā mission compound, fearing they might be killed at a heiau. But Keōpūolani told her people, as her husband Kamehameha had, that no one should be sacrificed on any altar when she breathed her last breath, and Liholiho followed his mother's wishes. When she died on September 16, "Loud and repeated wailings were heard among the multitude for several days." She had asked her son to give her a Christian funeral, which Ellis conducted, without traditional mourning rituals, which led to the end of most funerary customs. She wanted some of the old ways to die with her.[15]

Hundreds of Islanders, ali'i and commoner alike, carried stones from an old heiau to Keōpūolani's grave, creating a wall around her tomb and a monument to her. Liholiho's heart seemed to be touched by his mother's final plea, and during the last two weeks of her life, he had remained sober, promising that he would never get drunk again. After her burial, though, some of his foreign friends offered the young king cherry brandy, which he had never tasted and may not have known was intoxicating. In no time at all, he was "beginning a dreadful revel."[16]

The baptism, death, and funeral of the Wahine Kapu profoundly affected Ka'ahumanu. A group of chiefs asked William Ellis and Charles Stewart to pray with them every evening at the Kuhina Nui's home, and Ka'ahumanu asked Ellis to lead a worship service at Waikīkī when they returned to O'ahu. After Keōpūolani's death, her husband Hoapili told the missionaries that he planned to marry Ka'ahumanu's sister Kalākua, and that he wanted a Christian ceremony. They were delighted to perform the wedding—and relieved that the groom did not plan to take additional wives. The marriage failed to launch a wave of church-sanctioned matrimony, but there were now 1,000 people in

Queen Kaʻahumanu of Hawaii

Lamentations for Keopuolani by William Ellis, 1823, engraved by S. Barter, from William Richards' *Memoir of Keopuolani, Late Queen of the Sandwich Islands*, 1825 (Wikimedia Commons).

worship in Honolulu most Sundays, a greater number than in nearly any sanctuary in the United States.[17]

Liholiho presided over ceremonies, but Kaʻahumanu controlled the government and the money that Liholiho needed to continue his dissipate life. As the kingdom's first written constitution explained, the Kuhina Nui conducted nearly all the business of the kingdom and was not supposed to act without the king's knowledge and approval (though she sometimes did), and he needed her approval to

Liholiho (Kamehameha II), artist unknown, after John Hayter, 1824 (National Portrait Gallery, Smithsonian Institution, gift of the Metropolitan Museum of Art, Joseph Verner Reed Collection).

Chapter 7—The New Kaʻahumanu

take action. Liholiho was drunk more and more often. When he and his friends took part in a parade during the annual feast in memory of his father, they were so inebriated that they could barely stay on their horses. Another time, in a drunken rage, he ordered the murder of a chief of whom he was jealous. Hiram Bingham despaired, "How unfit such a ruler to be the leader of a nation."[18]

Facing mounting pressure from American merchants to pay his debts and rumors that haoles and aliʻi were plotting to kill him, the king startled everyone by announcing that he planned to sail halfway around the world to London to meet King George IV. He hoped to forge closer ties with Beretania and hoped to bring back Church of England missionaries to counterbalance the American Calvinists. He would take with him Kamāmalu, the Favorite of his five tall, beautiful wives, Governor Boki of Oʻahu and his wife Liliha, and several other Hawaiian leaders. Jean-Baptiste Rives persuaded the king to take him as his secretary and translator. Rejecting a suggestion from the Mission—and indicating his true feelings toward it—he refused to stop in New England or take William Ellis, who wanted to return to England and hoped to exert a positive influence on the wayward monarch during the long sea voyage.[19]

The Council of Chiefs hastily gathered in Lāhainā and approved the trip. When the royal party sailed on November

Boki, Governor of Oahu of the Sandwich Islands, and His Wife, Liliha by John Hayter (drawn on stone from the original painting by John Hayter, London, 1824, printed by C. Hullmandel, C-020-009, courtesy Alexander Turnbull Library, Wellington, New Zealand).

Queen Kaʻahumanu of Hawaii

27, 1823, there was much wailing and crying, since many people loved their flawed, dissolute monarch and feared that he might not return. The king was disappointed, however, that no one tried to stop him from leaving; some seemed relieved to see him go.[20]

Liholiho named his young brother Kauikeaouli as the heir apparent, in case he did not return from England, and he designated Kaʻahumanu the Regent, as well as the Kuhina Nui. She would rule in his absence and in the future should Kauikeaouli take the throne while still a child. She, in turn, appointed her younger sister Nāmāhāna acting governor of Oʻahu while Boki was away. Without the erratic king, one local merchant noted almost immediately, the kingdom was better governed.[21]

After the royal party sailed away, the missionaries were startled to discover that the reins of power were in the hands of a woman. Hiram Bingham, a man of his times, had concentrated on converting Kalanimōkū, hoping to win the king through his prime minister. Despite the examples of Cleopatra, Queen Elizabeth, and Catherine the Great, Bingham was startled to see a woman exercising authority and confessed to not "knowing fully the standing and influence of Kaahumanu, and perhaps lost time and opportunities on that account...." The London Missionary Society (LMS) was even slower to grasp the situation. More than two years later, the LMS would still be reporting, incorrectly: "The islands are now subject to one government, consisting of a king.... The king is regarded as owning all the lands, and possesses unlimited power."[22]

In December 1823, though, the mikaneles celebrated a major achievement. On a small handpress they had brought on the *Thaddeus*, Elisha and Maria Loomis printed the first Hawaiian-language hymnal, filled with chants composed by Ellis—and, of course, "Owhyhee's Idols Are No More." Soon, the mission press was churning out schoolbooks, religious tracts, and portions of the Bible in Hawaiian. They also were overjoyed when Kalanimōkū ordered people on December 21 to observe the Sabbath strictly, not even lighting cooking fires, though it would prove as difficult then as it is now to compel piety.[23]

After Liholiho's departure, the Queen Regent began attending Christian worship more frequently, often with both of her husbands, which must have simultaneously encouraged and perplexed the Binghams. He suspected that her interest in this new faith grew out of a desire to enhance her power more than it did out of genuine piety, but he welcomed it nonetheless. How, though, could he ever convert a monarch who was married to a father and son, both of whom had been abducted?[24]

Chapter 7—The New Kaʻahumanu

Kaʻahumanu may have overturned the old taboos, but by the beginning of 1824, she was having second thoughts about abandoning the akua. When her brother Keʻeaumoku ʻOpio fell ill, it was thought that an enemy was trying to pray him to death. She ordered hogs and dogs to be sacrificed to lift the curse, but he died two and half months later.[25]

Then, she became sick herself, though, and Sybil Bingham nursed her back to health. Kaʻahumanu concluded that Sybil's prayers were responsible for her recovery. Almost overnight, she became the biggest supporter of the Sandwich Islands Mission, and Binamuwahine and her husband became advisors in matters both spiritual and governmental. Sybil succeeded where he had failed. She forged a friendship that won the monarch for the church. As Hiram Bingham acknowledged:

> As Mrs. B. sat down by the side of the sick queen, and with unfeigned sympathy for her sufferings and danger, bathed her aching temples, she bound a silken cord around her heart, from which I think she never broke loose while she lived.

These women forged this relationship despite cultural differences that remained vast. A year after Charles Stewart arrived, a kanaka whom Stewart considered an excellent prospect for conversion told him, "the Hawaiians thought us a very coldhearted people."[26]

The American Board intended to get Hawaiian women to conform to New England Christian gender roles, as part of their project to "civilize heathens," but paradoxically opened new avenues of work for American and European women. The success of missionary women likewise opened up new roles back home for women in the church, from teaching to preaching, from medicine to social reformation.[27]

The Binghams named a daughter after the Regent, calling her Elizabeth Kaʻahumanu Bingham—and the queen later took the child's name, Elisabeta, as her own baptismal name. She built a cottage for them next to Pukaomaomao (*Green Gateway*), her home in cool, upper Manoa Valley, where she spent an increasing amount of time. This cottage provided both a place for them to stay when they came to visit and an escape from hot, dusty Honolulu. Hers was a stately grass house with green shutters and doors, built on a stone foundation, and surrounded by ʻōhiʻa lehua trees and sweet-scented hibiscus. Several leading aliʻi built homes nearby, and Elisha Loomis noted a year later, "a kind of village is springing up around them, consisting already of 40 or 50 huts, the houses of the chiefs, a school house, and chapel." He called the view from Pukaomaomao "the most picturesque and romantic scenery I have ever beheld."[28]

Earlier, the Regent had spent much of her time playing cards, but when she grasped the power of the written word, she suddenly became far more interested in the palapala. Able to read within a few weeks, she urged her people to attend mission schools and worship services. Hawaiian women also began to accept invitations to female-only gatherings hosted by the missionary women. She also expressed interest in forming a choir, and joined other chiefs in learning how to sing Christian hymns in the Hawaiian language.[29]

More than 500 students took part in quarterly exams in the spring of 1824. As each class chanted together what they had learned, Ka'ahumanu grew more and more excited. She then walked to the Binghams' house and announced, "I am ready now to be sprinkled with water in the name of the Lord." Her government also enacted a new law on March 29, 1824, to control drinking of alcohol and public drunkenness, which pleased the Calvinists. By the end of the year, there were nearly 2,000 pupils in the mission schools.[30]

Earlier, the chiefs had opposed literacy for the common people, declaring, "If the palapala is good, we wish to possess it first ourselves; if it is bad, we do not intend our subjects to know the evil of it." On April 13, 1824, however, the chiefs gathered to debate whether "it is proper that all the people should attend to the palapala and learn to read"—as opposed to only ali'i being instructed. Ka'ahumanu and Kalanimōkū said that "all their people from Hawaii to Kauai should be instructed...."[31]

Commoners were slow to convert, but they did show up for worship. missionaries soon were preaching to thousands of people at a time. Some Hawaiians walked all day each Saturday to attend services. They came in droves to prayer meetings, too, and thousands of Hawaiians joined lay groups promoting Christian living. At these "moral societies" or "kapu meetings," they discussed the state of their souls, confessed their sins, and promised to turn away from immorality. These groups set a high standard for moral improvement; even taking too much pleasure in one's piety was considered sinful. After three years, the Sandwich Islands Mission disbanded them, not because they failed to reform the behavior of their members, but because they did not inculcate sufficient humility, explaining, "Their influence, we found, was to foster pride and self-righteousness."[32]

Ka'ahumanu and many chiefs thought Christianity might supply new rules to replace old taboos. Other ali'i were not so sure. They

Chapter 7—The New Kaʻahumanu

wanted to first hear from Liholiho about how this religion was practiced in the lands that haoles called "the Christian nations" before they embraced it themselves. Despite the skepticism of some chiefs, class attendance grew by leaps and bounds. There were now schools in every district of every island, with seven of them on Niʻihau, where only a few hundred people lived—at a time when there were few tuition-free schools in the United States or England. By 1825, 20,000 people in the kingdom could read. By the end of the decade, one-third of the population was in school.[33]

There were not nearly enough teachers for them, but they found it relatively easy to understand the simplified Hawaiian alphabet that the First Company taught, despite the initial lack of any books printed in their language. Many students became teachers themselves, fanning out across the Islands. For them, reading and writing were exciting. In one school on Kauaʻi, students used surfboards as seats and writing tables. Eager to learn, they crowded around the few books that were available. Some learned to read equally well upside down. Within 10 years, most adult Hawaiians could read; soon, the literacy rate exceeded that in the United States or Europe. It was higher, in fact, than in any other nation except for Scotland. The kingdom had the most literate working class of any nation, and those who went abroad to labor sent home detailed reports on the people whom and places that they visited. Writing in Hawaiian, kanakas preserved more of their oral literature in written form than almost any other indigenous people.[34]

Literacy, however, was not universally welcomed. Some Hawaiians who feared Western ways and some haole merchants who were concerned mostly with making quick profits warned that if Hawaiians spent time reading and writing rather than fishing and farming, they would end up poor, sick, and starving. They also blamed foreign disease on missionaries and their schools—rather than on sailors and prostitution. William Richards reported sadly that 30 chiefs had died in the past two years, and "some say it is the *palapala*."[35]

Early in 1824, the Regent built a New England–style home in Honolulu for her once-abducted-but-now-beloved Kaumualiʻi but had little time to enjoy it with him. Already sick when they moved in, he grew steadily weaker. Disgusted with his son Humehume's behavior, he dictated a will that largely disinherited him, leaving Kauaʻi and Niʻihau to Kaʻahumanu and Kalanimōkū to hold in trust for Liholiho and fulfilling the promise he made to Kamehameha. Then, Kaumualiʻi slipped into a coma and died on May 26.

Queen Kaʻahumanu of Hawaii

Kaʻahumanu gave her husband a Christian funeral, with Ellis presiding, which may have offended some traditionalists. Some kanakas accused the missionaries of praying Kaumualiʻi to death, telling Charles Stewart that "soon there would not be a chief left on Oahu." The Sunday after his funeral, someone torched the church in Honolulu. Shaken by this arson, chiefs rebuilt it with their own hands.[36]

The death of Kaumualiʻi and the subsequent transfer of his lands, arms, and other property to Liholiho consolidated the Kamehameha dynasty's authority over the entire archipelago. It also revived tensions between the aliʻi from Kauaʻi and those from Maui and the Big Island. Humehume remained chief of one valley on the Garden Isle, but he seethed with resentment and suspicion. When Hiram Bingham called on him, he accused Kaʻahumanu of poisoning him and his father.[37]

Meanwhile, in Lāhainā, the Kuhina Nui and the Council of Chiefs gathered in June to discuss whether 9-year-old Princess Nāhiʻenaʻena might make a suitable bride for her brother, Crown Prince Kauikeaouli. The old religion had taught that a child would be filled with immense mana or spiritual power if its parents were high-ranking aliʻi and siblings, and few could have more mana than the children of Kamehameha the Great and his Sacred Wife, Keōpūolani.

As Elisha Loomis noted in his journal, "It was well known here that the prince and princess for a considerable time past have lived in a state of incest"—at least as the mikanele defined incest. The missionaries adamantly opposed sibling marriage. Many kanakas, however, hoped the royal children would wed, including Kaʻahumanu and the young king's spiritual advisor, John Papa ʻĪʻī. Kalanimōkū asked Elisha Loomis whether such a match was proper. Loomis answered that it was immoral and risked producing children with serious birth defects. Far from securing the Kamehameha dynasty, Loomis warned, such a union was likely to produce few children and sickly ones at that.[38]

Elisha Loomis and William Richards rushed to the meeting of aliʻi. They asked the assembled chiefs if they knew any children born out of such a marriage. Told that Keōpūolani's parents were brother and sister, Loomis and Richards pointed out that she had been in poor health most of her life and had died young, but few were persuaded by their argument. The chiefs approved the match and held a traditional banquet that got nearly everyone in Lāhainā roaring drunk. Raucous celebration spread throughout the kingdom.[39]

Kauikeaouli (*placed in the dark clouds*) and Nāhiʻenaʻena (*hot fires*) undeniably were attracted to each other. They had been raised in

Chapter 7—The New Ka'ahumanu

isolation as the most sacred children in the kingdom and had lost their parents at a young age, driving them even closer together. They probably were having sexual intercourse by 1824, even if some missionaries refused to believe this. The Prince chafed at the attempts of the mikanele to control him, while the Princess spent her short life wavering between obedience to the new faith and loyalty to the old ways.[40]

Meanwhile, on Kaua'i, some ali'i who had rejected Christianity were angry about the distribution of Kaumuali'i's lands. Egged on by his haole friends, Humehume revolted against the government of Lohploho and the Kuhina Nui. The rebel forces may have been enthusiastic, but they were inexperienced and poorly trained. Kalanimōkū, on the other hand, commanded a well-equipped, well-organized army supported by a vastly superior navy. The rebels launched a Sunday-morning surprise attack on Fort Elizabeth at Waimea, hoping to seize its cannon and hundreds of muskets that were stored there. Led by the sword-wielding widowed queen, Deborah Kapule, forces loyal to the government repelled Humehume's ragtag army, and he managed to seize only about 100 muskets and one small field piece. Ka'ahumanu immediately proclaimed a day of fasting and prayer "to supplicate the divine on the people at Kauai, that the war may cease and effusion of blood be stopped and that even Humehume may be spared from death."[41]

Kalanimōkū turned to William Richards for advice as to how Christians should conduct warfare. Richards replied that Christians fight only when no other course of action is possible, only when their lives are in danger, and with as little bloodshed as possible. Captives should not be executed, Richards insisted, even though this had long been the custom in Hawai'i unless someone such as Ka'ahumanu intervened to spare their lives.[42]

This restraint was both good ethics and excellent strategy. By moving slowly and cautiously, the prime minister built a wide coalition of supporters—and an overwhelming military force that outnumbered those of Humehume 10-to-one. In August, Kalanimōkū's army triumphed in a decisive battle on the south coast of Kaua'i. After hiding in the mountains for nearly two months, the rebel leaders finally were captured. Humehume's life was spared, and he spent the rest of his days in exile on O'ahu with his wife and child, free but broken in spirit. Kalanimōkū pardoned nearly all of the other rebels, telling them to go home, dwell in peace, cultivate their fields, study the palapala, and worship the Christian God.[43]

Elisha Loomis lamented:

Queen Kaʻahumanu of Hawaii

> Like all wars, this has brought with it a train of evils. Burning homes, destroying the crops of kalo and potatoes and such ... have been practiced to a considerable degree, and considerable plunder taken from the innocent inhabitants has already arrived at this place.

There were casualties and some retribution after the fighting ended, but Bingham noted with approval,

> it was a matter of thanksgiving and an indication of the ameliorating influence of Christianity on the minds of the leaders of the nation, to find the queen, Kaʻahumanu, and her high chieftains so free from any charge of barbarity or cruelty in subduing those who had risen up against them.[44]

This victory convinced many kanakas that the Christian God was stronger than their old akuas. Restive chiefs on Kauaʻi were replaced by aliʻi from Oʻahu and Maui who were loyal to Liholiho and Kaʻahumanu. She sailed from Lāhainā to Kauaʻi "to maintain the newly-restored tranquility." Even after this triumph, however, Kamehameha's widow (and Kaʻahumanu's sister), Nāmāhāna Piʻia, found the current king lacking in comparison with his father, telling Otto von Kotzebue, who had returned to the Islands for a third time, "we shall never have such another King." Kotzebue thought, by contrast, that Kaʻahumanu "seems to have been born for dominion."[45]

The government proclaimed another national day of fasting from dawn to sunset on August 27. It ordered there to be no "eating, cooking, bathing, playing in the surf, drinking rum, singing, dancing and everything except prayer and the exercises of the Gospel." European and American governments might suggest a day of prayer for the nation, but it was inconceivable that they would ban eating, drinking alcohol, working, and relaxation. In the Hawaiian Islands, this use of royal power seemed perfectly natural. Charles Stewart insisted that this fast was not the missionaries' idea. The chiefs came up with it on their own, he insisted.[46]

Having suppressed another traditionalist uprising, the Kuhina Nui faced a new disturbance. The Prince and Princess observed the first anniversary of their mother's death with a drunken "heathenish" revel in Lāhainā that lasted a week. Kaʻahumanu finally acted to stop brawls that had been sparked by drinking alcohol, boxing, and gambling. On September 23, she sent messengers throughout the kingdom, forbidding drunkenness, theft, and murder and urging people to honor the Sabbath, build schools, and study the palapala. She and her young husband, Kealiʻiahonui, spent nearly four months on Kauaʻi, urging people to

Chapter 7—The New Ka'ahumanu

learn how to read and write under the tutelage of newly trained, native teachers.[47]

Her people listened politely, but many remained devoted to their traditional gods. Kotzebue found that when he visited the Big Island in January, his Hawaiian guides were afraid to lead them more than halfway up Mauna Loa, "from fear of the spirits which haunt the summit." In January 1825, Kalanimōkū told Kotzebue that Liholiho should not have overturned everything his people held sacred when he abolished the kapus. He feared, the prime minister confessed, that a unified realm "probably will not survive me."[48]

In March 1825, the Kuhina Nui and her people were stunned to receive terrible news. Halfway around the globe, the royal expedition to London had met disaster. Liholiho arrived in England only to learn that the government of the United Kingdom had no idea that they were coming.

King Liholiho, Queen Kamamalu, Madame Boki of the Sandwich Islands by J. W. Gear, 1824 (National Portrait Gallery, Smithsonian Institution).

Queen Kaʻahumanu of Hawaii

Liholiho led his delegation to the theater and out on walks through the capital, but King George IV, who may have been addicted to laudanum and shared his father's mental afflictions, refused to meet Liholiho and Kamāmalu, whom he ignorantly dismissed as "a pair of dammed cannibals." The British press at first debated whether or not they were monarchs or "savages" but soon became fascinated with them.[49]

The royal party had barely landed, however, before several of them contracted measles. With no resistance to this haole disease, Kamāmalu died on July 8. Six days later, her grief-stricken husband followed her. It took eight months for the sad news to reach the Islands.

Elisha Loomis feared Liholiho's death would plunge the kingdom into civil war, as the demise of high chiefs often had, but the nation calmly accepted the decision of the Council of Chiefs confirming Kauikeaouli, the only surviving son of Kamehameha and Keōpūolani, as the new king. He would reign as Kamehameha III until 1854, longer than any other Hawaiian monarch. Kaʻahumanu continued as Regent and Kuhina Nui. Because of the boy's youth and inexperience in government, it was she who actually ruled the realm. Boki, who had led the royal party after Liholiho's death in London and had met with King George IV, now enjoyed even greater prestige than he had before the ill-fated trip.[50]

To lose a young monarch who had boasted, "I am God myself" was a further blow to those who remained loyal to the old faith. People mourned their king in a restrained manner, in stark contrast to their uncontrolled grief when his father died. Kaʻahumanu turned for consolation to the mikanele. Within weeks, Charles Stewart noted, young Kauikeaouli and "every chief of any importance" took part in Christian worship regularly. Nāhiʻenaʻena asked the regent and the prime minister to raise her and her brother, and he pleaded, "It is not good for us to be without parents." In the end, William and Clarissa Richards became their foster parents. The missionaries would not give up their own children to be raised by kanakas, but they would raise the royal orphans.[51]

George Canning, the British Foreign Secretary, sent the bodies of Liholiho and Kamāmalu home with full honors on a big, 46-gun frigate, the *Blonde*, along with newly appointed Consul Richard Charlton—while the United States continued to be represented only by a part-time consular agent, the lowest rank in the Foreign Service. The *Blonde* had an impressive commander, George Anson Byron, brother of the famous poet and British politician. Kaʻahumanu sailed with Lord Byron from Hilo to Honolulu. There, the Britons gave the royal couple an elaborate

Chapter 7—The New Ka'ahumanu

Queen Kamamalu, Her Attendant, and Boki by Julia Swinburne, about 1825 (Yale Center for British Art, Paul Mellon Collection).

Queen Kaʻahumanu of Hawaii

Christian funeral in June 1825, read by the *Blonde*'s chaplain from the Church of England's *Book of Common Prayer*, even though neither had joined the Anglicans—or any church. The dignified, stately ritual made a deep impression on many Hawaiians.[52]

Liholiho and some chiefs had worried that Beretania might object to the presence of American missionaries in the Sandwich Islands. Boki reported that King George supported their work, but also pointed out that Christianity was practiced somewhat differently in England than from how the Calvinists said it was practiced in New England, particularly when it came to such matters as laws enforcing Sabbath observance. The next Sunday, Kaʻahumanu, her sister Nāmāhāna Piʻia, Prime Minister Kalanimōkū, and more than 100 other aliʻi publicly declared their faith in Christ, asked to be baptized, and began a six-month period of probation—after which, the Sandwich Islands Mission would decide if they were worthy of membership in the church.[53]

Having kept the mikanele waiting to see if they might settle in her realm—and not granting them permission to stay permanently until four years later—the Kuhina Nui now found herself waiting for the Calvinists to accept her. Conversion to Christianity was not sufficient to make one a member of the church, she was told. When Hiram Bingham informed her that she could not be baptized until the missionaries had scrutinized her behavior for several months, she stormed out of his house in a huff. She felt insulted by this period of probation, but wait she did.

Lord Byron took Kaʻahumanu and other chiefs back to Hilo to "encourage the missionary labors of the station there." Upon her arrival, she repeatedly asked the local pastor, Samuel Ruggles, to come see her. He refused, an extraordinary insult to a prospective member of the church, let alone a queen, because he "thought her imperious and heathenish." When he finally relented, he "found that he had misjudged the case."[54]

Aliʻi asked Lord Byron what he thought of the new laws proposed by Kaʻahumanu. He refused to interfere in Hawaiian affairs but made two suggestions: Capital punishment should be imposed only very seldom (though many were sent to the gallows in England), and those accused of a crime should have the right to be tried by a jury. Kaʻahumanu accepted both ideas with relief, having grown reluctant herself to order executions. At the end of June 1825, the aliʻi outlawed drunkenness, theft, and violations of the Sabbath. Exposure to Western disease also prompted Kaʻahumanu to try something else that was new: Western

Chapter 7—The New Ka'ahumanu

Left: Kauikeaouli (Kamehameha III) by Robert Dampier, 1825. *Right:* Nāhi'ena'ena by Robert Dampier, 1825 (both courtesy Honolulu Museum of Art, Gift of Eliza Lefferts Cooke, Charles M. Cooke III, and Carolene Alexander Cooke Wrenn in memory of Dr. C. Montague Cooke, Jr., 1951).

pharmacology. On July 12, 1825, she received a prescription from William Davis, the *Blonde*'s surgeon, the first one ever written by a European physician that was given to a Hawaiian. This in turn made her subjects more open to the ministrations of haole doctors.[55]

Robert Dampier, the artist on the *Blonde*, painted striking portraits of young king Kamehameha III and Princess Nāhi'ena'ena, which captured how young the two were, dressed in traditional clothes and looking adrift in the world. Dampier did not see the courage it took for Ka'ahumanu to embrace new ideas. He wrote,

> It must be known that this Old Dame is the most proud, unbending Lady in the whole island ... she possesses unbounded authority and respect, not any of which is she inclined to lay aside for any occasion whatever. To submit therefore to my will for an hour or two was a severe trial of her pride....[56]

Dampier's annoyance suggests his arrogance. It is difficult to imagine him expressing the same disdain for an English monarch who displayed any pride.

Dampier may have seen Ka'ahumanu as unbending, but James Macrae, a Scottish botanist on the *Blonde*, was struck with the queen's playfulness, watching how she delighted in being pulled up a small rise in her four-wheeled cart—itself a novelty in the Islands—and gleefully coasting downhill. Macrae was not fond of the Mission, however. When Lord Byron arranged a magic lantern show (a precursor of projected slides), the first ever seen in the Islands, he complained that "owing to the religious fanaticism of the American Methodists, the king was prevented from being present," dismissing the missionaries as "illiterate mechanics."[57]

Like many other visitors, Macrae could not imagine that kanakas made decisions for themselves. The Calvinists objected to entertainment on the Sabbath but had no power to bar the king from it, and he often disregarded their wishes. They may have come from a lower social class than Macrae, but they were neither Methodists nor illiterate, not even in the older sense of being poorly schooled. Many had undergraduate degrees from Yale or Princeton Universities and had done graduate work at Andover or Princeton Theological Seminary. The mission women were uncommonly well-educated for their time and were accomplished writers, as can be seen in their letters and journals. Sybil Bingham had worked as a schoolteacher for nine years in New England. Once-enslaved Betsey Stockton had studied at Princeton Theological Seminary and knew enough science to recognize that a shark harpooned while the *Thaddeus* was en route to Hawaii had a cartilaginous skeleton rather than a bony one of a true fish—something unknown to many people, then or now. She quickly learned Hawaiian and started the first school for maka'āinana in the kingdom, a widely admired one that became the celebrated Lahainaluna High School.[58]

As for Macrae's charge of fanaticism, there was at least a bit of rigidity in the Mission's rules, though. The Regent and her husband asked the missionaries to marry them in a church wedding, but the Calvinists urged them to separate instead. First, the mikanele opposed the Kuhina Nui's marriage to a son and father at the same time. Now, after Kaumuali'i had died, Binamu still remained repulsed by her polyandrous marriage, and he no longer needed Keali'iahonui's help to prevent Humehume from inheriting his father's kingdom. It was hard to understand the attitude of these mikanele, particularly when one's language lacked any word for *adultery* or *illegitimate child*, since both concepts were unknown.[59]

For their part, Hiram Bingham and his colleagues were simply applying to Islanders the standards they expected of themselves. Any profession of faith had to be matched by a public commitment to build the rule of God on earth that Jesus preached. They did not expect candidates for church membership to understand fine points of theology

Chapter 7—The New Ka'ahumanu

but did demand that they "exhibit signs of a true conversion over a period of time." In the coming months, the Regent, with the support of most chiefs, banned prostitution, public drunkenness, theft, and nearly everything that the Calvinists thought violated the sanctity of the Sabbath. They also enacted new port regulations to corral sailors who jumped ship in the Islands and caused trouble.[60]

As David Chappell has observed, these efforts did not end the trade in sexual services but merely degraded its status. What had begun as voluntary, amicable relationships between wahines and haoles came to resemble prostitution in Europe and the United States. The New Englanders' belief that women should be submissive made it difficult for them to understand that kanakas saw sexual intercourse as a casual form of recreation. Far from being corrupted by foreigners, they often initiated these liaisons. What Calvinists recognized before most kanakas or other Europeans, however, was that many sailors treated women with contempt, as well as exposed them to myriad diseases. Slowly, the ali'i came to believe that the sex trade was debasing their people. For their part, sailors and merchants often blamed the Calvinists for decisions made by the chiefs, while the mikanele blamed sailors and merchants for oppressing women who had sexual intercourse with haoles quite willingly.[61]

Missionaries and merchants vied for the new king's support, while Boki and Ka'ahumanu each sought to mold him. Boki, who had been chosen by the boy's father to govern O'ahu and had traveled all the way to London, must have seemed to the young king to know more than the Regent about the ways of the world. Boki taught him to drink alcohol, smoke, gamble, and try every imaginable sexual union. Kauikeaouli frequently attended worship, but he preferred drinking, riding horses, and playing billiards on the Sabbath. The Calvinists saw this as the boy's moral weakness; many Hawaiians concluded that the new king rejected Puritanism.[62]

The Regent regularly toured the Islands to assess the needs of her people. Seeing how some nobles exploited commoners, she prohibited ali'i from increasing taxes or making people travel to distant fields to work for them without pay. She put an end to an ancient love game in which married couples switched partners for a night. Husbands and wives were not supposed to be jealous unless a couple stayed together past daybreak. She found these laws regulating personal morality difficult to enforce, however, as have many governments since. One missionary feared that foreigners, who seemed to resent the new rules more than kanakas did, would rise up in rebellion.[63]

Queen Kaʻahumanu of Hawaii

Otto von Kotzebue was dismayed to see Islanders observing the Sabbath in an austere, Calvinist manner, though as William Ellis observed, he was dismayed by nearly everything about the Sandwich Islands Mission and considered himself to be an instant expert on the Islands. Ellis ridiculed him for thinking "a few days residence ... all that is needful (notwithstanding he knows not a word of their language) to render him, in his own opinion, historiographer of a country...." Kotzebue lamented that on Sundays:

> The streets, formerly so full of life and animation, are now deserted; games of all kinds, even the most innocent, are sternly prohibited; sinning is a punishable offense; and the consummate profligacy of attempting to dance would find no mercy ... the whole day is devoted to prayer.

Despite the encouragement of the Regent, some Islanders resisted the new ways. Kotzebue met an elderly man who carried a book with him and explained with a laugh, "Don't think that I am learning to read. I have only bought the book so that I may look into it, that Kahumana may think I am following the general example...." Even those who sought to understand the new religion she had embraced sometimes missed the point of Christian piety. When they prayed, some aliʻi issued orders to the Almighty rather than reporting for duty.[64]

As her months of probation wore on, Kaʻahumanu and other probationers could not understand why Binamu would not baptize them. Despite her taking actions that pleased him immensely, some mikanele suspected that she embraced Christianity for political purposes, not out of genuine piety. Hiram Bingham explained, without really explaining anything, "though all these had, for several months at least, given much evidence of conversion, we still hesitated to baptize them...." Levi Chamberlain recognized, however, that the Kuhina Nui and her government were taking a major risk in attempting to keep women from visiting ships in now-bustling ports. In Honolulu alone, 20 to 30 wahines left their foreign lovers, which outraged dozens of haoles. A new path, she said, was required to bring ke ola hou (*new life*) to the nation.[65]

Having once found her haughty, Mercy Whitney now reported, "She wishes us to tell her how she should conduct herself, at home and in church...." Whitney realized how often the two women had misunderstood each other. When she gently reproved the Regent for sitting in worship with her back to the preacher, she was told that it was the custom in Hawaiʻi for royalty to face the people. No one had ever suggested to her that things were done differently among Christians. Her behavior had changed so completely that her people now called her "Ka'ahumanu hou" (*the new Ka'ahumanu*).[66]

Finally, on December 4, 1825, after eight months of probation, the missionaries accepted Ka'ahumanu's expression of faith and admitted her into church membership, along with Kalanimōkū, her former husband Keali'iahonui, four other prominent chiefs, and one commoner. She took Elisabeta (*Elizabeth*) as her baptismal name—the name of both a woman who played a pivotal role in the birth of Jesus and England's strongest queen—and received the sacrament of communion for the first time. The mikanele called her "the first fruit" of Kawaiaha'o, the "Westminster Abbey of the Pacific."[67]

Many foreigners suspected Ka'ahumanu converted because it served her political purposes, but whatever her motives, this was a great victory for the Sandwich Islands Mission. A few weeks later, 1,000 people came to worship at the new sanctuary in Honolulu, and services had to be held outdoors. Soon, there were 3,000 or 4,000 people worshipping on many Sundays. When Binamu preached at Waimea on Kaua'i, a quarter of the island's population showed up.[68]

CHAPTER 8

New Rules, New Riots

The American Board had ordered the Sandwich Islands Mission to abstain "from all interference and intermeddling with the political affairs and party concerns of the nation," but when Kaʻahumanu asked Hiram Bingham which sort of laws her realm needed, he did not hesitate to tell her what he thought. There had never been any separation of religion and politics in the archipelago—and not much of one in Massachusetts—so they assumed the faith that she embraced should be the faith of her people. Foreign merchants and sailors thought that the missionaries were meddling in their personal business when they preached against prostitution or drunkenness, but many kanakas thought this was fair criticism of lecherous drunks. As one American, Mrs. A.P. Cummings, noted with chagrin,

> It is a humiliating fact that the only opposition with which our missionaries have ever had to contend, in their self-denying labors in the Sandwich Islands, has been caused by the influence of foreigners, and too often by those who boasted the same American origin....[1]

Within days of her baptism, the Kuhina Nui gathered the principal chiefs and suggested that they base the laws of Hawaiʻi on the Ten Commandments, which had been translated recently into Hawaiian. As historian Walter McDougall explained, "Kaahumanu had not abolished kapu because she had ceased to believe in moral laws but because she had ceased to believe the old laws were moral." Embracing a new faith, she sought to impose a new morality. When she and Governor Kuakini attempted to close grog shops and gambling dens, an Englishman objected, "They do not prohibit these things in England or America."

"We do not rule there," Kaʻahumanu replied, "but these islands are ours and we wish to obey the word of God."[2]

Governor Boki claimed to support the laws that Kaʻahumanu proposed, but said he wanted their government to be modeled on Great Britain's Parliament, not America's presidential system. Aliʻi heatedly

Chapter 8—New Rules, New Riots

debated new laws and governmental structures. In the end, they agreed on only one thing: They had to control the bars and bordellos in Honolulu and Lāhainā.

The chiefs soon discovered how difficult a task this would be. Some foreigners who settled in Hawai'i were enterprising and industrious. Anthony Allen, for example, escaped slavery in Schenectady, New York, made his way to Boston, where he became a mariner, and eventually reached O'ahu. There, he married a local woman, raised a family, and became one of the first foreign merchants in the Islands. By the early 1820s, he was one of the wealthiest residents of the Island. Many, however, came ashore after months at sea, got drunk, and went looking for wahines. If they could not find willing women, they often seized girls by force and tried to keep them as sex slaves. This was not illegal in the United States and would not become so for nearly a century. When the Sandwich Islands Mission published the Ten Commandments in Hawaiian, an American captain was so outraged at this interference in his men's pleasure that he confronted Samuel Ruggles, brandished a dagger, and threatened "to bathe his hands in the heart's blood of every missionary who had anything to do with it."[3]

This sort of violence, the ali'i also agreed, had to stop. The Council of Chiefs banned the sale of both sex and alcohol, despite the fact that Governor Boki himself operated a tavern in Honolulu, wanted to lease out a farm to grow sugarcane for rum production, and sought to raise revenue by licensing prostitution. Ka'ahumanu prevented him from leasing his land to the distillery and had it planted with potatoes instead. She also ordered anyone caught engaging in prostitution in Honolulu to carry heavy stones to build a new church, making an enemy of the governor and fueling resentment of the Calvinists.[4]

A few years earlier, visiting English missionaries had hoped that Christianity would lead to the end of prostitution, as it had in the South Pacific, but they recognized that the faithful would pay a price for its prohibition. In the Christianized islands of the South Pacific, the Rev. William Ellis noted,

> the gospel and its other triumphs are evil spoken of by many Christians (falsely so called) who visit these seas, and are filled with rage, disappointment, and malice when they find they cannot riot in licentiousness, as former voyagers did....[5]

Most Hawaiians supported the new kapu on prostitution, but many foreign residents opposed it. Consular Agent Jones and Consul Richard

Queen Kaʻahumanu of Hawaii

Charlton went together to see the king. They claimed, incredibly, to know the governance of the kingdom better than he did, insisting that the prime minister and the Kuhina Nui had no right to make such a law. When sailors learned that they could no longer buy the sexual favors of wahines, they were outraged. On October 4, 1825, about 20 crew members of an English whaleship had come ashore after a long cruise in the North Pacific and marched on the Binghams' house, demanding to know why women were barred from his ship. Hiram Bingham explained that this was the decision of the chiefs, not the missionaries, neglecting to note that he supported it wholeheartedly—at which point they marched to Kaʻahumanu's home. Elisha Loomis noted in his diary:

> The sailors insisted that they must have their girls and would seize and carry them off by force. Kaahumanu said that if they did not retire peaceably, she would inform their officers. They replied that they were encouraged by their officers to come and demand the removal of the taboo. We have no reason to doubt the truth of this statement.[6]

When the Regent explained that they simply were trying to do what was right, "The sailors said they did not come to talk about religion but came after women and if they could not get them by fair means they would catch them where they could and drag them on board ship—they said this measure would be borne out by their captains and officers." The sailors dispersed only when Kalanimōkū threatened to arrest them. Holding the missionaries responsible for the new laws, most merchants stopped speaking to them.[7]

An even more serious conflict with whalers had begun in March, when Capt. William Buckle brought the British whaleship, *Daniel IV*, into the harbor at Lāhainā. He soon became infatuated with a 16-year-old aliʻi named Leoiki, one of the Mission's star pupils, and wanted to take her with him while he sailed to the South Pacific. The girl's kahu, the chief Kahakuhaʻakoi Wahinepio, a one-time governor of Maui who initially embraced Christianity but then returned to her old akua, took 16 gold doubloons from the captain to allow him to take a reluctant Leoiki as his "temporary wife." This was a common practice among mariners—the Whitneys estimated that more than 90 percent of them did so in the Sandwich Islands. However, Leoiki sent three messages asking William Richards for help, but he was unable to enlist any chief who had enough power to stop Wahinepio.[8]

Richards then accused Buckle of buying Leoiki as a sex slave, a hangable offense in the Royal Navy, even though the captain may have

Chapter 8—New Rules, New Riots

considered Leoiki to be his real, if temporary, wife. He may have deemed the money that he gave her kahu to be not for the purchase of chattel, but rather a dowry or bride-price, which was perfectly legal in England in the early 19th century. During this era, prostitution itself was common in Britain and the United States. British officers were expected to bring prostitutes on board to live for a time, and when ships visited ports in the West Indies, officers were expected to arrange with plantation owners to send enslaved women aboard to service their crew. The Admiralty even warned one pious captain, Robert Wauchope, that he would forfeit his commission if he barred prostitutes from his ship. Sailors received little pay, endured terrible living conditions, and were prone to desert when they reached port. Bringing women aboard was intended to retain their labor, prevent mutiny, and curb homosexual relationships among the crew. The British bore a profound antipathy toward homosexuality, which also was a hanging offense in the Royal Navy.[9]

Kahakuhaʻakoi Wahinepio promptly confessed that she had done wrong. Both the mikanele and their converts supported Richards' accusation against Buckle, unjust though it may have been. Hiram Bingham wrote that haoles were robbing Islanders of their wealth and destroying their health by selling them into sin. Foreign residents threatened, in response, to horsewhip him, but kanakas rallied to his defense. Bingham noted, "the native members of the church stood their ground well, and the number of candidates officially announced for admission to full communion [i.e., membership in the church] was greater than usual...."[10]

When Buckle returned Leoiki to Lāhainā as promised on October 3, 1825, he learned that Governor Hoapili was attempting to restrict prostitution and had declared wahines off-limits to sailors. The captain blamed the missionaries rather than the chiefs for this deprivation and threatened to kill both William and Clarissa Richards unless Hoapili lifted the ban immediately. The governor refused. Forty sailors armed with knives and pistols then set out in search of Richards, saying they intended to kill him. Hoapili sent 200 Hawaiians armed with muskets, bayonets, and spears to drive them away.[11]

Disgusted by this captain who claimed to be a gentleman and a Christian, the Sandwich Islands Mission sent Buckle a letter admonishing him privately for his actions. Outraged, he published their letter and said he was seeking "an opportunity to beat some of the missionaries in the street." Storming into the Binghams' home, he declared, "I want an apology for that letter, and if I don't get it, I'll *kill* you." Buckle raged for two hours, said that his Unitarian church did not care what Calvinists

Queen Kaʻahumanu of Hawaii

thought of him, blasted Calvinists for burning Unitarian theologian Michael Servetus at the stake for heresy—in Switzerland in 1553—and then stomped away.[12]

Into these troubled waters sailed the U.S.S. *Dolphin*. An 88-foot, 12-gun schooner, she was the first American warship to visit the kingdom. She was commanded by Lt. John "Mad Jack" Percival, an unfortunate choice for a delicate mission. Kaʻahumanu was favorably predisposed toward anyone who represented U.S. President John Quincy Adams, a Yankee from Massachusetts whose father was a founder and president of the new republic, but Percival managed to offend her from the start. As the *Dolphin* entered Honolulu Harbor on Saturday, January 14, 1826, her cannon fired a salute to the fort and received one in return. After the ship docked, American merchants came aboard to greet the captain and his crew, but the lieutenant was disappointed that no missionaries did so. Apparently seeking to pick a fight, Percival took the *Dolphin* out into the harbor the next day, a Sunday. He fired another salute to the fort, which was not returned, since it was the Sabbath. Percival was enraged, feeling that both he and his nation had been insulted.[13]

The stated purpose of this visit was to persuade the Hawaiian government to accept as its own responsibility the personal debts that chiefs had racked up with American merchants. Americans now controlled most of the sandalwood trade, but it was in decline, and the forests would soon be exhausted. The aliʻi owed foreign merchants

John Quincy Adams **by Francis Kearney, after Charles Bird King, 1825 (National Portrait Gallery, Smithsonian Institution).**

Chapter 8—New Rules, New Riots

huge amounts of money, but as the hills were stripped bare, the quality of the wood harvested declined, and the price paid for it in China fell. Despite this, his superiors expected Percival to get the Hawaiian government to pay up.[14]

But the young republic also was flexing its muscles on the world stage. Isaac Hull, commanding officer of the small American squadron in the Pacific, had secretly given Percival additional orders: to determine how the Hawaiian government felt toward the American government and to learn "whether the same privileges are granted to vessels of the United States as to those of other nations." Percival had heard that the harbor fort had fired a salute to British ships when they arrived in Honolulu the previous year and that women had sexual intercourse with English sailors, so he demanded the same. When kanakas refused, the lieutenant swore at them profusely and threatened to level Honolulu with cannon fire, unaware that many Islanders had developed scruples about Sabbath observance and prostitution.[15]

Percival received the king and regent on board his ship. First Officer Hiram Paulding thought, "All returned to shore delighted with their visit."[16] When the captain learned about the month-old ban on shipboard visits by prostitutes, however, he demanded a royal audience, claiming that denying his crew wahines was an affront to the American flag. This insistence was driven at least in part by the U.S. Navy's fear of homosexuality. Like the Royal Navy, the American brass thought prostitutes would prevent crew members from seeking same-sex partners.[17]

Ka'ahumanu found Percival both rude and morally repugnant, but responded by letter, personally delivered by Governor Boki, in an attempt to show the lieutenant courtesy. She noted that she had every right to proclaim laws for her own subjects. This law did not apply to foreign women, only to her subjects, and only her people were punished for violating it. She intended no hostility to the United States, she explained, and wished only to protect her people from degradation. By the way, she asked, were not visitors to the United States expected to obey its laws and customs?

Percival refused to write back to the Kuhina Nui, demanded to meet the rulers, and threatened to shoot Hiram Bingham if he saw him. He also insisted on dealing with the king, who was still a child, rather than the regent—a bit like Ka'ahumanu going to Washington, refusing to see the president, and attempting to negotiate with his teenage stepdaughter. Percival apparently never imagined that a woman could rule. When neither mikanele nor ali'i appeared at a party he hosted aboard the *Dolphin*, the lieutenant was further enraged. Mad Jack told his sailors it "would serve the missionaries right if they should pull down their homes."[18]

Percival became even more suspicious of the missionaries when Boki, who was no friend of the Calvinists, asked him if it was true that they were official representatives of the U.S. government. Boki knew that they were not and had never claimed to be, but the governor often played his rivals off against the British Consul. He grabbed the chance to do the same with this naval officer and the Mission. The lieutenant assured the governor that they did not represent the American government, and proceeded to condemn Bingham—without verifying Boki's charge—for misrepresenting himself as an ambassador.[19]

To make matters worse, Percival, Paulding, and other officers of the *Dolphin* bought "wives" from ali'i, even though most, including Percival, were married to women back home. New converts saw this as prostitution or worse: sex slavery. If this is allowed in the United States, one chief suggested, let the Americans bring women from there and leave Hawaiian females alone. In the meantime, they said, these temporary wives could carry stone for the new church—just like prostitutes. Mad Jack's "wife" promptly left him.[20]

By her lights, Ka'ahumanu tried to be reasonable. When a large crowd brought her a wahine whom they had seized after she disembarked one of the ships, a sailor followed the woman to the regent's home, begging permission to live with her. "If you marry her, you may," she replied, "but otherwise you cannot have her." Refusing "to make an honest woman" of the woman, the sailor left without her.[21]

Percival and two other officers made at least one diplomatic gesture, attending Sunday worship on February 19. And on February 22, Percival, "conversed very mildly" with a group of ali'i, at least mildly by his lights, "and advised them not be too severe with those who choose to follow the course of prostitution."[22]

But when the regent received the lieutenant, he laughed contemptuously at her suggestion that prostitution was sinful, and sneered when she explained that she was trying to follow the Word of God. "Who is the King?" he asked.

"The young king," she replied.

"And who governs the King?" Percival demanded.

She answered that the king ruled, but she governed him, under God's guidance.

Percival clenched his fists in rage. He may even have roared, as

Chapter 8—New Rules, New Riots

some accounts have it, "You lie...! Mr. Bingham governs you!" It is inconceivable that Percival would have ever accused his president of being controlled by his pastor—let alone swearing at him—but like many other foreigners, he assumed that Islanders lacked moral agency and did whatever others told them. He then threatened that if she did not supply women for his sailors the next day, he would turn them loose to attack missionaries and seize any women whom they found.[23]

On Sunday, February 26, Percival granted shore leave to about two dozen of his sailors. It is possible that he "admonished them to attend church, stay sober, and behave themselves," as he later claimed, but one of the crew recalled his instructions as "go to church first and ... then go and have their frolic." The sailors drank alcohol heavily, armed themselves with clubs, gathered another 125 drunken crewmen from whaleships in port, and marched to Kalanimōkū's home. There, they disrupted an afternoon worship service, smashed 70 windowpanes, seized Hiram Bingham, and demanded women. Bingham told one of them, "Put down your club if you wish me to talk with you," but the sailor swung at the preacher instead. A female chief deflected the blow with her arm, and the congregation leapt on the sailors. Only the intervention of John Papa ʻĪʻī and other converts saved Hiram Bingham from serious harm. Only Bingham's plea, "Thou shalt not kill!" stopped a kanaka from bashing in the sailor's skull. The new Christian reluctantly put down his rock and spared the assailant.[24]

Percival arrived on the scene and managed to restrain his unruly men, acting shocked that they had perpetrated an attack that he had encouraged. Rather than apologize, he blamed the riot on the missionaries and called the new law against prostitution an insult to the Stars and Stripes. His men had gone too far, he admitted, but he would not leave the Islands until they had sexual intercourse.[25]

First Officer Paulding claimed that the Kingdom of Hawaiʻi was not one of the "civilized countries" and that its people were not "prepared to receive Christianity"; many Hawaiians thought Percival, Paulding, and their crew were uncivilized and un-Christian. After the lieutenant left, Kaʻahumanu asked if Percival was a naval officer or a pirate.[26]

The next day, Hiram Bingham came to the *Dolphin* at Percival's invitation and identified several of his attackers. Jesus may have urged his followers to turn the other cheek, but the head of the mission muttered as he left the ship before the miscreants were flogged, "I hope they lay it on well." Which the officers proceeded to do. Dr. Abraham Blatchley, a physician in the Second Company who was called to treat the sailors, estimated that each received two dozen lashes, a brutal punishment.[27]

Fearful of further violence, and not inclined to please the mikanele anyway, Boki lifted the ban on prostitution for the duration of the *Dolphin*'s stay.[28] Boatloads of women promptly headed for ships, much to the dismay of the Ka'ahumanu and the missionaries. Percival was so pleased that he paid for the repair of homes that his men had damaged and clapped in irons the two most violent sailors, at least until they left port.

As his stay in Honolulu lengthened, the lieutenant became embroiled in one conflict after another with Hawaiians, American residents, and nearly everyone else who crossed his path. Stephen Reynolds noted in his journal on March 24, "Something comes to my ears almost every day concerning Percival—that goes to lessen the Americans, and sink the Reputation of the American Navy—and make him the object of Ridicule among the Islands. Pity. Pity he ever came here." Two weeks later, he wrote that Percival was "the basest—meanest of Men—I have ever known."[29]

When the *Dolphin* sailed away on May 11, Percival left behind seething resentment toward the United States. The American Board of Commissioners for Foreign Missions asked the American government to investigate his conduct in the Islands, and a Court of Inquiry was convened. The U.S. Navy court-martialed Percival, but Hiram Paulding went on to become a rear admiral. Boki, who owned a bar in Honolulu, continued to make money selling liquor and wahines to sailors. Visiting seamen soon found a way to get back at Calvinists. They spread the word that they preferred girls who attended mission schools.[30]

The only thing that saved Hawaiian-American relations may have been the equally bad behavior of British sailors. The same year that Buckle and his crew threatened missionaries, the crew of the *Wellington* introduced mosquitos into the Islands when they stopped in Lāhainā. They may have accidentally dumped larvae-infested water barrels in order to refill them with fresh water, but it was widely suspected that they deliberately retaliated against kanakas for denying them wahines. Mosquitos soon harassed humans and devastated local birdlife.[31]

Christian ali'i had greater success elsewhere in their attempts to regulate personal behavior. By late 1825, the Big Island had substantially reduced public drunkenness. A missionary who had found entire villages inebriated two years earlier when he toured the Island now happily reported, "In my whole tour I saw but only one man intoxicated." In

Chapter 8—New Rules, New Riots

1826, Governor Hoapili completely banned the manufacture, sale, and use of alcohol on Maui, Molokaʻi, and Lānaʻi—and backed up this prohibition with steep fines. From this point on, the chiefs managed to prevent most commoners from drinking alcohol, but the mission would continue to import wine and rum for the Lāhainā station for another two years.[32]

Having learned that laws alone could not reform her people, Kaʻahumanu purchased paper from Amelika to print 3,000 copies of the Sermon on the Mount (Matthew 5–7), newly translated into Hawaiian. She also led a tour around Oʻahu with Hiram Bingham, her sister Nāmāhāna Piʻia, Nāmāhāna's husband, and a large group of newly trained teachers. She provided horses, two wagons, and two canoes, but more than 300 people walked a100 miles around the Island to accompany her. Once, a new paramount chief would circle his Island, dedicating new temples along the way. Now, after the debacle with the *Dolphin*, the Kuhina Nui demonstrated her leadership by circling the island herself, stopping every few miles to tell a crowd about her new faith and the new laws she proposed. Instead of heiaus, she dedicated new schools. In the fall of 1826, she spent two months touring the Big Island with a group of missionaries. A crowd of 10,000 people gathered to welcome her, surprised by her affectionate manner toward them and the way this once-"haughty queen" greeted aliʻi and commoners with equal warmth.[33]

After Percival's extended stay in Honolulu, it took considerable diplomatic skill for another American naval officer to mend relations between the kingdom and the United States. Capt. Thomas ap Catesby Jones, commander of the U.S.S. *Peacock*, arrived in October, five months after the *Dolphin* sailed away, and many kanakas were none too pleased to see another American warship in Honolulu Harbor. Jones brought home two wahines who had been abandoned in Peru by an unscrupulous sea captain, and a kanaka whom he had rescued from an American brig there, which immediately built up some goodwill.[34]

Capt. Jones had heard that crime was rampant in the Islands, people were starving, and the rulers were inept, but he decided to have a look himself before believing any of this. Even by Percival's own account, Jones realized, his predecessor's visit had been a disaster. Unlike "Mad Jack," Jones treated Islanders with courtesy and respect. Soon, they were calling him "the kind-eyed chief."[35]

The captain gratefully accepted Kaʻahumanu's offer to stay in her home in Honolulu while she was away. He skillfully negotiated local

Thomas ap Catesby Jones by Auguste Edouart, 1841 (National Portrait Gallery, Smithsonian Institution; gift of Robert L. McNeil, Jr.).

Chapter 8—New Rules, New Riots

politics, which were being stirred by rumors that Boki, with the encouragement of British Consul Charlton and various haole merchants, hoped to replace Ka'ahumanu as regent. He also rounded up 30 deserters from American whaleships, to end their mischief-making, which the chiefs appreciated. He then wrote to the regent, who was away on Maui, explaining his mission. His letters persuaded her to return to Honolulu so that negotiations might begin with her and the 11-year-old king.[36]

Jones listened and learned for nearly a month before making any proposals to the Hawaiian government. Unlike Percival, he put his requests in writing, so that they could be carefully translated and so that both sides might study them at length and resolve any misunderstandings before beginning formal negotiations. He suggested, for example, a few additions to the port regulations to control the sailors who deserted in the Island, where they caused no end of problems for both their captains and kanakas. There should also be, he proposed, a new tax to settle the kingdom's debts to foreign merchants.

Merchants hoped that the U.S. government would curtail the influence of the Calvinists and stop the commercial activities of the Mission. Hiram Bingham insisted that the values of the mission were not those of capitalism, but he gladly recruited Hawaiians for new enterprises to pay for books for his congregation and homes for mikanele. In theory, the traders believed in free markets, but in practice, many resented this competition. Capt. Jones, a devout Christian of a conservative stripe, had no quarrel with missionaries or capitalists who happened to be clergymen.[37]

The merchants also had imagined that the United States would send a gunboat to coerce Hawaiians to pay their debts to the traders, which they claimed totaled $500,000—an enormous sum at the time. Instead, to their dismay, the captain studied the debts, estimated that they really were no more than $200,000, and quickly negotiated a deal. Despite the British Consul's attempts to block it, the kingdom's first written treaty with the United States, or any other nation, was signed on December 23, 1826, by Capt. Jones, Ka'ahumanu, Kalanimōkū, Boki, and other chiefs.

This agreement opened Hawaiian ports to free and open trade, settled the debts to American merchants, and took additional steps to round up sailors who jumped ship in the Islands. Jones thought it to be a fair deal, even though it meant that commoners had to pay for the extravagant spending of ali'i, particularly the outstanding bills that Liholiho and others had accumulated for the overpriced luxury goods, including rotting ships. The U.S. Senate never ratified the treaty, but both Hawaiians and Americans acted for a decade as if it were in force.[38]

To settle this obligation, Ka'ahumanu's new tax required every able-bodied citizen to pay one Spanish dollar or cut a half-picul of sandalwood (a Chinese weight equal to 67 pounds or 30 kilograms) for the kingdom to sell—but also gave them the right to cut an equal amount to sell themselves. For the first time, commoners gained something from the sandalwood trade, though this tax accelerated the destruction of forests. Slowly, she was learning how difficult it was to introduce new ways to her people. They needed some incentive to change.[39]

Unable to impose her will on randy foreign sailors, she urged her subjects to be faithful to their spouses. In 1826, a new law recognized as valid all marriages under the old customs of the Islands, but warned that future unions would be considered legitimate only if celebrated by clergy. Henceforth, those who lived together without a Christian wedding would be considered adulterers. Ka'ahumanu's also insisted that the ban on adultery applied to ali'i, and not just the maka'āinana, though she mostly punished adulterers who were her political opponents. In contrast with Europe and America, where women were blamed for adultery, Ka'ahumanu fined Boki twice as much as his lovers.[40]

The missionaries also were delighted to receive Princess Nāhi'ena'ena into church membership in 1826, but whenever they thought they were making progress, new disappointment appeared. Toward the end of the 1826–27 Makahiki season, many Islanders reasserted old customs, abandoning school and church for dancing, sports, and festivities. The young king studied the palapala more faithfully than Liholiho ever had and strongly supported education for his people, but he showed little interest in Calvinist worship. He once embarrassed Ka'ahumanu by galloping by a worship service, right after a horse race that Kalanimōkū had tried in vain to stop. A year earlier, Levi Chamberlain was delighted with the number of students in the Mission's network of 69 schools: "The evidences of improvement were obvious and pleasing." Now, dramatically fewer Hawaiians attended, and those who did go to class were doing worse in their studies.[41]

Early in 1827, American merchant Stephen Reynolds heard from the Kuhina Nui's physician that she had contracted a sexually transmitted infection by having sexual intercourse with a young man, but Reynolds was hardly an unbiased source of information. Doubting this—or perhaps fearing that this rumor might diminish her usefulness to the Mission—Binamu urged the doctor not to say anything about this.

Chapter 8—New Rules, New Riots

Outraged, the physician replied, "I do not know what religion you teach. The religion I have been taught directs me to tell the truth." Artemas Bishop reported that she was in such feeble health that he feared she would never return to the Big Island.[42]

She also was worried that her nation would have trouble with finding leaders in the future—and assumed that only high-born chiefs could govern. The number of ali'i was diminishing steadily as disease decimated the Hawaiian population, and many chiefs no longer were willing to marry only those of their own rank. As an old proverb said,

> He 'imi ali'i, he ali'i no ke loa'a;
> he 'imi kanaka, he kanaka no ke loa'a.
> *(When a chief is sought, a chief is begotten;*
> *when a commoner is sought, a commoner is begotten.)*[43]

Ka'ahumanu was particularly disturbed that Kīna'u was living with Kekūanāo'a, whom the Kuhina Nui considered beneath her niece. Kīna'u was second in status only to her half sister Nāhi'ena'ena, and Ka'ahumanu thought she should marry Kauikeaouli, as their father Kamehameha the Great had wished, to continue his dynasty. Kīna'u, though, who had already outlived two husbands, Liholiho, and a grandson of Kamehameha, was deeply in love with Kekūanāo'a. The missionaries, along with most ali'i, favored this match, because Kīna'u "refused to separate, but would consent to marry." Her aunt remained adamantly opposed.[44]

Ka'ahumanu attended their wedding, but she seethed with anger at her niece's defiance. Babies, however, often soften the hearts of stubborn elders, and when the marriage produced a potential paramount chief to continue Kīna'u's royal lineage, the Kuhina Nui and her niece reconciled. Kīna'u and Kekuanaoa even gave their first son, Prince David Kamehameha, to her aunt to raise as her hānai child.[45]

Ka'ahumanu's relationship with the mikanele also survived disagreement and scandal. They saw her as a penitent sinner struggling to remold her life—and they needed her support as a powerful convert. On September 23, she asked one of the Calvinists, Mercy Whitney's husband Samuel, "to tell her plainly when he saw her in fault" since she knew that "her heart was full of evil and falsehood." She often stayed with the Binghams, even though she had two homes of her own nearby. Sybil was surprised to find how deep their friendship had grown, never having expected to "know the comfort of loving and showing kindness to her as a Christian sister." The missionaries were equally

Queen Ka'ahumanu of Hawaii

impressed with the love that Ka'ahumanu displayed toward her adopted children.[46]

The Calvinists also appreciated her attempts to curtail alcohol abuse, despite the fierce resistance of Boki and foreign residents. The governor had immense prestige, which made him a dangerous adversary and a constant threat to the regent's power. Kamehameha himself had named Boki the governor of O'ahu, and Boki had sailed all the way to England with Kamehameha's son. Early in 1827, she thwarted his attempt to manufacture rum with four haole partners, a business he hoped would allow him to repay his debts to British and French merchants. To soothe his resentment, she entrusted him with the guardianship of Kauikeaouli as his kahu—but only after the governor "acknowledged Kaahumanu as regent and his brother Kalanimōkū as superior to himself in the government" and offered at least token support to the mission. After Kalanimōkū died on February 7, there was widespread violation of Sabbath restrictions by those who enjoyed rum, cards, and the hula. As Jonathan Osorio observed, "Church attendance was not mandatory, but observance of the Christian Sabbath was." This, in turn, raised concerns that civil war might break out between the governor and the Kuhina Nui. Asserting her authority and commitment to Christian morality, Ka'ahumanu charged Boki, his wife Liliha, and several of the young king's friends with drunkenness, fornication, and adultery. Then she fined them all. In response, Boki made no effort to enforce the new Sabbath laws on O'ahu.[47]

CHAPTER 9

Law and Order, Church and State

In June 1827, Kaʻahumanu received the news that Roman Catholic missionaries were coming, uninvited, from France. She asked the American Board of Commissioners for Foreign Missions for advice as to what she should do if priests "who have another gospel" should arrive, indicating the hostility that existed at the time between two denominations.[1] On July 7, three priests—Fathers Alexis Bachelot (1796–1837) and Abraham Armand (born around 1776) from France and Patrick Short (1792–1870) from Ireland, disembarked on Oʻahu from the French ship, *Cométe*, along with Brothers Melchior Bondu and Leonard Portal (non-clergy members of the religious order) and seminarian Théodore Boissier, accompanied by French agricultural colonists and the French lawyer Philippe Auguste de Morineau. It was the first French mission to the Pacific.

Before this, kanakas had little experience of competing churches. Some had observed a Christian funeral, such as the one read by one of Cook's officers from the Church of England's *Book of Common Prayer*, at Napoopoo on the Big Island on January 28, 1779, the one for the captain himself soon thereafter, or the one for Liholiho and Kamāmalu that was led by the chaplain on the *Blonde*. Visiting Russian sailors may have worshiped here as early as 1791. Russian Orthodox colonists built the first Christian chapels in the Islands at Fort Elizabeth and Fort Alexander on Kauaʻi in 1815 but seldom used them. The first recorded Eucharist or communion service in the Islands was celebrated in 1816 by a Russian Orthodox priest who sailed with Kotzebue.[2]

Boki had been baptized by a Catholic chaplain during Louis de Freycinet's visit, and a few Islanders "were baptized and received into the Christian church" on board the *Blonde* in 1825 by Andrew Bloxam, the ship's naturalist who became an Anglican priest, but there were no Catholic or Anglican clergy living in the Islands to lead them. Besides occasional visitors such as the Methodist William Ellis and a few kahunas who still practiced the old Hawaiian religion in secret, the Congregational and Presbyterian missionaries had been the only religious leaders in the kingdom throughout the decade.[3]

There also were a handful of Unitarian Christians, whose liberal movement had finally separated from the Congregationalists in 1825. John Coffin Jones, Jr., had been conducting Unitarian worship services, as well as funerals for those whom the Calvinists refused to bury. He tried to persuade Unitarian leaders in Boston to send missionaries to the Islands but was unsuccessful in this effort, largely because he had children by two native women simultaneously "without benefit of clergy" and did not consider himself married to either. Seeing this as both bigamy and adultery, respectable New England Unitarians were reluctant to support him, and the Calvinists sought his removal as Consular Agent.[4]

In addition to these Christian denominations, there were a few Chinese living in the Sandalwood Mountains by 1788; they probably practiced Buddhism, Taoism, Confucianism, or some combination of these traditions. Some Japanese had been there since at least 1804, practicing both Buddhism and Shinto, but no other foreign religion had clergy in the Islands. Kanakas who had worked abroad had encountered a variety of faiths. Humehume, for example, had met Buddhists, Hindus, and Muslims during his travels as a sailor. But many who signed on to a ship's crew to see the world never returned to the Islands, which reduced any secondhand acquaintance with other religions that their friends and relatives might have gained.

Nor did the Calvinists have much experience with religious diversity. Upon arriving on Kaua'i, Samuel Ruggles mistakenly thought that he was the first Christian to ever speak to anyone there and also the first to offer a Christian prayer. Charles Stewart observed Russian Orthodox worship in February 1825 on Otto von Kotzebue's ship, apparently a first for him. Stewart noted that the service was in Slavonic but thought the chaplain and liturgy were Greek, apparently unaware that the Greek and Russian Orthodox belonged to different—and rival—denominations. Kotzebue had a public-worship service every Saturday evening when he was in port, but few Hawaiians, or haoles for that matter, could have understood it. In June of that year, the Stewarts worshiped in a Church of England service on the *Blonde* as they sailed to Hilo, but there would not be any resident clergy from the Anglican or Episcopal Church for another four decades.[5]

Chapter 9—Law and Order, Church and State

The French Mission counted on support from an influential local Catholic, Jean-Baptiste Rives, but he proved to be an unreliable champion. Described as an "adventurer, wanderer, and an enigma," he took several local wives, which did not exactly make him a model Catholic. In 1819, Louis de Freycinet and his adventurous young wife Rose de Freycinet (who had snuck onboard in men's clothing and short hair to journey around the world with him) dismissed Rives as "a blaggard and a rascal." Suspected of stealing the king's watch and a large sum of money en route to England, he now was persona non grata. Upon arriving in London, Rives promptly fled to France and angered the Kuhina Nui and many other kanakas by failing to accompany home the bodies of the king and queen. In Paris, he persuaded the French government and Catholic hierarchy to sponsor a colony and mission in Honolulu, and he signed a treaty ostensibly on behalf of the kingdom, which promised huge profits to French investors, an agreement he had no authority whatsoever to make.[6]

As Ralph Kuykendall observed, in France at this time, "Church and State were in close alliance in consequence of the ascension of the clerical-minded King Charles X." A reactionary, unpopular, ultra-royalist Bourbon monarch bent on colonial expansion, Charles X supported the French colony—but would soon be driven into exile. The religious mission was led by "a young and zealous religious order," the Sacred Hearts of Jesus and Mary, who are often called the Picpus Fathers. It was France's first mission in the Pacific, and from the first, the erstwhile evangelists confronted enormous difficulties.[7]

Stopping in California on his way back to the Islands, a sea captain warned Rives that he was now roundly hated in Honolulu, adding, "if he valued his life, he ought to give up any project of going to the Sandwich Islands." Rives once again decided that discretion was the better part of valor, this time abandoning the Catholic mission that already was en route to Honolulu.[8]

When the French mission stopped in California, they were informed that they, too, would not be welcome in the Islands, but they had decided to continue anyway. Rives had promised Alexis Bachelot, the head of the mission, that he would meet them in Honolulu, provide homes for them, and smooth their way with the government. Instead, they learned, the government had no idea that they were coming, and Rives had abandoned them and his two daughters, whom Kaʻahumanu raised. Rives, Morineau concluded, "had become odious to the natives" and the only knowledgeable businessman in their company had died en route to the Islands. Rives also had promised to pay the captain of the *Cométe* for their transportation, who in turn demanded payment from Bachelot, who had almost no money. The king visited the Catholics onboard the *Cométe*, but the captain, furious about not being paid, refused to let the missionaries eat at his table and threatened to seize their baggage, agricultural implements, and other tools until the bill was settled. "Our adversaries were already long-established," Morineau realized. "We could not have arrived under worse auspices."[9]

Perhaps someone such as Kalanimōkū, who had been baptized by a Catholic chaplain, might have built bridges between the denominations, but he died four months before the French mission arrived. His brother, Governor Boki, was glad to see them come, but he was a problematic ally, and Don Francisco de Paula Marín was an equally difficult one. Marín had assisted the First Company but eventually found that some of their teachings—such as monogamy—did not suit him. But he could not conform easily to Catholicism, either. He had baptized a number of people before the Calvinists arrived and baptized his children himself rather than ask Protestants to do so, which the Catholic church permits laypeople to do in the absence of a priest. But he also had adopted some pagan beliefs, had at least four Hawaiian wives, and did not object to them continuing to worship the old gods. He sympathized with the Picpus Fathers but wanted to maintain a good relationship with Ka'ahumanu, and therefore, was reluctant to oppose her. When Father Bachelot asked if they might live on some of his land, Marín replied that he could do nothing to help them.[10]

The Picpus Fathers had no idea what to do next. American Consular Agent Jones, no friend of the Calvinists, invited the Catholics to dinner with Boki. The governor agreed to seek permission for them to stay. As the chiefs considered this request, Bachelot managed to rent three huts and a small plot of land, unload their cargo, and celebrate Mass on July 14. The Picpus Fathers wisely kept a low profile as they studied Hawaiian and started translating the catechism they would use, benefiting from the work the Protestants had done to transcribe the language into written form and to translate Scripture into Hawaiian. Father Short learned the language quickly and soon was able to function as a translator. The French gladly met with visitors to their compound but did not venture out to seek converts.[11]

The Sacred Heart mission arrived with a bit more tolerance of the local culture than the Calvinists had. "If polygamy were allowed," Father Patrick Short said, Marín "could pass for a patriarch." They were

Chapter 9—Law and Order, Church and State

woefully ignorant, however, of their new mission field. They thought the Calvinists had not managed to teach Hawaiians anything much about God or Christianity and that human sacrifice had continued for three years after their arrival. They believed Boki was regent and kept referring to him as such—for years—which cannot have pleased the actual regent. Never grasping her authority, Father Bachelot described Ka'ahumanu as being "under an illusion, but she means well." They knew so little about Hawaiian culture that they believed these poetry-composing, history-reciting, singing, dancing people "had no idea of the arts." The French government had even offered to send someone to teach handcrafts to the natives, some of the most accomplished artisans on earth.[12]

The Picpus Fathers also were under the misimpression that kanakas had thrown themselves into the arms of the Calvinists: "We have no religion, give us another one. We are waiting for you to teach us." They believed that the Protestant mission was preoccupied with commercial ventures, rather than having an often-strained relationship with merchants and other capitalists—and ignoring how much their own project depended on the success of the French commercial enterprise. Hiram Bingham "preferred governing to preaching," they claimed, and he dictated the decisions of the rulers of the Hawaiian Islands, which he might have been happy to do but often could not.[13]

The Calvinists had arrived earlier, and they taught an appealing doctrine that encouraged everyone to learn to read and interpret Scripture for themselves, even if they hoped their students would end up interpreting it more or less the way they did. They had educated thousands in basic literacy and had won some important converts.

In stark contrast, Catholic insistence on priestly celibacy seemed perverse to kanakas. The presence of women in the First Company convinced Islanders that the American missionaries had not come to conquer; these priests arrived without women—and claimed only unmarried men could lead their faith. Why should they listen to anything these new haoles said about marriage or sex? How could these priests represent the same religion as Sybil Bingham, Mercy Whitney, Maria Loomis, Lucy Thurston, and Nancy Ruggles?

Many kanakas were predisposed toward religious tolerance. Kū and Pele had different priests who led vastly different rituals but generally coexisted amicably. They easily could have seen Calvinists and Catholics as two traditions within a single, larger religion and might have welcomed the elaborate pageantry of the latter as a welcome alternative to the austere simplicity of the former. The devotion of these French

Queen Kaʻahumanu of Hawaii

Christians to hundreds of saints might have reminded them of the lesser Deities and household gods of their own tradition. But unlike the occasional rivalry among kahunas, the leaders of these different churches seemed to loathe each other deeply.

Two weeks after the Catholics landed, Kaʻahumanu asked them to meet with her. They never responded, an extraordinary insult to a monarch. Bachelot also refused to meet with the Protestant clergy, even though the Americans made gestures to welcome them and said there was plenty of work for all of them to do in the Islands. The French mission gladly used the translations the Calvinists had made but would not allow Hiram Bingham to borrow a copy of the catechism that they planned to use for religious education, which only deepened the Protestants' suspicion of Catholic teaching. Hiram Bingham offered Brother Melchior a job in his printshop, but Melchior "declined from reasons of conscience," apparently thinking it would be sinful to work with a Protestant.

The Picpus Fathers emphasized similarities between the old religion and their version of Christianity. While this often has proven an effective strategy elsewhere, it did not work well in a land whose people had gleefully torched their temples—and only made the Kuhina Nui and other chiefs suspicious of Catholicism. The government did not object to the Catholic priests ministering to foreigners who were Catholic. Nor was anyone troubled much when Islanders expressed interest in seeing a Mass. But when Hawaiians reported that Catholics worshiped statues of Mary and the saints, many aliʻi were alarmed. Having sought to eradicate images of the akua, Kaʻahumanu and most chiefs thought that when Catholics prayed to icons or statues, they were practicing idolatry: "their worship is like that which we have forsaken." She told the Picpus fathers,

> We do not want you. We have put away our idols and abandoned our old system of religious forms and penances. We have received the Word of God by the hand of teachers whom we love, and with whom we are satisfied. Our kingdom is a little one. We do not wish the minds of our subjects distracted by any other sect. Go away and teach destitute countries, which have not received the Bible.[14]

Wanted or not, they refused to leave.

It is difficult today to imagine how badly divided Christians were two centuries ago. Today, most Protestants and Catholics see each other as fellow Christians who disagree over a few key issues; in 1827, they often saw each other as heretics headed for hell. One Catholic told Kīnaʻu that unless Hawaiians were baptized by Catholic priests, rather

Chapter 9—Law and Order, Church and State

than Calvinist clergy, "they cannot be saved." Catholics claimed that baptism was not a sacrament for Protestants, when in fact it and communion (the Eucharist) are the only sacraments for them, rather than the seven sacraments of Catholicism. And Protestants who defended the Catholics often referred to them as members of a religion distinct from Christianity.[15]

Father Short called the Americans "pseudo-missionaries." The Picpus Fathers knew so little about their rivals that they thought they were Moravian Brethren or Methodists, even though Jean-Baptiste Rives had reported that they were Calvinists. The French Catholic journal, *Annales de la Propagation de la Foi*, sometimes identified them correctly and other times called them Moravians. This mistake persisted in France for another 80 years and in Ireland for 120 years.[16]

The Calvinists, for their part, kept calling the new arrivals "Jesuits"—members of the Society of Jesus—even though they belonged to an altogether different religious order. Hiram Bingham claimed they were "false teachers" and that "[t]he Romish system sanctions the killing of men for repudiating her dogmas," without admitting that Protestants had persecuted Catholics with equal fervor. They thought the Catholics were trespassing on their territory, as the number of Protestant denominations had reached comity agreements. The missionaries of one denomination would work in this nation; another church, in another country. The Calvinists resented the Catholics as interlopers who were engaged in ecclesiastical poaching, even though the Vatican never struck any such deal with Protestants.[17]

In this era, there was hardly any nation where church and state were entirely separate. France would not establish religious toleration until 1830—and then would repeal it in 1848. In much of Europe, disagreeing with whatever denomination the state supported raised suspicions of disloyalty. The captain of a British ship told young Kamehameha III that Catholics had slaughtered his ancestors in England: "If Catholics gain much influence here, you may expect your islands to be filled with blood...." Irish Catholics said the same about British Protestants. Every official in England from mayor to prime minister was required by law to receive communion according to the rites of the Church of England. Catholics, Calvinists, and other Protestant dissenters were excluded from government positions, English universities, and many professions until 1828. Exceptions were often made for Protestant dissenters, but Congregationalists were decidedly second-class citizens, and Catholics fared still worse.[18]

Queen Kaʻahumanu of Hawaii

In the United States, the First Amendment to the U.S. Constitution promised freedom to practice whatever religion one chose, without the government taking sides in religious conflicts, but this constrained only the federal government. Courts would not consistently apply this standard to the states until a century later. In Massachusetts, Congregational churches were directly funded by the government, and their Sabbath rules were enforced by "blue laws" that dictated the behavior of both their members and those who did not belong to the denomination. In New Hampshire and North Carolina, only Protestants could be elected to public office, despite the constitutional ban on religious tests for public office. Until 1821, Catholics in New York had few political rights unless they denounced allegiance to the Pope in all matters political or religious, the latter of which would render them no longer Catholic. Kaʻahumanu assumed her people should practice her religion, but she did not jail Catholic priests upon arrival, even though she saw them as representing another faith, not Christianity.

The First Company may have arrived uninvited, but they brought home an aliʻi, a long-lost prince no less, along with three other kānaka maoli. They waited patiently to meet the rulers of the Islands, politely requested permission to stay, accepted a year's probation, and worked for four years before finally receiving approval to stay permanently. The Picpus Fathers never even asked. They disembarked and then refused to meet with either the king or the Kuhina Nui. As Father Bachelot later admitted, "it never came into my mind to ask for it till it was too late."[19]

If a boatload of foreign priests had landed uninvited in Boston in 1827, they might have been jailed or shipped home immediately. Had Congregationalists sent missionaries to France, they might have met a similar fate.

The French colonists refused to leave, at least in part, because they believed that the American missionaries had imposed this decision on the government. It embarrassed and angered Kaʻahumanu that they defied her, and Boki's support for the French mission made her all the more suspicious. Within weeks of their arrival, rumors reached the young king that she planned to depose him—fears which Boki stoked. When John Coffin Jones, Jr., attended Catholic Mass, her concerns about the new missionaries increased.[20]

In comparison to most people of this era, the American missionaries were fairly tolerant of other denominations. They accepted the validity of Kalanimōkū's baptism by a Catholic priest, for example. They also welcomed him at communion, even though Catholics barred Protestants

Chapter 9—Law and Order, Church and State

from receiving the Eucharist in their churches, both then and now. The French colonists, from the beginning, saw themselves as being persecuted by Protestants, whom they thought were jealous of the Catholics. But the Calvinists initially showed little fear of these rivals, confidant that kanakas would embrace their version of Christianity. Hiram Bingham's memoir scarcely mentions the Catholic mission for several years, and they really were little threat to Binamu. The promised second shipload of French farmers never arrived, and without any French trading company ever being established in Honolulu, the commercial side of the colony collapsed. Within months, two of its agricultural colonists returned to France; Morineau treated the Kuhina Nui with disrespect while seeking "to gain the confidence of the young prince," which naturally only alienated her further. He left soon thereafter.[21]

The kingdom's rulers, however, were anxious about the Catholic mission and worried about foreign incursions in general. The Picpus Fathers arrived at a time when they felt increasingly vulnerable to haoles who defied their laws. The *Dolphin* was a relatively small warship, but its cannons nonetheless had threatened the tiny harbor fort in Honolulu. When Governor Hoapili learned in October 1827 that women from Lāhainā were having sexual intercourse with the crew of *John Palmer*, an English whaler, in violation of his edict, he asked Capt. Clark to turn them over to him, fearing that Clark might sail away with the wahines. The captain refused, and Hoapili had Clark arrested. Holding the missionaries responsible for the government's decision, the *John Palmer* crew fired half a dozen cannonballs at the home of William and Clarissa Richards, who fled to the cellar for safety, along with their visiting guests, Hiram and Sybil Bingham. Missionary women faced the same perils as their husbands.[22]

Pastor Richards persuaded the governor to release Clark, who promptly sailed the *John Palmer* to Honolulu, taking the women with him. Hoapili wrote to Kaʻahumanu, expressing his confusion. Did this captain truly represent a civilized nation? Should Christians surrender when confronted by a show of force?[23]

Then Capt. William Buckle, who was once again in the Islands, learned that Richards' accusation of sex slavery had been published in newspapers from New York to London. Buckle had published himself the Mission's private admonition, but now he threatened to sue for libel. Having previously said that he wished to murder Richards, he now demanded the preacher's execution. If the government did not do this, the captain swore, he would shell Lāhainā. The chiefs shipped Richards off to Honolulu to stand trial. Some aliʻi were willing to knuckle under to appease Buckle. Others thought the pastor had misunderstood Leoki's relationship with the captain and had done the latter an injustice. Facing the possibility of capital punishment, William Richards accepted the authority of the Hawaiian government to decide his fate: "We have left our country and can not now receive the protection of its laws.... With you is my life and with you is my death." Richards pointed out that Britons had violated the laws of the kingdom, but he refused to concede any possibility that he might have misconstrued Buckle's actions. Davida Malo, an advisor to the Kuhina Nui and an ardent Calvinist, persuaded Kaʻahumanu to spare the missionary's life. This did not lead to a new bombardment of Maui but did infuriate the British Consul, foreign merchants, and Governor Boki.[24]

On December 8, Kaʻahumanu convened a meeting of chiefs in Honolulu to discuss Boki's suggestion that they not enact any law without the consent of the United Kingdom—which George Vancouver had promised would protect the Islands from any other outside power—and send a governor to London with a code of laws for British ratification—even though Great Britain had never ratified and had completely forgotten Vancouver's treaty. Alternatively, Boki suggested, they could submit proposed legislation to the British Consul in Honolulu. Kaʻahumanu sharply asked whether the king of England had suggested this to him when he met the monarch. No, Boki admitted, he had not—at which point she added that Carlton had already demonstrated that he could not be trusted. Furthermore, she argued, "If England gives us laws, she will send men to see that they are executed. Our harbors will be filled with ships of war...." Boki's suggestion was quietly shelved.[25]

The chiefs also discussed whether or not the French colonists should be expelled forcibly. Governor Kuakini, who had started the construction of the first church in the Islands, Mokuaikaua in Kona, but had not joined it himself, argued that the Picpus Fathers had conducted themselves well since their arrival. Marín's Catholicism created no problem for the realm, he pointed out. Then Kuakini suggested that the kingdom try something new: Let people judge for themselves which version of faith they preferred.[26]

Marín assured Kaʻahumanu—wrongly—that the Picpus Fathers had no intention of converting kanakas, but she continued to fear that competing denominations could plunge her nation into civil war, a concern that the captains of Yankee whalers raised with her. "I do not like two sorts of religion among my people," she told Father Bachelot. "This will make them quarrel."[27]

Despite her misgivings, she let them stay. In January 1828, they opened a small chapel in their Honolulu compound and began baptizing the children of foreign residents, including those of Consular Agent Jones and American merchant Stephen Reynolds. Then they started baptizing Hawaiians, both adult converts and their children.[28] With Unitarian services led by Jones and Mass celebrated by Catholic priests, the Islands experienced religious pluralism for the first time.

The Calvinists felt that at least they were making progress against prostitution, with sea captains now restraining sailors who sought wahines. They also were overjoyed by the conversion of Kekupuohi, who had been married to King Kalaniʻōpuʻu and Prince Kaʻiana, and something like 38 other men, who joined the church in 1828 and became an exemplary member. The Protestant mission also was strengthened by the arrival of the Third Company on March 30, 1828, even if the new recruits arrived with little more understanding of Hawaiian culture than the Pioneer Company had. Laura Fish Judd was shocked at the amount of native flesh on display and stunned when kanakas laughed at the hot, stiff New England clothes she wore, which they thought hilariously ill-suited to the tropics.[29]

The new missionary may have been inappropriately dressed, but Kaʻahumanu was eager to give her hānai daughter Ruth Keʻelikōlani a Western education and a solid grounding in Christianity, so she asked Judd to raise and educate the young princess as she would her own child. Judd felt unable to undertake this, but it alarmed Boki and his allies that the regent was determined to make Ruth into a good Protestant. When Boki heard that Kaʻahumanu had remarked on several occasions, "Perhaps when my grandchild is grown, she may become ruler," he began plotting to kill the regent.[30]

The Kuhina Nui's worries about foreign intervention were prescient. For the rest of the century, one hostile warship after another from England, France, and the United States would descend upon the archipelago. In the end, Americans would overthrow and annex the Hawaiian Kingdom. And foreign residents continued to meddle in local politics. Foreigners even encouraged Boki and his wife Liliha to seize the throne. In July 1828, Charlton, the none-too-diplomatic British Consul, told Boki he would "cut Kaʻahumanu's head off" and that all the foreign residents of the Islands "were ready to join in it." American merchant Stephen Reynolds doubted that many would join Charlton in taking up arms against the regent, but Boki gathered a small army at Waikīkī.³¹

Her supporters took up arms, too, preparing for battle. Going to Boki herself, Ka'ahumanu told him to kill her rather than start a civil war. Boki swore he never wanted to harm her—and quietly squelched his rebellion. The Kuhina Nui was strong enough and confident enough to remain calm. As Hiram Bingham remarked, "She, however, in her dignity and wisdom, appeared quite undisturbed...."³²

Charlton's interference reduced Beretania's influence in the Islands. His friend Alexander Simpson admitted,

> No doubt, had the British representative been a man of tact and diplomatic talent, the influence could not have so completely fallen into the hands of the Americans. But, ... he did not possess the qualifications necessary for a diplomatist—coolness, discretion, and an abstinence from party heats and personal animosities.³³

In August 1828, Ka'ahumanu issued an edict forbidding kanakas from attending Catholic Mass. Some refused to obey and were punished, while others resigned themselves to waiting for the aging regent to meet her Maker. They expected fun-loving Kauikeaouli, who surrounded himself with a boisterous group of aikānes and had sexual relations with his sister Nāhi'ena'ena, to reject Calvinism. Auguste Bernard Duhaut-Cilly, captain of the French ship, *Héros*, who spent two months on O'ahu during the summer of 1828, observed, "the adherents of the young king were being patient while awaiting the death of Kaahumanu, which they expected soon...." Both Kauikeaouli and Nāhi'ena'ena studied in Protestant schools, sang in Calvinist choirs, and attended the dedication of the first Congregational church in Honolulu. She had been a member since 1826, but he never joined the church.³⁴

Duhaut-Cilly thought that the attitudes of the king and Kuhina Nui toward Calvinists and Catholics were shaped by whom they loved, and whom they feared, more than it was influenced by their faith:

> One of Kauikeaouli's principal grievances against the American missionaries was that they were opposed to his marriage to his sister [Nāhi'ena'ena] whom he loved very much. Such unions that are repulsive to us are common in the archipelago of the Sandwich Islands, but Kaahumanu, fearing the power and influence of a young and beautiful queen, used religion as a pretext to block this marriage ... and separated the two young people by sending the Princess to the island of Maui....³⁵

Paul-Émile Botta, the surgeon-naturalist on the *Héros*, lamented the influence of missionaries, saying they represented "the most fanatical

Chapter 9—Law and Order, Church and State

and austere sect" of Christianity. Unlike his captain, he correctly identified them as Independents or Congregationalists, not Methodists, but inexplicably called his own countrymen Jesuits. Botta thought, and hoped, that the Protestant missionaries might be expelled after Kaʻahumanu died. In the short-term, though, he recognized that she was "the most influential person in the islands, the one who really governs them...."[36]

Others may have prayed for her demise, but Kaʻahumanu was in no hurry to leave this earth. Each year brought something new to try: governing a nation, playing cards, learning to read. She also enjoyed the latest fashions from abroad, adapting them to her considerable frame. While most commoners dressed in traditional kapa in 1828, she wore satin. She delighted in riding her expensive, imported gig (a light, two-wheeled, one-horse carriage)—though she switched to a slower, steadier donkey cart after driving the gig into a kalo patch and landing in the mud.[37]

By the beginning of April, Honolulu was rife with rumors. On the one hand, it was said that "a powerful party" wanted to put Kīnaʻu on the throne and make her son the heir-apparent. It also was rumored that Boki planned to attack the regent when she returned to Oʻahu. For weeks, the young king was afraid to go anywhere near Kaʻahumanu. The next month, she sailed to the Big Island to assert her authority in a new way. She went to Hale o Keawe, the burial house of ancient chiefs at Honaunau, took their bones, reburied them with Christian ceremony at Kaʻawaloa, and burned down the charnel house. The mikanele admired her dramatic action, but Boki called them blasphemous and treasonous, a desecration of royal ancestors.[38]

She also transferred from Liliha to the Mission, over the objections of the governor's wife, 200 acres of verdant land mauka (*uphill*) from Honolulu to provide both a permanent home and farmland for the Binghams and other mikanele. This allocation included a natural spring called Punahou. She had thatched cottages for herself and the Binghams built around Punahou, which eventually became the name of the school built there to educate the children of chiefs and missionaries.[39]

Initially, the Picpus Fathers had limited their work to haoles and their children, but in the summer of 1829, they began seeking converts among the kānaka maoli, just as the Calvinists had from the start. They particularly sought out those denied membership in the congregational church and people who had been admitted but then excommunicated. Soon, they had baptized 65 kanakas—and some Calvinists began saying the priests should be deported. An American and a Briton, hoping to weaken the Calvinist influence among the chiefs, urged 14-year-old Princess Nāhiʻenaʻena to marry her brother, claiming such unions were common in Europe and the United States. But Consular Agent Jones, no friend of the congregational church, told her that this was untrue and such a marriage would hinder the kingdom's relations with other nations. There was widespread support, though, among kanakas for them marrying and ruling together. Kaʻahumanu herself told Hiram Bingham that she saw the princess "as the future partner of the throne," though it is not clear whether she meant as the young king's wife or as the next Kuhina Nui. Boki, however, tried to turn this against the regent. He asked Nāhiʻenaʻena for permission to kill Kaʻahumanu so she could marry her brother and rule the kingdom with him. Alarmed, the child fled from the governor. The king, for his part, said that he was listening to Kaʻahumanu, not Boki.[40]

Both Binamu and Binamuwahine warned Kaʻahumanu that she was moving too fast, cautioning her that supporting Protestants was fine, but persecuting Catholics was not. It would be better to expel the Picpus Fathers, the American missionaries felt, rather than to punish kanakas who became Catholic. She chose the latter course, ratcheting up their persecution. She posted guards outside Catholic Mass to prevent Islanders from attending, ordered Marín to stop hosting Catholic worship in his home, and warned the priests that they would be ejected from the kingdom if they defied her ban.[41]

Late in the summer of 1829, Kaʻahumanu journeyed to Maui, Molokaʻi, and little Lānaʻi. On the last of these Islands, she preached at Kahalepalaoa, near the ancient Naha fishponds, six years before any mikanele visited the Island. There, she urged the residents of Lānaʻi to convert to Christianity and "listen to the word of God." On September 12, she lost an important ally when her sister, co-wife, and fellow convert Nāmāhāna Piʻia died, "one of the earliest, most constant, and efficient friends of the missions," but Kaʻahumanu's religious zeal remained undiminished. Kuakini, her only surviving brother and governor of the Big Island, was soon received into the membership of the congregational church in Kailua, and both Kīnaʻu and her husband announced their desire to join also.[42]

In October, Richard Charlton flew into a rage when a kanaka shot one of Charlton's cows, which the consul allowed to wander wherever they wanted, destroying gardens and fields across Honolulu. Charlton responded by throwing a noose over the farmer's head and dragging

Chapter 9—Law and Order, Church and State

Andrew Jackson by John Henry Bufford, after Ralph Eleaser Whiteside Earl, 1831–1832 (National Portrait Gallery, Smithsonian Institution).

him from a horse, nearly killing the man. Outraged at this near-murder, Ka'ahumanu and the ali'i issued a proclamation that foreigners were subject to Hawaiian law. Charlton, infuriated, boasted—bluffing—that he had 500 men under arms, ready to overthrow the government.[43]

Just then, the American warship, *Vincennes*, arrived with a letter from the Secretary of the Navy, which in turn conveyed a message from President Andrew Jackson:

> Our citizens who violate your laws, or interfere with your regulations, violate at the same time their duty to their own government and country, and merit censure and punishment. We have heard with pain that this has sometimes been the case; and we have sought to know and to punish those who are guilty. Captain Finch is commanded diligently to inquire into the conduct of our citizens, whom he may find at the islands; and, as far as he has the authority, to insure proper conduct and deportment from them.[44]

The president also endorsed the work of the New England missionaries. The First Company had arrived during the first term of James Monroe, who was nominally an Episcopalian but left no evidence of his religious beliefs. "Mad Jack" Percival had assailed the Calvinists during the presidency of John Quincy Adams, who was a theologically articulate Unitarian at a time when Unitarians were breaking away from the Congregationalists to form a new denomination. Neither of these predecessors opposed the American mission, but Andrew Jackson, a Presbyterian, openly supported it.

Charles Stewart, the member of the Second Company who returned on the *Vincennes* as a naval chaplain, reported that when Capt. W.C.B. Finch delivered the letter, along with gifts for the Islands' rulers, including a silver vase inscribed with the coat of arms of the United States and her name,

> I never before saw Kaahumanu more excited ... her eyes were filled with tears. "Maitai—maitai no!" "Good—good indeed." ... was the hasty comment of the king.

Stewart recognized that many of the foreign residents would oppose nearly any law:

> I believe I am warranted by facts in saying that in general, they have been decidedly opposed to the establishment of all defined public laws, even for the government of native subjects, under a pretense that if laws were formed, they would be made by the missionaries; but in reality, I fear, because [they] wished the whole nation to remain lawless....[45]

Haole residents blamed the American mission for legislation that inconvenienced them, but Finch reported that these accusations were false. His admiration for their work, the captain noted, had nothing to do with denominational loyalty. He was an Episcopalian.[46]

Foreign merchants often viewed Hawaiians as a backward people, but Stewart saw progress:

Chapter 9—Law and Order, Church and State

An entire moral reformation has taken place in the vicinity of this station.... Instruction of every kind is eagerly and universally sought; and only last week, not less than ten thousand people were assembled at the examination of school.

The mission house is daily crowded with earnest inquirers in every right way; evil customs and atrocious vices are abandoned....

Many of the scholars, both [m]ale and female, write well; quite as much so as most persons of common education in our own country; and all manifested as full an understanding ... as would be found among scholars at a similar exhibition at home.

In the year 1820 the people might justly have been denominated a nation of drunkards and gamblers—without letters, without morals, without religion, and without hope.... Now no nation probably is more temperate or less addicted to gambling; their language has been reduced to writing; morals have been improved, and the Christian religion established on a firm basis; old and deep-rooted habits of evil have been, in thousands of instances, broken up ... schools have been everywhere established; and about 30,000 of the inhabitants, perhaps *more* brought under instruction.[47]

Unfortunately, this moral reformation did not include religious liberty. What protection Boki had given Catholics came to a sudden end in December, when he sailed away to Vanuatu (New Hebrides) in the South Pacific in search of sandalwood to pay off his debts, after nearly all the timber on Oʻahu had been cut. Boki had long been a thorn in the regent's side. Levi Chamberlain thought that "she would gladly have removed him could she have done it without endangering the peace of the nation," but now he removed himself voluntarily, taking hundreds of aliʻi and sailors who supported him and opposed the Kuhina Nui. Before departing, he named his wife Liliha acting governor. The king begged him not to go, but Boki replied that he would not return until one particular "great chief is dead."[48]

Liliha immediately turned over control of two forts on Oʻahu to her current lover, which enraged Kaʻahumanu, who responded with new attempts to legislate morality. The regent banned the singing of joyful olis and humorous, often-sarcastic meles, many of which she had written herself. She now found them too risqué. A renowned hula dancer in her youth, she tried to ban the dancing of any "lewd and lascivious hula," though this edict was widely ignored. Then, she ordered couples, both Hawaiian and haole, to separate if they had not been married in a Christian ceremony, a blow to Kauikeaouli and Nāhiʻenaʻena and countless others. These new laws, Jonathan Osorio observes, "criminalized not just ordinary behavior, but also ʻhula, the culture's highest artistic expression.'"[49]

Queen Ka'ahumanu of Hawaii

By the end of 1829, it was clear that the Picpus Fathers were violating the conditions under which Ka'ahumanu allowed them to remain on O'ahu. They could open a chapel to foreigners only so long as kanakas did not worship there. She summoned Father Alexis Bachelot, who told her, "Your highness, we cannot refuse instruction in the only true religion to those who ask for it."[50]

The Calvinist missionaries offered her mixed advice. Hiram Bingham said that the biblical law against idolatry did not apply to Catholic worship, but also insisted that the government could expel whomever it wished—and claimed the priests were "enemies in our midst." He urged the government not to persecute kanakas who embraced Catholicism, but when they were punished, his "protests were seemingly very mild indeed." Levi Chamberlain and Ephraim Clark, who had just arrived with the Third Company, argued on the other hand that "there should be no compulsion in matters of faith."[51]

On January 3, 1830, Ka'ahumanu ordered Hawaiians who had embraced Catholicism to surrender their crucifixes (small statutes, often worn on a necklace, which showed the execution of Jesus on a cross), which she incorrectly considered to be small ki'is (*tikis*). Those who refused were threatened with exile, hard labor, or imprisonment. Several Islanders were arrested while attending Catholic Mass. The punishment meted out was less severe than the sentence might have been under the old religion—death—but harsh enough to horrify haoles. Next, she summoned Hawaiian Catholics and asked them to reject their denomination and become Protestants. Not one spoke a word in reply.[52]

Sometimes Ka'ahumanu tried gentler forms of persuasion. She took into her home a Catholic woman, Luika (*Louisa* or *Louise*) Kaunaka, hoping to make a good Calvinist out of her. Luika, who was now in her 40s, had sailed to Guam and Californian when she was younger, had become more or less Catholic, and had returned to the Islands, calling herself its priest—a title the Vatican would never have given her. Despite pressure from Ka'ahumanu, she refused to become a congregationalist, and the queen finally sent her away.[53]

Any hope Catholics may have had for their persecution easing after Boki returned was dashed when news reached Honolulu that he had been lost at sea, and that only a dozen of the hundreds of kanakas who accompanied him had survived. Meanwhile, in Paris, what little chance the Picpus Fathers might have had for support from France vanished when the July Revolution of 1830 overthrew the conservative House of

Chapter 9—Law and Order, Church and State

Bourbon, drove Charles X into exile, and put liberal, anti-clerical Louis Philippe on the throne.[54]

On January 8, 1831, Kaʻahumanu, the king, the Council of Chiefs, and the governors of Kauaʻi, Maui, and the Big Island concluded that these "Jesuits" were "a danger to the State and religion, an obstacle to the progress of civilization and instruction, enemies of morality and Christ." They told the Catholic missionaries:

> Leave at once from this land. You shall not stay here in the Hawaiian archipelago because your doctrine opposes and is different from that which we observe.... When you arrived here, we did not invite to stay, but you took up residence and for that we are expelling you.... We are giving you three months for you to prepare for your departure. If you are not gone within three months, then your assets shall be seized by us.... If you stay a fourth month, you will be imprisoned, and we will treat you in the same manner as rulers of all lands do when their rule is not respected.[55]

Father Armand had already returned to Europe because of illness, but the other two priests refused to go. How could they abandon their converts? How could they leave them without the sacraments, without the Bread of Life? Instead, they stalled for time. After months of waiting for them to find their own transportation, the government marched them onto the government brig, *Waverly*, and sent them to California, which was Mexican territory and predominantly Catholic. British Consul Charlton and American Consular Agent Jones protested, providing written testimony in December that the Picpus Fathers had behaved admirably in the Islands, but support from these two hardly helped their cause. Finally, in December, the priests were marched aboard the *Waverly* under armed guard. The king explained, "At seven times we gave them that order.... Therefore we put them on board our own vessel, to carry them to a place where the service is like their own." Governor Kuakini took pains to state that they were being deported not because of what they believed, but rather because they never sought permission to remain in the kingdom.[56]

Only laybrothers of the order were allowed to stay. Taking a parting shot at the Protestants, Father Bachelot told Hawaiian Catholics, "Beware of eating the bread of sacrilege in partaking of the Lord's Supper with the Calvinists." At least this time, he identified his adversaries correctly.[57]

Brother Melchior, who was left in charge of the Catholic Mission, offered a prayer in the forlorn little grass hut that had served as their chapel, the altar no longer holding the chalice of communion wine or the plate of consecrated bread:

Queen Ka'ahumanu of Hawaii

Dear God, look upon these beautiful islands and give them Your blessing. May these kindly people open their hearts to Your love, and grant that these pinpoints of land out here in mid-ocean may be blessed again and forever by Your Sacramental Presence. Send back Your priests, and may the day come when we can guild churches, hospitals, and schools, and through them reap a glorious harvest of souls for Eternity![58]

Who was responsible in the end for their expulsion? Ka'ahumanu told Luika, "I did not banish them. Binamu did."[59]

Chapter 10

Going Where the Mansions Are Ready

There were now more than 50 American missionaries in the kingdom, facing no serious competition from any other denomination. When the Calvinists toured remote areas where no congregation had been established yet, they sometimes preached to 5,000 listeners. And a new generation of local leaders had been trained within a decade. There were now 20 worship services on Maui each week that were led by kanakas, though the mission still would not ordain any of them as pastors. The Hilo congregation was the largest Protestant church in the world.[1]

Kauikeaouli never embraced the Calvinist code of Christian conduct, but he enthusiastically supported the mission schools and urged his people to attend them. By 1831, there were more than 52,000 students attending more than 1,100 schools scattered across every island in the kingdom. About 40 percent of the population had studied in them. With a growing demand for teachers, Ka'ahumanu and other chiefs donated land on Maui to the American Board of Commissioners for Foreign Missions to establish Lahainaluna Seminary, the first high school west of the Rockies. Growing out of Betsey Stockton's school for commoners and dedicated to training Hawaiian educators, clergy, and government agents, it became one of the finest schools in the Pacific.[2]

But all was not well. Liliha, who enjoyed strong support among both kanakas and haoles, was plotting rebellion. Toward the end of February 1831, she heard rumors that the Kuhina Nui intended to replace her as governor and began assembling an army. Rumors swirled through Honolulu and Lāhainā that Liliha's army would strike when the king, the regent, and many of the leading chiefs were making a tour of other islands with Protestant missionaries. "There will be no peace," Liliha was rumored to have said, "until the heads of Kaahumanu and Mr. Bingham are taken off."[3]

Queen Kaʻahumanu of Hawaii

Kīnaʻu wrote to her aunt, who was meeting with other chiefs in Lāhainā, to warn her that Liliha had gathered troops and was preparing for war. Liliha's father, Hoapili, rushed from Maui to Honolulu and persuaded his daughter to surrender, preventing bloodshed. On April 1, 1831, the young king formally gave Kaʻahumanu control over all land, laws, and forts on Oʻahu. She, in turn, promptly stripped Liliha of her office and her land, redistributing it to aliʻi who were loyal to her and the king. Then, she appointed her brother Kuakini, already governor of the Big Island, as acting governor of Oʻahu, too.[4]

The first Hawaiian to read English and the first to master the written form of his own language, Kuakini was widely admired for these accomplishments, for the roads he built on the Big Island, and for the successful businesses he launched there. On Oʻahu, he immediately formed a "temperance society" whose members promised to stop drinking alcohol or selling hard liquor. As in the United States, Calvinists in the Islands moved only quite slowly from opposing public drunkenness to encouraging Christians to swear off alcohol completely. The Sandwich Island Mission did not commit itself to complete abstinence until December of that year. Long before temperance leagues thrived in the United States—Americans still consumed on average seven gallons of pure alcohol per year—Kuakini's group took in 1,000 members almost overnight. The young king, however, was not among them.[5]

The acting governor, unfortunately, did not allow time for persuasion to work. Rather than rely on personal pledges to abstain, he imposed prohibition, which turned out no better in Honolulu than it did a century later in Chicago, Illinois. The very day that Kaʻahumanu appointed him to replace Liliha, Kuakini banned liquor sales, billiard halls, and gambling houses on Oʻahu. He then sent armed patrols out to suppress the sale of rum, break up gambling houses, and enforce respect for the Sabbath, including a ban on Sunday horseback riding. A group of haoles protested, saying these were not only an infringement of their freedom, but also an attack on non–Calvinists. Kuakini insisted, however, that those who defied his laws would have their property seized. His soldiers fought with merchants in the streets of Honolulu, but alcohol still flowed freely in a now-clandestine network of hotels and other underground purveyors of alcohol.[6]

The Kuhina Nui, as zealous as her brother, supported his attempts to impose morality. She even agreed with Hiram Bingham's plea to ban the hula completely—though the young king, who loved to dance,

Chapter 10—Going Where the Mansions Are Ready

ignored her edict. These prohibitions produced widespread resentment, making it increasingly difficult to maintain order.[7]

Even some people who admired their attempts to lead Hawaiians away from alcohol abuse thought the methods they employed were overly harsh. General William Miller, a British officer serving in the Peruvian Army, visited Honolulu in 1831 and urged the Hawaiian government to ease its laws regulating drinking and Sunday observance. Kuakini's approach to law enforcement, Miller claimed, came more "from sectarian enthusiasm, not to say intolerance, than from justice or sound policy." Some mikanele thought the governor was too zealous in applying what they taught and that he was going too far in attempting to legislate morality. Sheldon Dibble, who arrived with the Fourth Company on June 7, 1831, conceded that the missionaries had not entirely restrained the sexuality of the locals: "For a man or a woman to refuse a solicitation for illicit intercourse was considered an act of meanness."[8]

Many of her attempts to change behavior by force of law failed, but Ka'ahumanu did manage to correct some injustices. She eased the economic burdens that ali'i had placed on ordinary people, for example, by prohibiting chiefs from collecting heavy taxes or requiring forced labor. Rather than lord it over her subjects, she gave up the elegant clothing she loved and wore simple, loose-fitting white dresses instead of expensive satin robes. She moved out of her extravagant, European-style wooden house and into a simple Hawaiian hut. Her identification with the maka'āinana did much to regain their loyalty, which had been sorely tested by her moralizing.[9]

In September 1831, she wrote to the American Board, praising "the kindness of our Lord Jesus Christ in aiding us by [sending] several new teachers," though she noted that they would need to study the Hawaiian language for some time before they could teach anything—more than 15 years after Henry 'Ōpūkaha'ia had begun compiling a Hawaiian dictionary, grammar book, and spelling book to prepare future missionaries. That same month, she made a final tour around O'ahu, both to reassert her authority after Liliha's attempted rebellion and also to visit her people one last time. In February 1832, she sailed to Maui and the Big Island. In Lāhainā, people from all over Maui paid homage to her by cutting and carrying stone for a fort to control unruly whalers. It was an impressive fortress, with walls measuring 12 feet thick. As the sun fell, a guard would blow a shell trumpet to warn sailors to return to their ships. Any sailor caught ashore after sunset would be locked in the fort until first light the next morning.[10]

Queen Ka'ahumanu of Hawaii

As Kauikeaouli approached adulthood, Ka'ahumanu often delegated minor decisions to him—and retained her wry sense of humor. In the middle of discussing whether a particular haole could take passage with Captain William Sumner on the government brig, she dismissed herself, letting the boy decide and telling Captain Clark of the *John Palmer*, who stopped to bid her and the young king farewell before sailing away, "Salute the British." When Clark explained that he was not sailing to Beretania but rather hunting whales, she replied jauntily, "Salute the whales!" and left.[11]

She could not bend the young king to her will, however. Many ali'i wanted him to marry High Chiefess Kamānele so that their children might be undisputed heirs to the throne, but in 1832, he fell in love instead with Kalama, daughter of the lesser chief Naihekukui, who had been admiral of the royal fleet. Knowing that Ka'ahumanu's days were few, the king urged his lover to come to him without fear of the Kuhina Nui's wrath, saying that he was "no'u na wahi a pau" (*the master everywhere*). Eventually, he would make Kalama his queen. She would be queen consort and dowager queen until 1870.[12]

Ka'ahumanu returned to O'ahu in spring 1832 quite ill. Neither kahunas nor missionary doctors knew how to treat her, but they suggested "a change of air." She was carried, bed and all, on the shoulders of her friends for five miles up to Pukaomaomao, her summer home in cool Manoa Valley. With its beautiful view of farms, streams, and Diamond Head, it was a pleasant place to end her days. Two hundred grass houses were hastily built nearby to house her staff and guests.[13]

In failing health, she welcomed the Fifth Company on May 18, immediately after their arrival from New England. One of the new missionaries, Dr. Alonzo Chapin, joined Dr. Gerrit Judd, who had arrived with the Third Company, in diagnosing her illness as dysentery, a disease that neither knew how to treat. Judd told her, "You will soon die; soon, you will triumph over death."

Thousands of Hawaiians flocked to Manoa and camped out there to wait with their monarch for her death. Her pastor, Hiram Bingham, told her, "Elisabeta, this perhaps is your departure. Stay yourself on Jesus: he is your Physician, your Savior."

Ka'ahumanu replied, "I am going where there is a house prepared for me.... I will go to him and be comforted." Bingham rushed a copy of the New Testament, printed in Hawaiian for the very first time. It was hot off the presses and beautifully bound in leather with her name stamped in gold on the front cover. It represented serious scholarship,

Chapter 10—Going Where the Mansions Are Ready

translating ancient texts from their original languages into a modern tongue that only recently had been expressed in written form. With great pleasure, she clasped the gift to her chest.[14]

News of her impending death spread rapidly throughout the Islands. The newly arrived missionary Lorenzo Lyons wrote of the young king on June 4,

> The people say in tones of deep anxiety, "We hope he will become o ke kanaka maikai (*a good man*)."[15]

Ka'ahumanu grew weaker just before dawn on June 5, 1832. Friends and relatives surrounded her, with Sybil Bingham holding her hand. They bent over her to hear what she whispered faintly. One of the last things they caught were a few lines of a favorite hymn,

> "Now will I go to Jesus,
> Here am I, O Jesus,
> O, smile upon me now."

A few moments later, she died peacefully and painlessly.[16]

Newly arrived mikanele Richard Armstrong noted, "The people are overwhelmed with sorrow in consequence of the death of the regent Kaahumanu." Lorenzo Lyons reported that a great wail of, "Auwe! Auwe!" arose "in slow protracted tones, united with the plaintive and solemn touches of the drum," but the missionaries were relieved that there was no rending of clothes or knocking out of teeth. The young king sought to maintain a dignified composure, but as Betsy Lyons observed, "he has manifested an unfeigned sorrow."[17]

Ships in Honolulu harbor flew flags at half-mast. Hiram Bingham said, "We have lost a warm friend, an able supporter of our cause, a distinguished reformer of her nation. She has finished her course, she has fought a good fight. She has kept the faith."[18]

Davida Malo wrote a song of lamentation, one of the first Hawaiian kanikau (*funeral dirges*) ever published:

> Miha lanaau i kuakahiki ka newa na, Ke kaha na ka leina aku nei liuliu,
> Liua paia aku nei i Kuanalia,
> I analipo i analio....
> Ke halelu ia la ilaila,
> Iloko o ka Paredaiso nani,
> I kea o mau loa o ka Haku e, ia, ko kakou mau Haku no ia,
> O ka Haku mau no ia, oia no.
> O ka Haku mau no ia, oia no.
> (*Her spirit glides away to the far regions*

Queen Kaʻahumanu of Hawaii

beyond Kahiki. She flies; averting her eyes,
he fades away in the wild mists of the
northland, the deep, dark, mysterious north....
She sings praise-palms of joy in
the paradise of glory, in the everlasting daytime
of the Lord. He is our Lord, the everlasting
Lord, he indeed, in truth.)[19]

Even some who had been skeptical of the regent's conversion finally admitted her sincerity. Henry A. Peirce, who often was critical of the Calvinists, concluded,

> She died a Christian. It has always heretofore been my opinion that her adherence and adoption of the Christian religion was from policy ... but I have lately been convinced from the piety displayed during her sickness and at the hour of her death that she really believe in and practiced the principles of the Christian religion.[20]

On June 7, Hiram Bingham presided over Kaʻahumanu's funeral at Kawaiahaʻo, his church and hers in Honolulu. He preached in Hawaiian, and the Rev. Lorrin Andrews, part of the Third Company, came from Maui to preach in English. Thousands thronged around the solemn procession that carried Kaʻahumanu's body from her Manoa home to the church. Binamu chose as his sermon text the triumphant words of 2 Timothy 4:7–8: "I have fought a good fight, I have finished my course, I have kept the faith."[21]

After the service, thousands marched with her one last time to a burial site on the grounds of Iolani Palace—a far cry from the way Kamehameha's bones had been hidden in a cave in the dark of night. Later, her coffin was moved to the Royal Mausoleum in Nuʻuanu Valley to rest beside Liholiho, Kamāmalu, and other rulers. Later, some said, Governor Kuakini led eight strong Hawaiians to the Royal Mausoleum one evening at midnight. They quietly opened his sister's casket, lifted her kapa-covered body onto a surfboard, and carried it down to a secluded beach east of Honolulu Harbor. There, they met a silent group of elderly Hawaiian men and women and the crew of a double-hulled canoe. The kapa bundle was gently laid on the canoe, which was paddled to the Big Island, to reunite Kaʻahumanu with her beloved Kamehameha.[22]

Kaʻahumanu had performed her duties so well that there was little doubt that someone needed to replace her and continue the power sharing she had inaugurated. Her 27-year-old niece, Kīnaʻu, eldest daughter of Kamehameha the Great and half sister to Kauikeaouli, became the new Kuhina Nui, an office she exercised until her death, taking the title of

Chapter 10—Going Where the Mansions Are Ready

Ka'ahumanu II. Yet another niece would succeed Kīna'u in 1839. Kīna'u also would serve as regent until the king came of age. Nine months after Ka'ahumanu's death, he declared himself ready to rule without a regent. He was only 19 years old but already more self-controlled and dignified than his older brother had ever been.[23]

Together, and often at odds with each other, the new king and the new Kuhina Nui steered the kingdom through times of tremendous change. As had been the case with Ka'ahumanu and Liholiho, their divided powers helped move their people away from absolute rule. Kauikeaouli would rule longer than any other Hawaiian king, leading his nation into constitutional monarchy.

Kīna'u quickly assured her people that she would govern much as her aunt had, but she also learned from Ka'ahumanu's mistakes. Hula dancing resumed almost immediately. Kīna'u, whom Bachelot had called "our greatest enemy," did not immediately embrace freedom of worship, but she set free Catholics who had been imprisoned for practicing their faith, and she generally eased their persecution. The chapel that her aunt had tried to crush became the site of Our Lady of Peace, the oldest continuously operating Catholic cathedral in what is now the United States. Today, nearly one-third of the state's population is Catholic.[24]

The children whom she raised took distinctly different paths in adulthood, as did the people whom she led as Kuhina Nui. Liholiho was trained in the rituals of the old akua but overturned them at the urging of his kahu and his mother; Ruth Ke'elikōlani, her hānai daughter, became a staunch defender of ancient Hawaiian customs and traditions. Ka'ahumanu remains a controversial figure among kānaka maoli. Did she liberate her people from oppressive kapus or betray their traditions? Perhaps a little of both. She steered her nation through revolutionary change, making mistakes, learning from some of them, and leaving a legacy of empowered women, courageous leadership, and openness to the future.

Places to Visit

On Maui, a slow, winding, picturesque road leads to the little town of Hāna. In 1830, Kaʻahumanu identified the spot on Kaʻuiki Hill where she hid with her mother as a child. From the pier at Hāna Bay, a path leads up to the cave. The path is marked by a plaque, though erosion often makes the going difficult. Most temples were destroyed after the kapus were overturned, but Piʻilanihale Heiau near Hāna, the largest in the archipelago, remains intact. It was said to have been built by Paramount Chief Piʻilani in 1400 for human sacrifice, but an archeological excavation in 1990 led to carbon dating the original construction as late as the 13th century. Covering nearly three acres, with five terraced levels, it overlooks a magnificent stretch of coastline and is surrounded by Kahanu Garden, one of five places in the National Tropical Botanical Garden system. You need to make arrangements in advance for a guided tour.[1]

While on Maui, you also can attend the Kaʻahumanu Church on High Street in Wailuku. In 1832, Kaʻahumanu visited the simple shed that initially served as a sanctuary and asked the congregation to build a more permanent structure, which they did, naming it in her honor. As with most congregational church buildings, it resembles a New England sanctuary of the 19th century. Not far away, you can see a stunning, 8-foot-tall bronze statue of Kaʻahumanu created by Tom Faught and Dan Skinner in 1996, at the Queen Kaʻahumanu Center in Kahului. The two-day Queen Kaʻahumanu Festival takes place each March at the mall, which is perhaps an appropriate place to honor a monarch who loved nice clothes. At the end of Market Street in Lāhainā, just behind the public library, you can see the restored foundation of the Brick Palace that Kamehameha constructed for his Favorite Wife.

On the Kona coast of the Big Island, you can tour Puʻuhonua o Hōnaunau (*City of Refuge*), which was spared during the iconoclasm of 1819, due to its connection with the Kamehameha dynasty. A national

Places to Visit

Ka'ahumanu Church, Wailuku, Maui (Eric Chan, Flickr).

Places to Visit

historical park today, three temple platforms and the 1,000-foot-long Great Wall have been preserved. One heiau has been reconstructed, along with a thatched house, a wooden fence, and huge statues of gods made from ohia wood. You can also see the Pohaku o Ka'ahumanu (*Ka'ahumanu Stone*), behind which she is said to have hidden to spy on Kamehameha after a quarrel, only to be discovered by his four-legged companion.

At the north end of Kailua Bay on the Big Island, near Kailua Pier, you can see Hale o Lono (which earlier was called 'Ahu'ena Heiau), a two-thirds-scale replica of the temple where Kamehameha spent a great deal of time in prayer, much to the dismay of his Favorite Wife, who could not enter it. The stone platform, thatched buildings, and wooden statues, and a canoe landing site, have been restored by the Hawaiian royal societies. If you happen to be there on May 8, you might witness the commemoration of the anniversary of Kamehameha's death by the Hawaiian royal societies, including the 'Ahahui Ka'ahumanu (*Ka'ahumanu Society*).

Kailua-Kona is also where Kamehameha died, where Ka'ahumanu and Keōpūolani prodded Liholiho to break the kapus, and where the First Company was granted permission to come ashore. A marker indicates the spot where the missionaries landed, "Hawai'i's Plymouth Rock," and nearby Mokuaikaua Church, the oldest Christian sanctuary still standing in the Islands. The latter was built on the site of the first Calvinist church in Kona. Originally constructed with a wooden frame and a thatched roof in 1823, it was replaced with a stone structure, in the style of New England but made from lava rock taken from the heiau that had stood on the site.

On O'ahu, you will find a judiciary building named after the Kuhina Nui, at Punchbowl and Halekauwila Streets in Honolulu, a fitting tribute to the woman who shaped the first written laws of Hawai'i. The school at 1141 Kina'u Street in Honolulu also is named after her, paying homage to a leader who also championed education, and the street itself is named after her successor.

If you stop at the site of Ka'ahumanu's summer home in upper Manoa Valley, at the intersection of Kumuone and Loulu Streets, you can see how beautiful of a location it was.[2] You can visit her tomb at the Royal Mausoleum of Hawaii in lovely Nu'uanu Valley—though perhaps her casket lies hidden on the Big Island alongside the bones of Kamehameha. Also called Mauna 'Ala (*Fragrant Hills*), it is now a state park, located at 2261 Nu'uanu Avenue, mauka (*uphill*) from downtown

Places to Visit

Honolulu, just off the Pali Highway. The tombs of Liholiho, Queen Kamāmalu, Kauikeaouli, Kīnaʻu, and other rulers of Hawaiʻi also can be seen there.

The Bishop Museum (1525 Bernice Street in Honolulu), the state museum of natural and cultural history, has silver spoons that Capt. W.C.B. Finch of the *Vincennes* gave her, a fish trap associated with her, the Bible she received on her deathbed, and many of the songs and hulas she composed. They also have the feathered image of the war god, Kū, which Kalaniʻōpuʻu placed under Kamehameha's protection, a rare surviving kiʻi (*tiki*) that was not consigned to the flames. They also display the mahiole (*feather helmet*), said to be the finest in existence, which her second husband, Kaumualiʻi, brought to Oʻahu after he was kidnapped. The museum also has portraits of Hawaiian royalty and the elegant silver teapot engraved with her name and the royal coat of arms that George IV gave to Kaʻahumanu. In 2020, Te Papa Tongarewa (*the Museum of New Zealand*) permanently repatriated the beautiful ʻahu ʻula (*feather cloak*) and mahiole (*feather helmet*) that King Kalaniʻōpuʻu gave to Capt. James Cook, both of which can be seen now at the Bishop Museum.

You can attend Sunday worship at the church that Kaʻahumanu joined, Kawaiahaʻo, in downtown Honolulu. There were four consecutive thatched sanctuaries before this two-story, coral-stone structure was built in 1842. The church has a memorial plaque dedicated to her and a portrait of her in its Aliʻi of Hawaiʻi display. Services regularly employ both Hawaiian and English. Kawaiahaʻo has an austere, New England-style sanctuary, but it is filled with color for Aliʻi Sundays about nine times each year. The annual service honoring Kaʻahumanu is usually held in March.[3]

St. Andrew, the Episcopal cathedral in Honolulu, has 8 a.m. Aliʻi Sunday services in Hawaiian half a dozen times or more a year, celebrating a different set of leaders. Other churches also have occasional Aliʻi Sundays. In nearly any congregation, you can see how, despite the initial misgivings of Calvinists, churches in the Islands eventually incorporated aspects of indigenous culture. United Methodist worship may begin with a Hawaiian creation chant or the blowing of a conch shell and close with "the Queen's Prayer" or the hymn, "Hawaiʻi Aloha." Catholic worship on the beach at Waikiki often features a hula interpretation of part of the liturgy. As was the case everywhere else, Christianity changed in this "Crossroads of the Pacific" as it interacted with people who came to the Islands from many other lands and cultures.

Near Kawaiahaʻo, you can tour the Hawaiian Mission Houses, which

Places to Visit

includes Hale Laʻau, built in 1821, the oldest surviving wooden structure in Hawaii. This was the home of the Binghams and other members of the First Company, where Kaʻahumanu was a frequent visitor. It housed up to four families, with 12 adults and 12 children living under one roof and sharing meals, and sometimes as many as 50 people crowded around a common table. You can also visit the 1831 coral-block Ka Hale Kamalani, which served as both Levi Chamberlain's home and the Mission's communal storehouse. The mission houses preserve photographs, journals, letters, furniture, and other artifacts of the first missionaries, and its library has the largest collection of Hawaiian-language books in the world.

Near Waimea on Kauaʻi, at Russian Fort Elizabeth State Park at Pāʻulaʻula, you can visit the site of the Schäffer's ill-fated attempt to conquer islands for the Russian Empire—or perhaps himself. The Friends of King Kaumualiʻi have erected a memorial to him there, including an 8-foot bronze statue by Saim Caglayan, Kaumualiʻi: Last King of Kauʻi.

On Lānaʻi, you can visit Kahalepalaoa, where Kaʻahumanu preached in 1829, near ancient fishponds, heiaus, and petroglyphs. Nearby is Kaunolū, the well-preserved ruins of an ancient fishing village, including Halulu Heiau, a place of refuge. Kamehameha visited the area often during deep-sea fishing trips and found it to be a convenient place to rest during trips between the Big Island and Oʻahu. The roads there are unpaved and unmarked, so it would be wise to book a guided tour.[4]

You also can see Kaʻahumanu's legacy at any gathering of family and friends in the Islands. Boys and girls, women and men mix freely, usually across generations and ethnic lines. And you can share the spirit of ʻai noa at any lūʻau, where everyone can enjoy the delicacies once reserved for men, such as lomi-lomi salmon, laulau cooked in an imu, and haupia (*coconut pudding*). The food is ʻono—*delicious*—and ʻai noa is maikaʻi—*good*.

Glossary

The once-declining Hawaiian language has been undergoing a major revival in recent decades. Hawaiian spelling is not entirely standardized and continues to evolve over time, as is the case with English and every other living language. The same is true of pronunciation: tomayto, tomahto, potayto, potahto. When missionaries expressed spoken Hawaiian in writing for the first time during the 1820s, they did not use any diacritical marks, but in recent years, it has become common to employ the ʻokina (ʻ) to indicate a break in a word and the kahakō (ā ē ī ō ū) to indicate that a vowel is lengthened. These diacritical marks both indicate how to pronounce a word and can distinguish it from another word that might otherwise be spelled and pronounced the same. Some controversy remains, however, as to exactly where they should be used. In street signs? In Hawaiian words which have become part of local English?[1]

It also is becoming less common for Hawaiian words to be printed in italics, since they are not foreign in Hawaiʻi. In this book, italics are used for Hawaiian words, and diacritical marks are omitted only in quotations where the original source did so.

aikāne: intimate companion and lover of the same gender

ʻāina: land

akua: a god or goddess; Christians used the word for their God, the Creator

aliʻi: royalty, the nobles, the ruling class

aliʻi aimoku: the high chiefs, those who ruled a district

aliʻi nui: the paramount chief of an island or large district, sometimes called mōʻī (*king*)

aloha: love, hello, or goodbye, much like *ciao* in Italian, *shalom* in Hebrew, or *salaam* in Arabic

Haole: foreigner or someone from someplace strange, used today for Euro-Americans; other words are used for Asians, such as pākē for Chinese

Glossary

heiau: temple

hula: a graceful Hawaiian dance that tells a story through chant and motion

kahu: an adult who cares for a child or adolescent as a guardian; today, a pastor

kahuna: an expert or professional, such as a priest, teacher, or doctor

kanaka: a human being, later used for Hawaiians, or more generally for Polynesians or Pacific Islanders

kānaka maoli: native Hawaiians (also called *kānaka 'ōiwi* or *Hawai'i kānaka*), descendants of the first seafaring settlers of the Islands

kane (plural, *kāne*): man or husband

kapa: cloth or paper made from the bark of the mulberry tree

kapu: sacred; because most people could not do anything that was kapu or taboo, it also came to mean "restricted" or "forbidden"

Kuhina Nui: co-ruler

maka'āinana: commoner, as opposed to ali'i

Makahiki: the period lasting up to four months, roughly from October to January, when crops were harvested, games and celebrations were held, and warfare ceased

mele: a poem or song of praise or rejoicing, usually chanted to the beat of a drum or gourd and accompanied by a hula dance

mikanele (or *mikionale*): missionaries

nui: great, important, much, big

palapala (or *pala*): Originally, patterns made on kapa or symbols carved on rocks; later, reading and writing

poi: a nutritious paste made from the steamed root of kalo (taro)

wahine (plural, *wāhine*): woman or wife

Timeline

Year	Event in Ka'ahumanu's Life	Event Elsewhere
1768	Possible year of her birth	First Spanish settlement in California
1778	Capt. Cook visits	France aids the American Revolution
1779	Capt. Cook returns and dies	First iron bridge built in England
1783	Law of the Splintered Paddle	First balloon flight in France
1785	Possible year of marriage to Kamehameha	First steam-powered cotton mill
1789	Kamehameha invades Maui	George Washington becomes first U.S. president
1795	Kamehameha rules Hawai'i to O'ahu	Catherine the Great dies in Russia
1804	Her father dies	Louis and Clark's expedition begins
1807	She and Kamehameha move to Waiiikī	Robert Fulton's steamship *Clermont*
1816	She becomes Liholiho's *kahu*	Argentine independence from Spain
1819	Kamehameha dies; *kapus* overturned	First steamship crossing of Atlantic
1820	Arrival of first missionaries	Britain colonizes South Africa
1821	She marries Kaumuali'i and his son	Greek War of Independence
1823	King Liholiho sails to London	Mary Anning discovers Plesiosaurus
1824	Kaumuali'i dies; revolt on Kaua'i	Bolivar defeats Spanish army in Peru
1825	She joins the church	Erie Canal opens
1826	Confrontation with Lt. Percival	First U.S. railway

Timeline

Year	Event in Kaʻahumanu's Life	Event Elsewhere
1827	Catholic priests land	First matches invented
1829	She bars Hawaiians from Mass	Typewriter invented
1830	She prohibits the hula	Revolution in France and Belgium
1831	Liliha's rebellion	Charles Darwin sails on the *Beagle*
1832	She dies in Manoa	Cholera epidemic in Europe

Explore Further

Cahill, Emmett. 1999. *The Life and Times of John Young, Confidant and Advisor to Kamehameha the Great.* Aiea, HI: Island Heritage Publishing.
Cahill, Emmett. 2004. *The Dark Decade, 1829–1839: Anti-Catholic Persecutions in Hawai'i.* Honolulu: Mutual Publishing.
Chang, David A. 2016. *The World and All the Things upon It: Native Hawaiian Geographies of Exploration.* Minneapolis: University of Minnesota Press.
Chun, Malcolm Nāea. 2011. *No Nā Mamo: Traditional and Contemporary Hawaiian Beliefs and Practices.* Honolulu: University of Hawai'i Press/Curriculum Research & Development Group.
Grigg, Richard W. 2012. *In the Beginning, Archipelago: The Origin and Discovery of the Hawaiian Islands.* Waipahu, HI: Island Heritage Publishing.
Guttman, D. Molentia, and Golden, Ernst. 2011. *African Americans in Hawai'i.* Charleston, SC: Arcadia Publishing. PBS. 2020. *Islands of Wonder: Hawaii.* https://www.thirteen.org/programs/islands-of-wonder/.
Kalakaua, His Hawaiian Majesty David, 1990. *Legends and Myths of Hawaii.* Honolulu: Mutual Publishing.
Kneubuhl, Victoria Nalani. 2002. "The Conversion of Ka'ahumanu," *Hawaii Nei: Island Plays.* Honolulu: University of Hawai'i Press.
Loomis, Albertine. 1951. *Grapes of Canaan: Hawaii 1820, the True Story of Hawaii's Missionaries.* New York: Dodd, Mead (reprinted Woodbridge, CT: Oxbow Press, 1999).
Moore, Susanna. 2015. *Paradise of the Pacific: Approaching Hawai'i.* New York: Farrar, Straus and Giroux.
Thigpen, Jennifer. 2014. *Island Queens and Mission Wives: How Gender and Empire Remade Hawai'i's Pacific World.* Chapel Hill: University of North Carolina Press.
Thompson, Christina. 2019. *Sea People: The Puzzle of Polynesia.* New York: HarperCollins.
Vowell, Sarah. 2011. *Unfamiliar Fishes.* New York: Riverhead Books.
Warne, Douglas. 2008. *Humehume of Kaua'i: A Boy's Journey to America, an Ali'i's Return Home.* Honolulu: Kamehameha Publishing.

Website Resources

http://www.hawaiihistory.org, website developed for anyone who wants to learn more about Hawai'i.
http://www.hokulea.com, the Polynesian Voyaging Society website.
http://www.kumukahi.org, website with Hawaiian history, culture, and language from the Kamehameha Schools.
http://kaiwakiloumoku.ksbe.edu/digital-collections, website with more history and culture from the Kamehameha Schools.
https://www.nps.gov/puho/index.htm, Pu'uhonua o Hōnaunau National Historic Park website.

Explore Further

http://imagesofoldhawaii.com, website with Peter T. Young's extensive collection of pictures and short historical vignettes.

http://www.fortelizabeth.org, website with materials on King Kaumuali'i and the history of the Garden Isle.

http://Ulukau.org, website with resources on Hawaiian language, culture, and history, with most information available in both Hawaiian and English.

Chapter Notes

Chapter 1

1. Grigg, 12–13, 23, 37. Meiji is now a guyot, a submerged island. The older islands, guyot, and atols at the northwestern end of the archipelago are now in the Hawaiian Islands National Wildlife Refuge, the largest marine conservation area in the world.

2. Grigg, 76.

3. Barth, 8. Sadly, fewer than 42 of Hawai'i's unique bird species survive today, all but 11 now threatened or endangered—Richard Coniff, "Hawaiian Honeycreepers," *New York Times*. April 23, 2017. Even Hawai'i's state bird, the Nene goose, found only in the Islands and once common, nearly disappeared in the 1950s, but conservation efforts have subsequently saved the species from extinction. The white tern almost vanished 60 years ago, too, but has since rebounded.

4. Grigg, 55–56, Herman, 2020.

5. When people first colonized the Hawaiian Islands is not known. Several decades ago, it was generally thought to be around 800 CE, or even 500 years earlier. Recent radiocarbon dating and other evidence, however, has led to an emerging consensus that the first settlers probably arrived around 1000 CE from the Marquesas, certainly not much before 900, with later settlers coming from the Society Islands—Kirch and McCoy, 2007; Kirch, 2011; Kirch, 2018; La Croix, pp. 17–20. David Lewis, 53, points out that calling their voyaging vessels *canoes* is misleading. They were catamarans, some longer than *Endeavour*, Cook's earlier ship on an earlier voyage. Any doubts that Polynesians could have colonized the Islands intentionally, during an era when European sailors seldom sailed beyond sight of land, were laid to rest in 1976 when *Hōkūle'a*, a recreated double-hulled craft, reached Tahiti, using only ancient navigation techniques.

Euro-Americans often call the area bounded by the Hawaiian Islands, Rapa Nui Nui (*Easter Island*), and New Zealand *Polynesia*, but many scholars today think this term exaggerates the differences between these cultures and those that outsiders have labeled Melanesia and Micronesia. Today, many prefer to call the entire region, including Australasia, Oceania, and its indigenous people, Pacific Islanders.

6. Thompson, 273. In recent years, *Hōkūle'a* has sailed around the world. The possibility that Pacific Islanders reached the Americas before Columbus has been debated for two centuries. Jones, Stacy, *et al*, 263–276, summarize the evidence of early expeditions, suggesting Chile, Ecuador, and Santa Barbara as the most likely landing sites, perhaps using the Hawaiian Islands as a staging area for the last of these. New DNA studies indicate that Polynesians and Native Americans first made contact and shared offspring sometime around 1200 CE, either as a result of Polynesians voyaging east or indigenous people from the Americas traveling the opposite direction, and that this was not the result of South Americans settling Rapa Nui (*Easter Island*) as Thor Hyerdahl and others had argued—Ioannidis *et al*, 2020.

7. Grigg, 81, 84–85; Kirch, 2007, 291, 2012, 293. Only later did Pacific Islanders discover and settle New Zealand, an even larger land mass.

Notes—Chapter 1

8. Kirch, 2007, 291.
9. McCoy and Graves, 104.
10. Schweizer, 79; Cordy, 2000, 49; Okihiro, 45–55; Kirch, 2007, 312; Thompson, 154; La Croix, 34; Greene, Chapter 1. Most pre-contact population estimates range between 200,000 and 800,000. Archer, 2018, 27–28, points out that if it were half a million, it was much greater than the pre-contact population of California, an area 25 times the size of the entire archipelago. Whatever the size of the population, the loss of life to foreign disease was catastrophic.
11. James, 1996, 38–40.
12. Kanalu Young, 4.
13. Hays, 31–33; Taylor, 1926, 54–56; Fuchs, 6.
14. Muirhead, 1–2; Finney, 23–34; Warshaw, 23.
15. Fornander, *Account of the Polynesian Race*, 2:150, 242. For more on the difference between Hawaiian and Western calendars, see Cahill, 1999, 56. Dates from this era are often uncertain, even where written records exist. Historians do not agree, for example, whether Alexander Hamilton was born in 1755 or 1757.
16. Silverman, 1. The date of Kaʻahumanu's birth is uncertain. The Kaʻahumanu Society observes March 17, 1768, as the most likely date, but it may have been as late as 1774.
17. Kameʻeleihiwa, 1992, 21; Speakman, 61–62; Taylor, 1926, 54; Silverman, 5.
18. Pukui and Varez, 219; Jarves, 66.
19. Hiram Bingham, 30; Withington, 1953, 135.
20. 20 McGregor and MacKenzie, 25–26.
21. Kirch, 2012, 7.
22. *Kauā* is sometimes translated as *slave*, but they did not form a permanent caste, and there was nothing like the chattel slave markets of Europe and the United States, nor anything like the horrific Middle Passage of the Transatlantic slave trade.
23. Holt, 1995, 2.
24. Taylor, 1926, 52; Beyer, 77–78; Archer, 2018, 27.
25. Moore, 34–35; Terence Barrow, 175–176.

26. Holt, 1995, 3; Kamakau, *The People of Old*, 10.
27. Callcott, 14–15; Pukui and Varez, 188.
28. Kamakau, *Ruling Chiefs*, 176–177; Hays, 32.
29. Maxine Mrantz, 1975, 4, observed that "in many ways, the Hawaiian woman was freer and more liberated than her wealthier foreign sister who lived in luxury," but in religion, "the Hawaiian woman came out second best."
30. Malo, 50–51.
31. Terence Barrow, 30–31. Cook and his crew spoke a little Tahitian they had picked up in earlier travels.
32. Tabrah, 1984, 17–18. Britons were not alone in these atrocities. When Ferdinand Magellan's crew landed on Guam in 1521, they saw exchange of gifts as theft, so they killed Chamorros with their crossbows, burned more than 40 huts, and named these *Las Islas de Ladrones*, the Islands of Thieves.
33. Greene; Tabrah, 1987, 21; Day, 1968.
34. Villiers, 256–257.
35. McCoy, 2018, 243.
36. Dibble, 1839, 26–27; Terence Barrow, 99–100, quoting Lieutenant James King; Haley, 3. As many as 3,000 canoes may have escorted the English ships into the bay—Jarves, 113; Kirch, 2007, 246.
37. Villiers, 269–270. See Borofsky. 420–442; Sahlins, 1989; Okihiro, 56–66, for the debate over whether Hawaiians saw Cook as the god Lono or someone else. Christina Thompson, prologue, suggests that they considered Cook to be only a temporary embodiment of Lono.
38. Samwell, journal entry for February 3, 1779, cited in Beaglehole, 2017, 1188; Villiers, 261–262.
39. Jarves, 118–119; Greene; Chapter 2; Terence Barrow, 105, 113–114, 127; Haley, 7–8.
40. Pukui and Varez, 18.
41. John Barrow, 418.
42. Kotzebue, 1830, 180; Terence Barrow, 135–136.
43. Jarves, 121; Terence Barrow, 137; Villiers, 264; Beaglehole, 1974, 661.
44. Beaglehole, 1974, 652, 662.

Notes—Chapter 2

45. Speakman and Hackler, 34–35.
46. Westervelt, *Hawaiian Historical Legends*, 108–110; Williams, 34–37.
47. Cahill, 1999, 61; Withington, 1953, 137; Terence Barrow, 168–171; Walter F. Judd, 1976, 92.
48. Chappell, 1992, 134.
49. Tupaia died in Batavia in 1777 before Cook reached Kaua'i. Lars Eckstein and Anja Schwarz have demonstrated that he made his wayfinding knowledge understandable to Cook's officers—see "The Making of Tupaia's Map: A Story of the Extent and Mastery of Polynesian Navigation, Competing Systems of Wayfinding on James Cook's *Endeavour*, and the Invention of an Ingenious Cartographic System." *Journal of Pacific History*, 54 (2019), 1–95, www.tandfonline.com/doi/full/10.1080/00223344.2018.1512369, and "The Making of Tupaia's Map Revisited," *JPH*, 54 (2019), 549–561, www.tandfonline.com/doi/full/10.1080/0022334 4.2019.1657500.
50. Jarves, 130; Desha, 224; Walter F. Judd, 1976, 45, 52–53; Silverman, 6.
51. Bennett, 117; James, 2002, 82; Judd and Lind, 11–13; Marchand, 410, journal entry for October 5, 1791.
52. Judd and Lind, 11–13; Day, 1968, 36–37.
53. *Haole* is not a compliment, but also not really an insult, the equivalent of *gringo* in the Southwest rather than *gabacho*. Euro-Americans usually refer to themselves as haoles in the Hawaiian Islands. Imagine how different cross-cultural relations might be on the Mainland if descendants of invaders and *auslanders* called themselves Palefaces or Gringos.
54. Bark, 14–16.
55. Klieger, 3.
56. Chappell, 1992, 134; 2015, 12, 17; Colnett, 186; Chang, 33; Speakman, 31; Okihiro, 2001, Tabrah, 1984, 33; Rosenthal, 3. For a biography of Kaumuali'i's son, see Douglas Warne's *Humehume of Kaua'i*.
57. Walter F. Judd, 1976, 81; Taylor, 1926, 193. Metcalfe massacred hundreds in response to the loss of a small boat, and ended up losing a ship and his son Thomas, ultimately delivering cannon into the hands of Kamehameha, who quickly learned how to use them—Carpenter, 15; Haley, 15–16.
58. Chappell, 2015, Chapter 1; Herman, 2020.
59. Hill and Converse, Introduction; Archer, 2018, 36.
60. Hill and Converse, 40, 70–71; Susan Bell, 1986, 12–13.

Chapter 2

1. Sinclair, 1982, 37–38. Fornander, *Hawaiian Antiquities*, "Fallen Is the Chief," Canto IV, 368–410.
2. D'Arcy, 2003, 46.
3. Kamakau, *Ruling Chiefs*, 311; Moore, 82; Chun, 304; Portlock, 78–79.
4. Silverman, 7; Warshaw, 24.
5. Finney, 41–42; Taylor, 1926, 53–54; Silverman, 7; Clark, 13.
6. Newell, 237; Clark, 68–69, 364.
7. Fornander, *Account of the Polynesian Race*, vol. 2, 320; Tregaskis, 139; Silverman, 7; Desha, 223. They may have married in 1785—Cahill, 1999, 56–57; Walter F. Judd, 1976, 62, 71. As for Kamehameha's age, Day, 1974, 5, reports that "a bright star shone over the baby's birth, and Halley's Comet was seen over the islands in 1758."
8. Malo, 93; Ledyard, 132; Hiram Bingham, 400; Haley, 84; Kamakau, *Ruling Chiefs*, 89; Westervelt, *Hawaiian Historical Legends*, 109–110; McKenzie, vol. 2, 72; Bettinger; Chun, 299–304.
9. Murray, 97–99; Morris Kapā'ihiahilina, 27; Wallace, 2003, 40–55; Moore, 2015, 20.
10. Haley, 84; Chang, 43–45, Morris Kapā'ihiahilina, 29–30. For more about arranged and forced marriages in England and wife-sales and wife-auctions that took place well into the 19th century, see Roy and Lesley Adkins, 17–18.
11. Ahlo, Walker, and Johnson.
12. Pukui and Varez, 113.
13. Van Dyke, 360; Kame'eleihiwa, 1992, 43–44; Bob Dye, *Merchant Prince*, 69–70. When the author was the pastor on O'ahu in the mid-1970s, two members of his congregation had been exchanged

Notes—Chapter 2

at birth by their parents to cement the friendship of two families. He also met a couple who had been given a hānai daughter while working in the Fiji as childless Peace Corps volunteers.

14. Klieger, 44–49; Choris, Cuvier and Chamisso, 88; Gunson, 147; Haley, 47–48; Richards, 11; Langlas and Lyon, 37–40, 42–43.

15. Campbell, 137; Westervelt, 1922, 29; Pukui and Varez, 45, 368.

16. Dale Morgan, introduction to Laura Judd, xxv; Campbell, 137; Westervelt, 1922, 29; Silverman, 20, 50–51.

17. Pukui, 194–196; Pukui and Varez, 102; The chant is said to be about Queen Kalama, but this is probably a misidentification of the object of Kamehameha's ardor.

18. Kamakau, *Ruling Chiefs*, 184–186; Mookini, 11; Anonymous, "Kapuka-amao-mao," 12; Silverman, 41.

19. Patterson, 68; Black, 33.

20. D'Arcy, 2003, surveys the considerable evidence that Western weapons helped Kamehameha but were not decisive in his victory. McGregor and MacKenzie, 128–132, suggest that his rise to power was based on his care for his people, which won their loyalty, both in war and in peace.

21. William Ellis, 1832, 124–125; Anonymous, "Kapuka-amao-mao," 12; Richards, 1825, 13; Joesting, 45–46.

22. Hiram Bingham, 41–42; Silverman, 8; Westervelt, 1916, 139–145. Herbert and Bardossi, 32–33; Pukui and Varez, chapter 2, 357.

23. Silverman, 8.

24. Kuykendall, 40.

25. Mookini, 11. Notions of male attractiveness have changed, too. John Sutherland and Amanda Vickery suggest that in Jane Austen's time, Mr. Darcy would have needed pale complexion, powdered hair, and thin, sloping shoulders to be deemed handsome—*New York Times*, February 15, 2017.

26. First-cousin marriage is legal in most of the world today, even if it has become less common since the 19th century. Hawaiian custom encouraged ali'i to have children by close relatives, whether married or not, and the offspring of a brother and sister, the Pio, had the greatest status. As a young man, Kamehameha the Great probably slept with his stepmother Kalola and his aunt Kānekapōlei, even though the latter was a wife of his ruler, Kalani'ōpu'u—Tregaskis, 138–139. The King of Thailand still has multiple wives simultaneously.

27. Mellen, 1949, 161. Ho'olulu is a valley in Kona.

28. Vancouver, 1142; Silverman, 14; Walter F. Judd, *Kamehameha*, 145–147. King David Kalākaua thought Ka'ahumanu's dalliance was with Ka'iana, but David G. Miller, 13, argues that Kamehameha's rage was kindled by another affair, and that Ka'iana was actually sleeping with Ka'ahumanu's mother at the time, which shocked no one.

29. Vancouver, 1160; Edward Bell, 121, log for February 6, 1794.

30. James, 2002, 150; Vancouver, 836, 846; Edward Bell, 120,122, 127–128, log for February 6 and 18, 1794; Speakman and Hackler, 42, Hackler, 1986; Gonschor, 22–23, Walter F. Judd, 155–156. It is sometimes said that he ceded his kingdom to Britain or made it a British protectorate, but such concepts were foreign to Hawaiians. Kamehameha probably had mutual assistance in mind, not becoming anyone's vassal.

31. Taylor, 1926, 154–155; McDougall, 109; Bern Anderson, 183.

32. Kamakau, *Ruling Chiefs*, 174; Susan Bell, 49–51; James, 2002, 46–47; Jackson, 11; Croft, 51. Keaka'ele'ele and "Mr. Miller" lived on O'ahu before 1795; both may have been fugitives from the Botany Bay penal colony.

33. Kamakau, *The People of Old*, 19; Moore, 112.

34. La Croix, 2; Trevelyan, 1966, 148; Cahill, 1999, 13, 94; Boit, 77, entry for October 16, 1795. For more about the enclosures and the level of poverty in rural England at the time, see Jo Draper, *Discover Dorset: The Georgians*. Wimborne, Dorset: Dovecote Press, 1998, 65–66.

35. Beamer, vol. 2, 2; Westervelt, 1922, 24–25; Walter F. Judd, *Kamehameha*, 1976, 104–105; Gerrit Judd, 33; Gowen,

Notes—Chapter 3

27–33; Moore, 106. This edict also is translated as "The Law of the Broken Paddle."
36. Walter F. Judd, *Kamehameha*, 107.
37. Warne, 2008, 3–6.
38. Barratt, 1981, 123.
39. Jarves, 191; Schweizer, 81; Croft, 64–65.
40. Kamakau, *Ruling Chiefs*, 317.
41. McGregor and MacKenzie, 28.
42. Walter F. Judd, 1976, 199; Kameʻeleihiwa, 2001, 78–79; Kamakau, *Ruling Chiefs*, 429–430; Kuykendall, 62; Joesting, 66.
43. Richards, 17; Klieger, 33.
44. Kotzebue, 1821, 247, 308; Seaton, 201; Walter F. Judd, *Kamehameha*, 162.
45. Kameʻeleihiwa, 1992, 8; Seiden, 8.
46. D'Arcy, 2003, 50; 2018, 192; Hiram Bingham, 51; Charlot, 1991, 123; Walter F. Judd, *Kamehameha*, 171.
47. Hays, 34; Moore, 99; Fuchs, 6; Delano, 399.
48. Walter F. Judd, *Kamehameha*, 200–201; Day, 1974, 25; Wyban, 96.
49. Turnbull, vol. 2, 59–60, 104.
50. Moore, 101.
51. John P. Wagner, 41–44; Haley, 30.
52. Whitman, 65–66.
53. Kamakau, *Ruling Chiefs*, 187–196; Schweizer, 81; Silverman, 51–52; Bradley, 1942, 9–10; Mills, 1996; Warne, 2008, 19–23; Barrère, 1975, 7; Pukui and Varez, Chapter 2, 378.

Chapter 3

1. Archer, 2010, 518; Silverman, 52; Rosenthal, 5; Soehren, 271–271.
2. Herman, 2020. There was no census until 1832: it counted only 130,313 kanakas, so their numbers had already declined 35 to 70%—Grigg, 88–89.
3. Titcomb; Turnbull, 65–66; Cahill, 1999, 62; Barrrow, 182; Kaeppler, 2008, 33–35.
4. Joesting, 59–60; Gerrit Judd, 37–38; Turnbull, vol. 2, 38. While haoles now called the archipelago the Sandwich Islands, Kamehameha preferred "the Islands of the King of Hawaiʻi."
5. Campbell, 119.
6. Silverman, 51–52; Corney, 16.
7. Kanahele, 1995, 101.
8. Kotzebue, 1821, vol. 3, 250; Kamakau, *Ruling Chiefs*, 194; Kanahele, 1995, 101; Clark, 443–444; Silverman, 53–54.
9. Campbell, 88; Chevigny, 118; Okun, 154; Day, 1969, 5–6; Walter F. Judd, *Kamehameha*, 230–231; Bolkhovitinov, 1987, 262.
10. Bishop and Roe, 144; Moore, 124; Chappell, 1992, 147.
11. Frierson, 122; Seaton, 196.
12. Kamakau, *Ruling Chiefs*, 180. Walter F. Judd, 1976, 184–185.
13. By Thomas Manby's 1791–1793 voyage with Vancouver, he found he could leave valuable items with Hawaiians for safekeeping and return to find none missing—Manby, 2223.
14. Walter F. Judd, *Kamehameha*, 136–137; Bennett, 121; Johnston, 181.
15. Alexander Simpson, 3–4; John P. Wagner, 45.
16. Whitman, 22.
17. Whitman, 30–31.
18. Croft, 118; Whitman, 22. Stephen Reynolds (1938, 47) reports that when the *New Hazard* arrived in Oʻahu on September 30, 1811, they found a kapu had been imposed to stop wahines from boarding ships.
19. Daws, 1968, 45, 57; Campbell, 136.
20. Nichol, 73.
21. Busch, 136–137; Daws, 1968, 45, 57; Ralston, 1984, 25–27, 32; Sahlins, 1985, 143–143.
22. Buck, 34–35; Joesting, 16.
23. Thurston, 71–72; Gunson, 147; Lisiansky, 117; Walter F. Judd, *Kamehameha*, 191–192; W.D. Alexander, 1917, 38.
24. Emerson, 255–256.
25. Campbell, 123–125; Asa Briggs, *The Making of Modern England, 1783–1867: The Age of Improvement*. New York: Harper & Row, 1959, 217.
26. Campbell, 99–100.
27. Pukui and Korn, 13; Charlot, 2004; Tengan, 55–56.
28. Sahlins, 1981, 46–47; Kameʻeleihiwa, 2001, 79; Moore, 142; Bushnell, 183; Daws, 1967, 77–79.
29. Black, 32; Kashay, 2012, 294.

Notes—Chapter 4

30. Sissons, 1, 63.
31. Croft, 78–80; Pierce, 1963, 60; Chevigny, 76. Schäffer's Russian name was Egor Nikolaevich Sheffer. His journal entry for March 26, 1816, and the statement of accounts he sent on April 222, 1819, to the Russian-American Company's home office in St. Petersburg show that he paid for the use of these lands. Kamehameha, Ka'ahumanu, and Kuakini did not give or sell them—Pierce, 1965, 135–137, 167. Rose de Freycinet, observed in 1819 (Bassett, 166) that Kamehameha rarely granted use of his land to haoles: "the lover of Europeans, loved his own land and people even more; he entrusted these white strangers with grounds for use only during their lifetime, never permanently." As Kame'eleihiwa, 1992, 51, points out, "Control of 'aina is not the same as ownership of 'aina..."
32. Day, 1969, 11; Schäffer, journal entries for March 26, May 16, and August 15, 1816.
33. Bolkhovitinov, 1973; Walter F. Judd, *Kamehameha*, 237. Louis Thiercelin, 1995, 285, 334, and 336, was told two decades later that the fort at Waimea had been built by Russian pirates. His translator thought Thiercelin was mistaken, but this actually was a fair description of this rogue operation.
34. Marin, 210; Mills, 2002, 99–107; Warne, 2008, 55–57; McDougall, 155–158; Mills, 2002, 20–25, 111–118; Pierce, 1963, 400–401; 1965, 9–18, 72; Walter F. Judd, 1999, 14; Croft, 84–85.
35. Schäffer, diary entries for January 1 and May 89, 1817; Owens, 256; Okun, 161–165.
36. Kotzebue, 1821, I, 14; Pierce, 1963, 402–403; Khlebnikov, 94; Schweizer, 75–76.
37. Barratt, 1988, 137.
38. Strauss, 24; Gonschor, 1.
39. John P. Wagner, 47; Haley, 32–33; Ralston, 1984, 22.
40. Kotzebue, 1821, I, 308.
41. Gunson, 146–147; Pierce, 1965, 8, 60, 137, 166–167; Kotzebue, 1821, I, 306, 330–331; Moore, 115.
42. Chamisso, 116, 123, 312.
43. Richards, 16.
44. Golovnin, 179, 209.
45. Kuykendall, vol. 1, 161; Busch, 187.
46. Jarves, 206; Alexander, 1917, 38; Campbell, 123; Chun, 169–170.
47. Holman, 24—diary entry for April 7, 1820.
48. Kanahele, 1986, 76–77; *Kame'eleihiwa*, 1992, 80–82.
49. Archer, 2010, 518; Haley, 33; Kuykendall, 67; Gerrit Judd, 21–22; Pukui and Varez, 135, 1242; Barrère and Sahlins, 20; Klieger, 3; McCoy, 2014, 73.
50. Walter F. Judd, 1976, 72.
51. McGregor, 31.
52. Roquefeuil, vol. 2, 342–343, author's translation.
53. Kotzebue, 1821, vol. 3, 249.
54. Day, 1968, 73.

Chapter 4

1. Marin, 230. Thiercelin, 1992, 116; 1995, 290–291, quotes an elderly local ship pilot called Old William. *Auwe*, which today usually is spelled *auē* or *auwē*, is used here to express despair or fear. It is used in other contexts to express wonder, scorn, pity, or affection.
2. Walter F. Judd, *Kamehameha*, 275–276.
3. Whitman, 26; Moore, 120; Archer, 2018, 130; Westervelt, "The Passing of Kamehameha I," 34; Silverman, 62; Levin, 422; Silva, 48; Linnekin, 70.
4. Marin, 230.
5. Kamakau, 1961, 224.
6. Webbs, 25.
7. Holt, 1985, 39; Tabrah, 1984, 34; Desha, 501; Kamakau, *Ruling Chiefs*, 220.
8. McDougall, 176; Haley, 49.
9. Joesting, 67, Linnekin, Kanahele, 1986, 403; Kameeleihiwa, 2001. Gunson, 171, notes four women who were ali'i nui before the 19th century: Kūkaniloko and her daughter Kalaimanuia in the 15th century on O'ahu, and Keakamahana and her daughter Keakealaniwahne in the 17th century on the Big Island. The last of these, the great-great-grandmother of Kamehameha I, entered heiaus, which otherwise were off-limits to women. Cordy, 2002, 19, 30–31 lists five women who ruled the O'ahu Kingdom.

Notes—Chapter 5

10. Taylor, 1928, 22; McGregor and MacKenzie, 141–152; Archer, 2018, 142; Dale Morgan, introduction to Laura Judd, xxv–xvi; Webbs, 25; Marin, 250–251.
11. Winne, 7–8; Kuykendall, 63–65.
12. Bassett, 161; Louis de Freycinet, 531.
13. Arago, 92, 144–145.
14. Dibble, 1909, 60, 126; Desha, 501.
15. Levin, 423.
16. Linnekin, 70.
17. W. D. Alexander, 1917, 40; Silverman, 63; Taylor, 1926, 117; Moore, 124; Archer, 2018, 143.
18. Silverman, 63.
19. McDougall, 176–177.
20. Kameʻeleihiwa, 1992, 78; Kalakaua, 436–437.
21. Kameʻeleihiwa, 1992, 78.
22. William Ellis, 1823, 111–112, noted that Liholiho's decision to break the eating kapu seems to have been motivated both by "a desire to ameliorate the condition of his wives, and the female in general, whom the *tabu* sunk into a state of extreme wretchedness and degradation, obliging them to subsist on inferior kinds of food" and also "a wish to diminish the power of the priests, and avoid the expenditures of labour and property which the support of idolatry required." Withington, 1937, 60–61, relates John ʻIʻi's horrified reaction to Liholiho's apostasy.
23. Linnekin, 70.
24. Laura Fish Judd, 146; Penrose C. Morris, 45.
25. Kalakaua, 437–438.
26. McDougall, 177; Moore, 127; Thurston, 27–28.
27. Richards, 15; Warne, 2008, 118.
28. Kamakau, *Ruling Chiefs*, 226.
29. Langlas and Lyon, 32; Kalākaua, 28.
30. D'Arcy, 2018, 216.
31. Jarves, 218–219; W. D. Alexander, 1917, 43; La Croix, 83–84; Langlas and Lyon, 32; Kuykendall, I, 69; Levin, 430.
32. W. D. Alexander, 1917, 44.
33. McDougall, 177; Sissons, 67. For more on the persistence of devotion to Pele, see H. Arlo Nimmo, *Pele, Volcano Goddess of Hawaiʻi*, Jefferson, NC: McFarland, 2011.
34. Silverman, 69.

Chapter 5

1. Piercy, 4–5.
2. Green, 234.
3. Hiram Bingham, 58; Morris, 3–5. The Foreign Mission School in Cornwall operated from 1817 to 1821. Nineteen of its students were from the Hawaiian Islands, a dozen of whom returned home.
4. Demos, 39.
5. Johnson, 7; Gerrit Judd, 40; Sandra E. Wagner, 67; Burlin, 231–240; Piercy, 13–15.
6. Piercy, 6; Dwight, 33–34; MacKinnon Simpson, 39; Gerrit Judd, 41.
7. Mercy Whitney, quoted in *The Friend* 95 (1925), 207; Hiram Bingham, 68; Piercy, 13–18. Scriptural inspiration for their socialism is found in Matthew 6:24, Luke 16:13, and Acts 2:44–45 and 4:32. Even the skeptical scholars of the Jesus Seminar believe these passages accurately represent the teaching of Jesus.
8. Warne, 2008, 49–50, 91–92; McDougall, 174; Strauss, 46; Bargatsky, 10–11; Sissons, 98–99; Demos, 96.
9. Warne, 2008, 22, 46–48, 83, 85, 90, 110–112.
10. Warne, 2008, 97, 102; Spoehr, 31; Susan Bell, 1976, 26; Morris, 3–5; Demos, 94. Each of the other returned kanakas was excommunicated at some point but later returned to the church. Ellis, Tyerman, and Bennet urged the Calvinists to license Thomas Hopu as a preacher, but the Mission refused to do so. Kanui was suspended periodically from the church, fell in with Kauikeaouli's retinue of merry libertines, then left for the gold fields of California. John Honoliʻi labored valiantly for the Mission but soon died.
11. Stewart, 1828, 26.
12. "Journal of the Missionaries," April 3, 1820, *The Missionary Herald* 17 (April 1821), 117; Johnson-Hill, 317; Taylor, 1926, 66; Vowell, 44.
13. Lemon, 18; Arago, 111; Croft, 91–94.
14. Kamakau, *Ruling Chiefs*, 247.
15. Hiram Bingham, 84.
16. Loomis, journal entry for March 31, 1820; Thigpen, 2014, 67–68.

Notes—Chapter 5

17. Thurston, 32, April 3, 1820; Thigpen, 2014, 65, 70–71.
18. Rohrer, 19; Thigpen, 2014, 1–2, 65–66, 70, 72.
19. Thurston, 80; Kashay, *HJH* 2002, 46; Desser, 464. For Sybil Bingham as an additional contributor, see James Rumford, editor, *The Hawaiian Language: Being Part of the Knowledge Gathered by the Missionaries Concerning the Language, as Copied in the Year 1823*. Honolulu: Manoa Press, 1993.
20. Hiram Bingham, 61–62.
21. Holman, 38–journal entry for September 18, 1820; Westervelt, introduction to *The Journal of Elisha Loomis*, 4.
22. Thigpen, 2014, 85.
23. Alfred Bingham, 8.
24. Day, 1968, 77; Moore, 158.
25. Alexander Simpson, 4; Taylor, 1926, 115–116, 251–252; Cahill, 1999, 127; Warne, 2008, 121.
26. Hiram Bingham, 88; Stewart, journal entry for May 24, 1823, *Journal*, 1830, 160–161; Joseph Tracy, 120; Eveleth, 90.
27. American Board of Commissioners for Foreign Missions, 1838, 27, 41–42. These instructions to avoid political interference were given to the First Company on October 15, 1819, repeated to the Second Company, and then published by the mission press in Honolulu.
28. Vowell, 47.
29. Hiram Bingham, 88.
30. *The Missionary Herald* 17 (April 1821), 114; Strauss, 49.
31. Perkins, 74.
32. Gast, 1976, 61; Thigpen, 2018. J. C. Jones visited the Sandwich Islands in 1818 or earlier. He mentions this trip in his letter accepting appointment as a consular agent, and in 1818 he presented an oil portrait of Kamehameha, painted by Ludwig (Louis) Choris in 1816 or 1817, to the Boston Athenæum. Serving as both a merchant and government agent is an obvious conflict of interest but was common in the 1820s—Hackler, 1969, 42.
33. Hiram Bingham, 164; Laura Judd, 26–27; Richards, 8; Langlas and Lyon, 32, DelPiano, 17–18.
34. Pukui and Valez; Schweizer, 41–42; Moore, 159.
35. Piercy, 21; Warne, 2008, 106–107; Haley, 82; Moore, 191.
36. Kamakau, 1961, 246–247; Greene, chapter 5; Cahill, 1999, 128; Taylor, 1922, 317; Allen, 129; Salazar, 14.
37. Samuel Ruggles, 26–27, journal entry for May 3, 1820; Samuel Whitney, journal entries for May 3 and 27, 1820, quoted by Damon, 1925, 205–206; Demos, 109–110.
38. Tabrah, 1987, 70–71. Kaumualiʻi married Kehaikkaakulou in 1817, who later took the name Deborah Kapule. Aliʻi continued for many years to ask missionaries to raise their newborn children. In July 1831, for example, Kīnaʻu was angry when the Judds refused to give her their daughter as a hānai child but somewhat mollified when they named her Elizabeth Kīnaʻu Judd.
39. M'Konochie; Gerrit Judd, 34; McDougall, 173.
40. Taylor, 1926, 228.
41. Holman, 20, entry for April 3, 1820; Haley, 56; Hiram Bingham, 131; Dibble, 1839, 77. Whitman, 26–31, provides an account from 1813–1815 of a woman's suffering when a kahuna tried to pray her to death.
42. Grimshaw, 61; Buyers and Noyes.
43. Daws, 2006, 46; Chun, 179–193.
44. Charlot, 2010, 29–31, 44; Kuykendall, 12.
45. Péron, vol. 2, 147; Kameʻeleihiwa, 1992, 138–139; Boit, Log of the *Columbia*, November 3, 1792, 262; Menzies, 105; Black, 34, 36.
46. Taylor, 1926, 250, citing the journal of Daniel Chamberlain; Sybil Bingham, journal entry for March 31, 1820; Holman, 25, entry for April 7, 1820; Hiram Bingham, 82.
47. Holman, 19–20, journal entry for April 2, 1820.
48. Piercy, 35–36; Holman, 32, journal entry for June 21, 1820. The Sandwich Islands Mission Account Books meticulously record donations of food to their Depository of common stock, https://hmha.missionhouses.org/items/browse?collection=216.
49. Bingham, 108–109; Coan, 9.
50. Thigpen, 2014, 78–80; Piercy, 37; Ashley, 121.

Notes—Chapter 6

51. Hiram Bingham, 137.
52. Hiram Bingham, 207–208.

Chapter 6

1. Warne, 2008, 133; Kashay, 2008, "From Kapus to Christianity," 36.
2. Tabrah, 1987, 78; Ballou and Carter, 9, 22. Both *tapa* and *kapa* are still used in the Islands.
3. Coan, 9.
4. Haley, 70; Hiram Bingham, 368–369; Haley, 71; Roy and Lesley Adkins, 43.
5. Mercy Whitney, journal entry, July 1820, quoted by Damon, 1825, 207; Del Piano, 17; Kuykendall and Day, 45; Hiram Bingham, 215.
6. Hiram Bingham, 103.
7. Bingham, 105, 113, Moore, 162; Thurston, 42; Tabrah, 1987, 71; Kameʻeleihiwa, 1992, 140.
8. Osorio, 1; Archer, 2010, 524; Lucia Holman's journal entry for June 21, 1820, 30; Mercy Whitney, journal entry for August 31, 1821; Warne, 2008, 126, 155; Thurston, 62 (October 7, 1821), 91. Lucia Holman became one of the first women to circumnavigate the globe.
9. *The Missionary Herald* (19) 1823, 183; Gerrit Judd, 51. Bassett, 159, notes that a few years earlier, a doctor on *L'Uranie* bled Rose de Freycinet, weakening her rather than curing anything, a good example of how Euro-American medicine was less advanced in many ways than the healing arts of Oceania. Drawing blood is used today to treat a few conditions, such as hemochromatosis, but is otherwise a bad idea.
10. Tabrah, 1987, 71; Hiram Bingham, 126; Thurston, 57–58; Gulick, 87–88. Missionaries were not allowed to settle permanently until four years after their arrival.
11. Allen, 129, 129, 135.
12. Sybil Bingham, journal entry for February 14, 1821; *the Missionary Herald* 17 (June 1821), 177; Taylor, 1928, 27; 30–31.
13. Allen, 135.
14. Hiram Bingham, 137; Ralston, 1978, 125–126; Laux, 39; Tabrah, 1987, 71–72; Daws, 2006, 47.
15. Kamakau, *Ruling Chiefs*, 252–253; Johnston, 67–69; Warne, 2008, 150–151. Earlier, Liholiho's yacht had been called *Cleopatra's Barge*.
16. Withington, 1953, 141; Warne, 2008, 163–165.
17. Allen, 136; Thigpen, 2018.
18. Mercy Whitney, journal entry for October 27, 1821.
19. JCP letter from Honolulu to Marshall & Wildes, October 5, 1821, quoted by Morison, 35; *the Missionary Herald*, December 1821, Eveleth, 116–117.
20. Marin, 259, journal entry for December 15, 1821; Hiram Bingham, 148–150; Barratt, 1988, 182.
21. Allen, 136; Silverman, 78–79; Hiram Bingham, 156–157. It is often said that the Calvinists banned surfing, but this is not true. They wished Hawaiians would wear more clothes in the water, but Hiram Bingham, 217–218, writes appreciatively about the grace and skill of surfers. Some mikanele rode the waves themselves—though never on Sunday.
22. Moore, 166; J. C. Jones, letters to Marshall dated November 20 and December 23, 1821; Ralston, 1978, 124; Daws, 2006, 48–49.
23. Klieger, 85.
24. Thurston, 102, 113, 210, letters to Goodell dated October 16, 1829, and to Mrs. Parkhurst dated November 14, 1832; Piercy, 58.
25. Hiram Bingham, 333; Partridge, 139–140. See also, Zwiep, 1990; Klieger, 116–117; Kashay, 1999, 90.
26. Ralston, 1978, 13–14.
27. Mrantz, 1976, 4, 9; Gerrit Judd, 47; MacKinnon Simpson, 97, Speakman, 77–79.
28. Shoemaker, Introduction.
29. Daws, 1967, 77–78; Day, 1968, 130–132; Michener and Day, 15.
30. Jeremiah Reynolds, 471 (J. C. Jones' letter to Commodore Downes); Hackler, 2008, 50–54.
31. Gene A. Smith, 60; MacKinnon Simpson, 79–80.
32. Gast, 1973, 20, 23; Stewart, 1828, 119, journal entry for May 24, 1823; Thurston, 68.

193

Notes—Chapter 7

33. Thurston, 45; MacKinnon Simpson, 44–45.
34. Shoemaker, 9.
35. Marin, 268, journal entry for August 29, 1821; Hays, 66; Daws, 1968, 68; McDougall, 180.
36. Piercy, 7–8; Loomis, 22, journal entries for November 17 and 19–20, 1824; Kashay, 2012, 290–291.
37. Sybil Bingham, diary entry for June 24, 1820.
38. Kashay, 2002 dissertation, 19–20, 140; 2012, 302.
39. William Ellis, 1832, 41–42.
40. Tyerman, 113; Hiram Bingham, 161; William Ellis, 1827, 15–16, 63–64, 85–86; 1832, 79. Belief in witchcraft was common in Dorset, for example, as late as the 1840s—Herman Lea, "Some Dorset Superstitions," *Memorials of Old Dorset*, 1907, T. Perkens and H. Pentin, eds., reprinted in *Monographs on the Life, Times, and Works of Thomas Hardy* 60, Guernsey: Toucan Press, 1969, 349–356; Jo Draper, *Thomas Hardy's England*. Boston: Little, Brown, 1984, 98.
41. Mathison, entry for June 25, 1822, 364–365, 372.
42. Eveleth, 122; Ellis, 1832, 43; Maude, 188–189, Barrère and Sahlins, 22–23.
43. Tyerman, 109, 116; William Ellis, 1832, 38–44; Del Piano, 18.
44. Mathison, entry for July 28, 1822, 428–429; entry for August 4, 1822, 432–433; *The Missionary Herald* (19) 1823, 100; William Ellis, 1832, 41; Zwiep, 173–174, 196.
45. Barrère, Pukui and Kelly, 26, 63; Silva, 29; Kame'eleihiwa, 1992, 142; Zwiep, 165.
46. William Ellis, 1832, 435–436.
47. Hiram Bingham, 162; Allen, 137; William Ellis, 1832, 45. See also the journal entry for June 4 by the Tahitian teacher Auna, quoted by Tyerman, 127–128. Only a few ki'i (*icons*) of akua survive, such as the statue of Ku, said to have been used by Kamehameha, at the Bishop Museum.
48. Tyerman, 122–123.
49. Kanalu Young, 107; Hammat, journal entry for June 1, 1823, quoted by Kirch and Sahlins, 66; Wyndette, 100.
50. William Ellis, 1832, 45.
51. Mathison, entry for July 26, 1822, 453, 455.
52. Bradley, 1942, 142; Grimshaw, 155.
53. Gulick, 96; Montgomery *et al*, Vol. 2, 87–88; Allen, 138; Hiram Bingham, 172; Kuykendall, 74–75; Wyndette, 100.
54. Allen, 138; Emory, 1928, 8; Tabrah, 1987, 74; Department of the Interior, "Hawaiian Islands National Wildlife Refuge Master Plan," August 28, 1984, section 3–25.

Chapter 7

1. Allen, 138; *Religious Miscellany* (Carlisle) October 31, 1823, 228, report from the Sandwich Islands dated January 22.
2. Yzendoorn, 23; Richards, 18; Chester Young, 167; Stewart, 1828, 121, diary entry for May 24, 1823; Liholiho's letter to Teuheiti dated February 18, 1823, Foreign Office & Executive Series, Archives of Hawai'i.
3. Hiram Bingham, 188.
4. Johnson-Hill, 312; Stewart, 1828, 64 and 75, journal entries for April 25 and 29, 1823; 1830, 156, journal entry for May 22, 1823.
5. Darwin's theory that all humans descended from common ancestors should not be confused with its bastard offspring, Social Darwinism, which claimed that the wealthy were more fit to reproduce than the poor. Its most pernicious and racist form, the Eugenics movement, was led by Darwin's cousin Galton. What began with sterilizing supposedly inferior races and classes ended with the slaughter of those deemed deficient during the Holocaust. For ore on this, see Stephen Jay Gould, *Rocks of Ages: Science and Religion in the Fullness of Life*, New York: Library of Contemporary Thought, 1999, 150–170.
6. Stewart, 1828, 103, journal entry for May 15, 1823.
7. Stewart, 1828, 125, 175 and 259, journal entries for May 26 and December 3, 1823, and February 8, 1825.
8. Piercy, 3.
9. Stephen Reynolds, 1989, xiv and 72,

Notes—Chapter 7

journal entry for March 20, 1825; Guttman and Golden, 7, 10; Stewart, 1828, 100, 119–120, journal entries for May 15 and 24, 1823.

10. William Ellis, 1827, 91, 99, journal entry for July 15, 1823.

11. Richards, 24–26; Kameʻeleihiwa, 1992, 143; Pfeiffer, 276.

12. Richards, 32; Stewart, 1828, 151, 158–159, journal entries for August 21 and September 16, 1828.

13. Scruggs, 60–62; Richards, 34.

14. Kameʻeleihiwa, 1992, 144; Gerrit Judd, 51; Zwiep, 210; Pfeiffer, 277–278.

15. William Ellis, 1827, 106–107; Sinclair, 1976, 77; Hiram Bingham, 196; Stewart, 1828, 166, journal entry for September 16, 1823; Kam, 21.

16. Stewart, 1828, 169–170, journal entry for September 24, 1823.

17. Eveleth, 126; Stewart, 1828, 169–170, 172–173, journal entry for September 24 and October 28, 1823.

18. Dale Morgan, introduction to Laura Judd, xxv; Eveleth, 46–49, Hiram Bingham, 180.

19. Jarves, 1843, 242; Ralston, 1985, 314–315; Corley, 2010, 6, 13.

20. Taylor, 1928, 23; Moore, 183; Daws, 2006, 55–56.

21. Kamakau, *Ruling Chiefs*, 258; Kuykendall, 117, 431. The exact date of Kauikeaouli's birth is not known.

22. Gast, 1973, 99; Hiram Bingham, 87; *Evangelical Magazine and Missionary Chronicle*, January 1826, 29–30.

23. Kuykendall and Day, 45–46; Levi Chamberlain, journal entry for December 21, 1823.

24. Pfeiffer, 277–278.

25. Levi Chamberlain, journal entry for January 2, 1824, and his letter to Jeremiah Evarts at the American Board of Commissioners for Foreign Missions (ABCFM), June 22, 1824.

26. Joesting, 73; Hiram Bingham, 149; Stewart, 1828, 205, journal entry for April 14, 1824.

27. Thigpen, 2014, 85.

28. Damon, 1941, 5–7; Grimshaw, 42; Sterling and Summers, 287–288; Loomis, 28, journal entry for March 5, 1825; Sahlins, 1992, 78. After graduating from Mount Holyoke, Elizabeth Kaahumanu Bingham returned to the Islands, where she taught girls at the Kawaiahaʻo Seminary and became its principal.

29. Laura Judd, 27; Thigpen, 2014, 94–95; Grimshaw, 157; Allen, 140.

30. Chamberlin, journal entry for April 3, 1824; Achiu, Kaʻowili and Akana-Gooch, 13–14.

31. Stewart, 1830, 179, journal entry for June 2, 1823; Levi Chamberlain, journal entry for April 13, 1824.

32. Wyndette, 112; Day, 1968, 90–91.

33. Eveleth, 144; Del Piano, 26; Joesting, 73; Kuykendall, 106; Tabrah, 1984, 44.

34. Kuykendall, 106–107; Laura Judd, 34; Joesting, 74; MacKinnon Simpson, 42; Chang, 6; Rosenthal, 5.

35. William Richards, letter to the ABCFM, quoted by Sinclair, *Nāhiʻenaʻena*, 57.

36. Stewart, 1828, 216–217, journal entries for May 28 and 30, 1828; McDougall, 180–181; Bradford Smith, 112; Warne, 178.

37. Hiram Bingham, 229–230; Warne, 179–182.

38. Sinclair, 1976, 57–63; Vowell, 122–123; Brown, 62, 67; Elisha Loomis, 15–16, journal entry for June 28, 1824; Loomis turned out to be right about the risk of sickly offspring: Nāhiʻenaʻena had a child, perhaps by Kauikeaouli, and the baby lived only a few hours. Nāhiʻenaʻena herself died at 21—Laura Judd, 38; Sinclair, 1969, 26.

39. Sinclair, 1976, 58; Daws, 2006, 78. Five years later, Charles Stewart still refused to believe reports of their sexual relationship, and the Regent and the Council of Chiefs formally, if disingenuously, protested these "rumors"—Stewart, 1831, II, 192–195.

40. Speakman, 71–72; Daws, 1966, 78.

41. Levi Chamberlain, journal entry for April 28, 1824; Stewart, 1828, 229, journal entry for August 10, 1824; Hiram Bingham, 238.

42. Levi Chamberlain, journal entry for April 28, 1824.

43. William Ellis, 1832, 162; Warne, 2002, 70; 2008, 193–194, 202; Demos, 236–237. See also, Elisha Loomis, "George

Notes—Chapter 8

Tamoree," *The Philadelphian*, April 25, 1828, available at http://obookiah.com/wp-content/uploads/2020/09/Loomis-death-of-Humehume.pdf.

44. Loomis, 20, journal entry for October 13, 1824; Hiram Bingham, 239; Taylor, 1926, 259.

45. Kameʻeleihiwa, 1992, 152–154; Kotzebue, 1830, 209, 232.

46. Charles S. Stewart, letter dated November 15, 1824, *Religious Intelligencer* (New Haven) 10 (February 18, 1826), 594.

47. Sinclair, 1976, 62; Stewart, 1828, 233–240, journal entries for September 6, 11, 16, and 23, 1824; Barrère, 1989, 77; McDougall, 177.

48. Kotzebue, 1830, 227–229, 245.

49. Daws, 1968, 73; Kuykendall, 77–78; Corley, 2008; Morrison, 1–2, 7–11.

50. Loomis, 29, journal entry for March 10, 1825; Mellen, 1963, 25.

51. Stewart, 1828, 262, 265–266, journal entries for March 10 and April 13, 1825; Gast, 1973, 104; Allen, 159; Kuykendall, I, 118; Sinclair, 1976, 78; Del Piano, 24; Kashay, 2002 dissertation, 248.

52. Macrae, 7; Woods et al, 151.

53. McDougall, 181.

54. Hiram Bingham, 271.

55. Helen Wong Smith, 87; Ehkle, McElhaney, and Tsutaoka, 87.

56. Dampier, 44–45.

57. Macrae, 38. 41.

58. Dickey, 19; Guttman and Golden, 7 and 10; Stockton, diary entry for December 31, 1822, published in *Christian Advocate*, May 1824, 232–236, and available at hmha.missionhouses.org/items/browse?collection=156. Betsey Stockton returned to the United States in 1825 and worked in Philadelphia, Princeton, and Canada. In 1829, U.S. Navy Chaplain Charles Stewart noted how warmly her former students in the Islands remembered her—Stewart, 1831, II, 159.

59. Piercy, 48.

60. Sandra E. Wagner, 69; Achiu, Kaʻowili and Akana-Gooch, 14–15.

61. Chappell, 1992, 132; Arista, 2019, 9.

62. McDougall, 183; Klieger, 6–7.

63. Bradley, 1942, 143, 174.

64. Ellis, 1831, 112; Kotzebue, 1830, II, 256–257, 259–260; Archer, 2018, 27.

65. Levi Chamberlain, 562, August 13, 1829, letter to Jeremiah Evarts; Klieger, 110; Hiram Bingham, 267; Daws, 2006, 63; Kaahumanu, letter dated December 20, 1825, published in *Ka manao o na alii*, 5; Archer, 2018, 162.

66. Silverman, 96.

67. Samuel Kamakau, quoted by Allen, 160.

68. Report of the American Board of Commissioners for Foreign Missions, 1827, 85; Paulding, 198–199; Bradley, 1942, 146–147.

Chapter 8

1. *The Missionary Herald* (29), April 1823, 108; American Board of Commissioners for Foreign Missions, 1838, 28 (instructions to the First Company, October 15, 1819); Cummings, 26.

2. McDougall, 182; Tracy, 258.

3. Tyerman, 111; Bradley, 1942, 38–39l; Loomis, 33, journal entries for April 28 and 29, 1824; Scruggs, 55–56; Bartlett, 9. Sex trafficking and sexual slavery was fairly common in the early United States and did not become a felony until 1910, when the Progressive movement and suffragists prompted Congress to pass the Mann Act. Predictably, perhaps, it was not the exploitation of native, enslaved, or colonized people that led to this legislation but rather the abduction of Euro-American women. The bill's name says it all: the White-Slave Traffic Act.

4. Marin, 303; journal entry for February 20, 1826; Hiram Bingham, 339–340; Day, 1968, 77.

5. William Ellis, quoted by Montgomery *et al*, Vol. 2, 20.

6. Tracy, 182; Loomis, 46, journal entry for October 4, 1825; Daws, 2006, 63–64.

7. Levi Chamberlain, journal entry for October 4, 1825; Kuykendall, 123–126; Bradley, 1942, 172–176.

8. Samuel Whitney, journal entry for June 17, 1821; Damon, 226; Tracy, 170–171; Creed and Hanson, "A Case Study of a Piracy Charge."

9. Stark, 10, 20, 29; Hoapili, his wife,

Notes—Chapter 8

Nāhiʻenaʻena, and Kekauonohi wrote to Kaʻahumanu on November 24, 1827, reporting that Leoiki did not want to go with Buckle and did so only because the captain had paid her chiefess (hmha.missionhouses.org/items/show/3142). Creed and Hanson argue in "A Case Study of a Piracy Charge" that Buckle was paying a bride-price, not buying a sex slave, since no aliʻi would enter into such a sale and the Royal Navy could have hung him for buying a slave. Leoiki seems to have gone with Buckle willingly, if reluctantly, as his temporary wife. Klieger, 116–117, suggests that what really appalled American missionaries in this episode was interracial sex.

10. Hiram Bingham, 319; Bartlett, 9.
11. Stephen Reynolds, 1989, 108, journal entry for October 8, 1825; Williston, 36.
12. Hiram Bingham, 276–277. The *Sir Andrew Hammond* visited the Islands with an American navy crew earlier during the War of 1812, but she was a captured British whaler, not an American warship.
13. Paulding, 196–197; McKee, 32–33; Long, 66–67.
14. Day, 1968, 60–61; Strauss, 24.
15. James Ellis, 56–57, 68.
16. Long, 69.
17. Long, 69.
18. James Ellis, 69; Hiram Bingham, 284–286; Long, 70.
19. James Ellis, 70–71.
20. Long, 70; McKee, 34, 86.
21. Arista, 2011, 47–48.
22. Levi Chamberlain, journal entries for February 19 and 22, 1826.
23. McKee, 34; Marin, 303; journal entry for February 22, 1826; Long, 70.
24. Long, 71; John Morris of the *Dolphin* crew, quoted by James Ellis, 70–71; Hiram Bingham, 287.
25. Hiram Bingham, 288.
26. Paulding, 196–197; Day, introduction to Paulding, xv–xvii; McKee, 32–33; James Ellis, 68–84, Long, 84.
27. Long, 72; Piercy, 69–70.
28. Silverman, 106–109.
29. Stephen Reynolds, 1989, 120, 123–127, 131, journal entries for February 20 and 26, March 6, 12, and 13, April 9, 1826.
30. Hiram Bingham, 289; McDougall, 182. John Percival may have received a private reprimand from the Court of Inquiry. If they had acquitted him, their decision would have been published—see Tracy, 184.
31. Day, 1968, 34–35.
32. Hiram Bingham, 292.
33. Hiram Bingham, 293; Moore, 81; *Report of the American Board of Commissioners for Foreign Missions* 1827, 92; Sahlins, 1981, 66; Artemas Bishop, 140–142.
34. Gene A. Smith, 53, 59. The word *ap* in Thomas ap Catesby Jones is Welsh for *son of*.
35. Day, introduction to Paulding, xvii; Gapp, 101.
36. Hiram Bingham, 302; Gapp, 104–105; Gene A. Smith, 60–61.
37. Bradford Smith, 150. Captain Jones was both a pious Christian and a plantation owner who enslaved others, though he did teach them to read and write at a time when most enslavers thought it easier to subjugate people if you prevented them from becoming literate.
38. Gene A. Smith, 61–63, 65–66; Gast, 1973, 112–113; Webbs, 48; Bradley, 1942, 178–180; Johnson, 11. Bradley, 1931, 24–26; Stauffer, 53–54, 81; Achiu, Kaʻowili and Akana-Gooch, 35–43. In 1818, Kamehameha made an earlier, unwritten treaty with the newly independent United Provinces of Rio de la Plata: Argentina and Uruguay, and part of Bolivia.
39. Stauffer, 41; Tabrah, 1984, 43.
40. Schmidt and Strombel, 271; Silverman, 117–118.
41. Sissons, 132; Klieger, 122; Levi Chamberlain, journal entries for April 20, 1826, and July 24, 1827.
42. Stephen Reynolds, 1989, 174, 188, journal entries for February 8 and June 19, 1827; Kashay, 2002 dissertation, 231; Artemas Bishop, 140–142.
43. Seiden, 8.
44. Levi Chamberlain, journal entries for July 17, September 15, and September 19, 1827.
45. Walter F. Judd, 1999, 52–53; Osorio, 111. Alexander Liholiho and Lot Kamehameha, the sons of Kīnaʻu and Kekuanaoa, ruled as Kamehameha IV and V.

46. Levi Chamberlain, journal entry for September 23, 1827; Zwiep, 276; Laura Judd, 26.
47. Hiram Bingham, 305, 308; Allen, 162; Daws, 1968, 83; Haley, 111; Ralston, 34; Osorio, 13.

Chapter 9

1. Klieger, 122.
2. Thrum, 181–182; Restarick, *Hawaii, 1778–1920*, 17–18; "The First Clergyman Resident in Hawaii"; Khisamutdinov and Lyovin, 1–3. John Howel, a.k.a. Padre Howell, was ordained in the Church of England, lived in the Islands in the 1790s, and tried to interest Kamehameha in Christianity, but he does not seem to have functioned as a cleric during this period.
3. Bloxam, 19.
4. Bob Dye, "Memoria of What the People Were," 55; Haley, 75; Hackler, 1969, 42–43; Gast, 1976, 19, 73–74. The American Unitarian Association merged with the Universalist Church in 1961 to form a new faith community, the Unitarian Universalist Association.
5. Samuel Ruggles, 26–27, journal entry for May 3, 1820; Stewart, 1828, 257, 280, journal entries for February 7 and June 13, 1825.
6. Bunson, 19, 22; Rives, 2003, 104–105; Wiltgen, 10–22; Alexander, 1906, 21; Corley, 2010, 28.
7. Kuykendall, 139; Johnson, 8; Joesting 78.
8. Cahill, 20; W. D. Alexander, 1906, 19–36; Lemon, 26.
9. Yzendoorn, 34–36; Cahill, 2004, 18–20; Stephen Reynolds, 1989, 190–191, journal entries for July 11 and 12, 1827; Morineau, "Notice Historique," 17–18, and "Precis Historique," 316–317, author's translations.
10. Lemon, 16–17, 30–31; Cahill, 2004, 5–7; Pietrusewsky et al, 69–70; Gast, 21–22; Lee, 16; Perbal, 143.
11. Yzendoorn, 34–35; Perbal, 116, 143; Bunson, 34–35.
12. Lemon, 17; Morineau, "Notice Historique," 22–23; Yzendoorn, 79; Bachelot, *Annales*, 1830, 267; Association de la Propagation de la Foi, *Annales*, 1828, 154, 156; 1830, 267, author's translation; Wiltgen, 19.
13. Male, 254–255.
14. Jarves, 280; Hiram Bingham, 422; Laura Judd, 122; Webbs, 53. The charge that Catholics worshiped idols persisted—see, for example, Levi Chamberlain's journal entry for December 31, 1828.
15. Levi Chamberlain, journal entry for March 4, 1828; Morineau, "Notice Historique," 24, author's translation; *Annales*, 1833, 104–105.
16. Wiltgen, 1–2; Yzendoorn, 36, 40–41; Lemon, 17; Cahill, 2004, 23–24; *Annales* 1828, 154; 1830, 270; 1833, 94 and 97; 1837, 366 and 502; 1907, 178; *L'ami de la religion* 69 (1833), 321; Carné, 297–300; Charlotte M. Kelly in "The Church in Hawaii," *Studies: An Irish Quarterly Review* 37 (1948), 335–336.
17. Hiram Bingham, 423. 150 years later, Congregational and Methodist leaders sometimes complained that Presbyterians and Disciples had "broken comity" when they established congregations there. No comity agreement assigned the kingdom to Methodism, but the denomination was founded there (as were the congregations the author served) not by Euro-Americans but by Japanese immigrants, who were not party to the denominational allocation any more than Catholics were.
18. Cahill, 2004, 31–32; Fraser, Antonia. *The King and the Catholics: England, Ireland, and the Fight for Religious Freedom, 1780–1829.* New York: Doubleday, 2018, 190.
19. *Annales*, 1837, 379.
20. Morineau, "Notice Historique," 21, 23; Levi Chamberlain, journal entry for August 1, 1827; Bob Dye, "Memoria of What the People Were," 55; Haley, 75.
21. McKee, 37; *Annales*, 1833, 93; Morineau, "Notice Historique," 25, "Précis Historique," 318–319, 326; Huetz de Lemps, 133; Bunson, 23, 36.
22. Hiram Bingham, 318–319.
23. Kashay, "Competing Imperialisms and Hawaiian Authority," 370; Char Miller, 1989, 2.
24. *The Missionary Herald*, February

Notes—Chapter 9

1827; Stephen Reynolds, 193, journal entry for August 4, 1827; Arista, 2009, 67–68; 2019, 2–3; Osorio, 17, 58; Dibble, 223–226; Clark, 444; Creed and Hanson, "A Case Study of a Piracy Charge."

25. Levi Chamberlain, journal entry for December 8, 1827.

26. Morineau, "Notice Historique," 24–25; Morris, 6.

27. *Report of the American Board of Commissioners for Foreign Missions* 1841, 210–211; Gast, 1973, 119–120.

28. Daws, 2006, 74.

29. David Miller, 14–15; Laura Fish Judd, entry for March 31, 1828, 9–10.

30. Levi Chamberlain, journal entry for June 17, 1826; Laura Judd, 26, 52; Tracy, 210; Hiram Bingham, 400–401; Zambucka, 17–19, Ka'ahumanu became the kahu of Princess Ruth Ke'elikōlani in February 1826 when Pauahi, one of Liholiho's widows, died in childbirth.

31. Stephen Reynolds, 1989, 230, journal entry for July 13, 1828.

32. Hiram Bingham, 342.

33. Alexander Simpson, 57–58.

34. Chester Young, 176; Stewart, 1831, II, 193; Klieger, 7, 11.

35. Duhaut-Cilly, 289, author's translation.

36. Botta, 144, 146, author's translation.

37. Stewart, 1831, II, 221, letter from Honolulu, dated November 5, 1829.

38. Stephen Reynolds, 1989, 258, 261, journal entries for April 1 and 21, 1829; Daws, 1968, 83; Gulick, 121–122; Klieger, 133.

39. Damon, 1941, 7–11.

40. Hiram Bingham, 345–346; Ralston, 1985, 316; Levi Chamberlain, journal entries for December 31, 1828, and June 9 and 10, 1829; Maria Ogden, a missionary teacher in the Third Company, letter dated June 17, published in *Christian Advocate* (Philadelphia) 8 (1830), 203; Stewart, 1831, II, 200–201, letter from Honolulu on November 24, 1829; *Annales*, 1833, 93; Gast, 1973, 120; Bradley, 1942, 184–185; Day, 1968, 106–107; Sinclair, 1976, 108–110; Daws, 1968, 84.

41. Cahill, 2004, 32–33.

42. Emory, 1924, 8; Linnekin, 175;

James, 2002, 167; Stephen Reynolds, 1989, 274, journal entry for August 9, 1829; Kuykendall, 142; Tracy, 225; Hiram Bingham, 363–364, 371, 375.

43. Jarves, 285; Williston, 42; Tracy, 225–226.

44. Stewart, 1831, II, 128–129, letter from Honolulu dated October 15, 1829.

45. Stewart, 1831, II, 130, 147, letters from Honolulu dated October 15 and 19, 1829.

46. Stewart, 1831, II, 278.

47. Stewart, 1831, II, 77, 130, 174, 259.

48. Laura Judd, 81–82; Hiram Bingham, 361–362; Brown, 69; Levi Chamberlain, letter dated December 5, 1831, quoted by Gulick, 127–128.

49. Brigham, 81; Silva, 29–30; Daws, 1968, 85; Osorio, 13.

50. Lemon, 34.

51. Allen, 184; Daws, 2006, 8.

52. *Report of the American Board of Commissioners for Foreign Missions* 1841, 210–211; Yzendoorn, 46–47; Allen, 184; Wyndette, 124; Perbal, 146.

53. Chappelll, 1992, 148. Braving periodic waves of persecution, Luika preached her version of her new-found faith and baptized converts in the area around Waialua on O'ahu's North Shore. Catholic doctrine permits laypeople to baptize in the absence of a priest, but was, and remains, opposed to female clergy.

54. *Annales de la Propagation de la Foi*, 1833, 93–97; Morineau, "Precis Historique," 327; *L'Ami de la Religion* 69 (1833), 321; Hiram Bingham, 373, 405–406; Kirch and Sahlins, 1, 159; Johnson, 10; Lee, 58–59. At first, King Louis Philippe did nothing to protect French priests or Catholic converts, but in 1839, he sent the warship *L'Artemise* to force the Hawaiian government to permit the denomination to establish a foothold in the Kingdom—Cahill, 2004, 80–85.

55. Proclamation dated January 8, 1831, signed by Kauikeaouli, Ka'ahumanu, Kaikioewa (governor of Kaua'i), Hoapili, Naihe (the national orator), and Kuakini.

56. Perbal, 144; Chester Young, 178; Klieger, 147.

57. Yzendoorn, 73–4; Cahill, 2004, 48–49; Joesting, 82–83; Chester Young,

Notes—Chapter 10

178. Fathers Alexis Bachelot and Patrick Short went to the small pueblo of Los Angeles, whose residents had been seeking a resident priest since 1810. Bachelot served for five years as pastor of the little parish church that grew into la Iglesia de Nuestra Señora de los Angeles (*Our Lady Queen of Angels Church*), before attempting, unsuccessfully, to return to Honolulu—Steven W. Hackel, *Southern California Quarterly* 94 (2012), 11.

58. Lemon, 113.
59. Yzendoorn, 80.

Chapter 10

1. Eveleth, 163, 169; Day, 1968, 106; Morris, 242. The Mission did not license kanakas to preach until 1842 and did not ordain any as pastors until 1847.
2. Klieger, 141–142; Eveleth, 144; Joesting, 73; Kuykendall, 106; Williston, 25–26; Speakman, 83–84. Lahainaluna served as the model for Hampton Institute, the teachers' school in Virginia for freed slaves that Booker T. Washington attended, which is today Hampton University.
3. Char Miller, 1989, 1, 5–6; Mary Ward, letter to Nancy Ruggles, February 1831, Hawaiian Mission Children's Society, hmha.missionhouses.org/files/original/95012d4e91bffa23f847f257fc7bbd03.pdf.
4. Gerritt Judd, September 10, 1831, letter to the editor of the *Western Recorder* (Utica, New York), excerpted in the Religious Intelligencer (16) March 17, 1832, p. 657; Hiram Bingham, 406–407; Bradley, 1942, 196–197; Daws, 1968, 88; 2006, 86.
5. Hiram Bingham, 338, 410; Bern Anderson, 103; Brown, 67; Kashay, 2012, 306.
6. Hiram Bingham, 408–409; Greer, 1994, 38, 41; Char Miller, 1989, 13–14.
7. Zwiep, 165; Sinclair, 1976, 124.
8. Chester Young, 174–175; Bradley, 1942, 198–202; Sheldon Dibble, quoted by Haley, 82.
9. Silverman, 134–135, 142–144.
10. Ka'ahumanu's letter to Jeremiah Evarts, dated September 11, 1831, https://hmha.missionhouses.org/items/show/30214; Hiram Bingham, 425; Allen, 184; Speakman, 66.
11. Hiram Bingham, letter to Jeremiah Evarts, Dec. 7, 1831, in Char Miller, 1988, 340; Klieger, 147.
12. Hiram Bingham, 1849, 428; Pukui and Varez, 255, 2345.
13. Bradford Smith, 177; Hiram Bingham, 429–430; Stirling and Summers, 287–288; Anonymous, "Kapuka-amaomao," 12; Sinclair, 1976, 126–127. Her home sometimes was called simply Pukamao.
14. Halford, 139; Silverman, 145; Betsy and Lorenzo Lyons, journal entries for May 18 and June 7, 1832—Doyle, 27–29, 35; Laura Fish Judd, 74; Joesting, 82.
15. Doyle, 32.
16. Letter from the Sandwich Island Mission published in *The Missionary Herald* 29 (May 1833), 165–168, and reprinted by the ABCFM in *Missionary Paper* 12 (1835), 26–28; Coan, 27.
17. Armstrong, 22, entry for June 5, 1832; Lorenzo Lyons, journal entry for June 5, 1832; Betsy Lyons, journal entry for June 8, 1832—Doyle, 34, 36.
18. Hiram Bingham, letter to Rufus Anderson dated June 5, 1832; Miller, 1988, 359–360.
19. Malo's "He Kanikau No Kaahumanu," quoted by Joesting, 1972, 152–153, was published in *Ka Lama Hawaii* on August 8, 1834. See also, Clark, 4, 6; Kaeppler, 2013, 73–76.
20. Pierce's letter dated June 11, 1832, Hunnewell MSS, quoted by Kuykendall, 133.
21. Kam, 38–40.
22. Betsy and Lorenzo Lyons, journal entry for June 7, 1832—Doyle, 35.
23. Kame'eleihiwa, 2001, 80; Laura Judd, 77; Tabrah, 1984, 46; Silverman, 146.
24. Silva, 29–30; Yzendoorn, 56; Schoofs, 27; Lee, 63; Cahill, 2004, 21; Lemon, 113. It is sometimes said that it was the King who ended the imprisonment of Catholics, but he was still a minor. Kina'u was both Regent and Kuhina Nui when the prisoners were released.

Notes—Places to Visit and Glossary

Places to Visit

1. James, 2002, 114–116.
2. Bouslog, 13.
3. Kawaiahaʻo was called the Great Stone Church, Honolulu First Church, and the King's Chapel before taking its current name. The memorial plaque and portrait of Kaʻahumanu can be seen at www.pbase.com/modbl/image/155353078 and www.pbase.com/modbl/image/152876386.
4. James, 2002, 154–155.

Glossary

1. Romaine, 190–191.

Bibliography

Achiu, Jason Kapena; Kaʻowili, Helen; Akana-Gooch, Kiele. 2005. "Na Kanawai o ke Aupuni Hawaiʻi, Mahele 1/Laws of the Hawaiian Government, Part 1," *Ka Hoʻoilina/The Legacy* 4, 14–43.
Adkins, Roy and Lesley. 2014. *Jane Austen's England.* New York: Penguin.
Ahlo Charles; Walker, Jerry; Johnson, Rubellite Kawena. 2016. *Kamehameha's Children Today.* Honolulu: Native Books, second revised edition.
Alexander, W. D. 1896. "An Autograph Letter, by Jean B. Rives," *Annual Report of the Hawaiian Historical Society* 4, 19–36.
Alexander, W. D. "Overthrow of the Ancient Tabu System in the Hawaiian Islands," *Annual Report of the Hawaiian Historical Society* 25 (1917), 37–45.
Allen, Gwenfread E. 1925. "Kaahumanu—A Study," *The Friend* (Honolulu) 95, 128–129, 135–140, 157–164, 182–185.
American Board of Commissioners for Foreign Missions. 1827. "Report of the American Board of Commissioners for Foreign Missions." Boston: Crocker & Brewster.
American Board of Commissioners for Foreign Mission. 1838. *Instructions of the Prudential Committee of the American Board of Commissioners for Foreign Missions to the Sandwich Islands Mission.* Lahainaluna: Press of the Mission Seminary.
American Board of Commissioners for Foreign Missions. 1841. "Report of the American Board of Commissioners for Foreign Missions." Boston: Crocker & Brewster.
Anderson, Bern. 1960. *Surveyor of the Sea: The Life and Voyages of Captain George Vancouver.* Seattle: University of Washington Press.
Anderson, Rufus. 1870. *History of the Sandwich Islands Mission.* Boston: Congregational Publishing Society.
Anonymous. July 1, 1932. "Kapuka-amao-mao, The Home of Kaahumanu," *Paradise of the Pacific* 45, 12.
Arago, Jacques. 1823. *Narrative of a Voyage Round the World in the* Uranie *and* Physicienne, Part II. London: Treuttel & Wurtz.
Archer, Seth. 2010. "Remedial Agents," *Pacific Historical Review* 79, 513–544.
Archer, Seth. 2018. *Sharks Upon the Land: Colonialism, Indigenous Health, and Culture in Hawaiʻi, 1778–1855.* Cambridge: Cambridge University Press.
Arista, Noelani. 2009. "Listening to Leoiki: Engaging Sources in Hawaiian History," *Biography* 32, 66–73.
Arista, Noelani. 2011. "Captive Women in Paradise, 1796–1826: The Kapu on Prostitution in Hawaiian Historical Legal Context," *American Indian Culture and Research Journal* 35, no. 4, 39–55.
Arista, Noelani. 2019. *The Kingdom and the Republic: Sovereign Hawaiʻi and the Early United States.* Philadelphia: University of Pennsylvania Press.
Armstrong, Richard. *Journal of Richard Amstrong.* Typescript at the Hawaiian Mission Houses Library in Honolulu, hmha.missionhouses.org/files/original/1cf84d3fd-6702cfe9f3137694853c48e.pdf.
Association de la Propagation de la Foi. "Mission des Îles Sandwich," *Annales de la*

Bibliography

Propagation de la Foi, 3 (1828) 152–159, 350–357; 4 (1830), 265–298; 6 (1833), 93–119; 10 (1837), 362–399, 501–512; 79 (1907), 176–181.
Ballou, Howard M., and Carter, George R. 1908. "The History of the Hawaiian Mission Press," *Hawaiian Historical Society Paper* 14, 9–44.
Bargatsky, Thomas. 1980. "Some Problems with Beachcomber Books: The Example of Samuel Patterson's Writings," *Hawaiian Journal of History* 14, 6–15.
Bark, Caroline O'Neill. 2011. *A Commentary on the Journal of Manuel Quimper Benitez del Pino.* Unpublished master's thesis, University of Hawai'i.
Barratt, Glynn. 1981. *Russia in Pacific Waters, 1715–1825: A Survey of Russia's Naval Presence in the North and South Pacific.* Vancouver: University of British Columbia Press.
Barratt, Glynn. 1988. *Russian View of Honolulu, 1809–1826.* Ottawa: Carleton University Press.
Barrère, Dorothy. 1975. *Kamehameha in Kona: Two Documentary Studies* (Pacific Anthropological Records 23). Honolulu: Bishop Museum.
Barrère, Dorothy. 1989. "A Tahitian in the History of Hawai'i: The Journal of Kahikona," *Hawaiian Journal of History* 23, 75–107.
Barrère, Dorothy, and Sahlins, Marshall. 1979. "Tahitians in the Early History of Hawaiian Christianity: The Journal of Toketa," *Hawaiian Journal of History* 13, 19–35.
Barrère, Dorothy; Pukui, Mary Kawena; Kelly, Marion. 1980. *Hula: Historical Perspectives* (Pacific Anthropological Records 30). Honolulu: Bishop Museum Press.
Barrow, John. 1993. *Captain Cook: Voyages of Discovery Compiled from the Authorized 18th Century Admiralty Editions and Documents.* Chicago: Academy Chicago Publishers.
Barrow, Terence. 1978. *Captain Cook in Hawaii.* Norfolk Island, Australia: Island Heritage.
Barth, Steve. 1995. *The Smithsonian Guide to Natural America: The Pacific—Hawai'i and Alaska.* New York: Smithsonian Books.
Bartlett, S. C. 1869. *Historical Sketch of the Hawaiian Mission.* Boston: American Board of Commissioners for Foreign Missions.
Bassett, Marnie. 1962. *Realms and Islands: The World Voyage of Rose de Freycinet in the Corvette Uranie, 1817–1820.* London: Oxford University Press.
Beaglehole, J. C. 1974. *The Life of Captain James Cook.* Stanford, CA: Stanford University Press.
Beaglehole, J. C. 2017. *The Journals of Captain James Cook on His Voyages of Discovery,* Volume III, Part II.
Beamer, Nona. 2001. *Na Mele Hula.* Lā'ie, HI: Institute for Polynesian Studies.
Bell, Edward. 1929–1930. "Log of the Chatham," *Honolulu Mercury* 1–2, 7–26, 55–69, 76–96, 80–91, 119–129.
Bell, Susan N. 1976. "Ohwyhee's Prodigal," *Hawaiian Journal of History* 10, 25–32.
Bell, Susan N. 1986. *Unforgettable True Stories of the Kingdom of Hawaii.* Kailua, HI: Press Pacifica.
Bennett, Guy Vernon. 1913. "Early Relations of the Sandwich Islands to the Old Oregon Territory," *Washington Historical Journal* 4, 116–124.
Bernice Pauahi Bishop Museum. 1892. *Preliminary Catalogue of Polynesian Ethnology and History.* Honolulu: Bishop Museum Press.
Bernice Pauahi Bishop Museum. 1915. *Bishop Museum Handbook. Part I. The Hawaiian Collections.* Honolulu: Bishop Museum Press.
Beyer, C. Kalani. 2010. "Past and Present Transformations of Hawaiian Religious Participation," in Kathleen J. Martin, Editor. *Indigenous Symbols and Practices in the Catholic Church: Visual Culture, Missionization and Appropriation.* Burlington, VT: Ashgate, 75–96.
Bingham, Alfred M. 1975. "Sybil's Bones: A Chronicle of the Three Hiram Binghams," *Hawaiian Journal of History* 9, 3–36.

Bibliography

Bingham, Hiram. 1849. *A Residence of Twenty-One Years in the Sandwich Islands*. Hartford: H. Huntington (reprinted Rutland, VT: Charles. E. Tuttle, 1981).
Bingham, Sybil. *Journal of Sybil Moseley Bingham*. Typescript at the Hawaiian Mission Houses Library, hmha.missionhouses.org/items/browse?collection=248.
Bishop, Artemas. August 1, 1827. "Visit of Kaahumanu to Hawaii" (letter dated Nov. 30, 1826, to the Corresponding Secretary of the American Board of Commissioners for Foreign Missions), *The Missionary Herald* 23, 140–142.
Bishop, Charles, and Roe, Michael. *The Journal and Letters of Captain Charles Bishop on the North-west Coast of America, in the Pacific, and in New South Wales, 1794–1799*. Cambridge: Hakluyt Society, Second Series, no. 131, 1967.
Black, William. 1959. *Voyage of the Raccoon: A "Secret" Journal of a Visit to Oregon, California and Hawaii, 1813–1814*. John A. Hussey, Ed. San Francisco: Book Club of California.
Bloxam, Andrew. 1925. *Diary of Andrew Bloxam, Naturalist of the "Blonde" on Her Trip from England to the Hawaiian Islands, 1824–1825* (Bernice P. Bishop Museum Special Publication 10). Honolulu: Bishop Museum Press.
Boit, John. 1981. *Log of the Union: John Boit's Remarkable Voyage Around the World, 1794–1795*. Edited by Edmund Hayes. Portland: Oregon Historical Society.
Bolkhovitinov, N. N. 1973. "Avantyura Doktora Sheffera na Gavayyakh v 1815–1819 Godakh," *Novaya i Noveyshaya Istoriya* 1 (1972). Translated by Igor V. Vorobyoff, *Hawaiian Journal of History* 7, 55–78.
Bolkhovitinov, N. N. 1987. "Russian America and International Relations," in S. Frederick Starr, editor. *Russia's American Colony*. Durham: Duke University Press, 251–270.
Botta, Paul-Émile. October-December 1831. "Observations sur les habitants des Îles Sandwich," *Nouvelles annales des voyages, de la géographie et de l'histoire* 53, 129–176.
Bouslog, Charles S. May 1983. "In Search of Ka'ahumanu's Cottage with the Green Shutters," *Historic Hawaii News* 9, no. 5, 13.
Braden, Whythe E. 1976. "On the Probability of Pre-1778 Japanese Drifts to Hawaii," *Hawaiian Journal of History* 10, 75–89.
Bradley, Harold Whitman. 1931. "Thomas ap Catesby Jones and the Hawaiian Islands, 1826–1827," *Hawaiian Historical Society 39th Annual Report*, 17–30. Honolulu: Hawaiian Printing Co.
Bradley, Harold Whitman. 1942. *The American Frontier in Hawaii: The Pioneers, 1789–1843*. Stanford: Stanford University Press (reprinted, Gloucester, MA: Peter Smith, 1968).
Brigham, W. T. 1903. *A Handbook for Visitors to the Bernice Pauahi Bishop Museum of Polynesian Ethnology and Natural History*. Honolulu: Bishop Museum Press.
Brown, Marie Alohalani. 2016. *Facing the Spears of Change: The life and Legacy of John Papa 'Ī'ī*. Honolulu: University of Hawai'i Press.
Buck, Elizabeth. 1993. *Paradise Remade: The Politics of Culture and History in Hawai'i*. Philadelphia: Temple University Press.
Bunson, Maggie. 1977. *Faith in Paradise: A Century and a Half of the Roman Catholic Church in Hawaii*. Boston: St. Paul Editions.
Burlin, Paul T. 2012. "Early Nineteenth Century Missionaries to Hawai'i and the Salary Dispute," Clifford Putney & Paul T. Burlin, editors. *The Role of the American Board in the World: Bicentennial Reflections on the Organization's Missionary Work, 1810–2010*, 227–243. Eugene, OR: Wipf & Stock.
Burlin, Paul T., and Putney, Clifford, editors. 2012. "We will banish the polluted thing from our house: Missionaries, Drinking, and Temperance in the Sandwich Islands," *The Role of the American Board in the World: Bicentennial Reflections on the Organization's Missionary Work, 1810–2010*, 287–311. Eugene, OR: Wipf & Stock.
Busch, Britton Cooper. 2009. *Whaling Will Never Do for Me: The American Whalemen in the Nineteenth Century*. Lexington: University Press of Kentucky.

Bibliography

Bushnell, Oswald A. 1993. *The Gifts of Civilization: Germs and Genocide in Hawai'i.* Honolulu: University of Hawaii Press.
Buyers, Elizabeth Kapu'uwailani Lindsey, and Noyes, Martha H. 2003. *Then There Were None.* Honolulu: Bess Press.
Cahill, Emmett. 1999. *The Life and Times of John Young, Confidant and Advisor to Kamehameha the Great.* Aiea, HI: Island Heritage Publishing.
Cahill, Emmett. 2004. *The Dark Decade, 1829–1839: Anti-Catholic Persecutions in Hawai'i.* Honolulu: Mutual Publishing.
Callcott, Maria Dundas Graham. 1826. *Voyage of HMS Blonde to the Sandwich Islands in the Years 1824–1825.* London: John Murray. Murray hired her to ghostwrite this, based on the diaries of Robert Dampier and Andrew Bloxam.
Campbell, Archibald. 1967. *A Voyage Round the World, from 1806 to 1812.* Charleston, SC: Duke & Browne, 1822, Third American Edition (first published in Edinburgh, 1816), facsimile reproduction, Honolulu: University of Hawaii Press.
Carné, Louis de. 1843. "Des intérêts Français dans l'Océanie," *Revue des deux mondes* 57/ new series 2, 288–301.
Carpenter, Edmund James. 1899. *America in Hawaii: A History of United States Influence in the Hawaiian Islands.* Boston: Small, Maynard, & Co.
Carter, Sybil Augusta Judd. 1893. "Kaahumanu: A Memorial." Honolulu: Women's Board of Missions for the Pacific Islands.
Chamberlain, Levi. *Journal.* At the Hawaiian Mission Houses Library, available at hmha.missionhouses.org/collections/show/173.
Chamisso, Adelbert von. 1986. *A Voyage Around the World with the Romanzov Exploring Expedition in the Years 1815–1818 in the Brig Rurik, Captain Otto von Kotzebue.* Honolulu: University of Hawaii Press.
Chang, David A. 2016. *The World and All the Things Upon It: Native Hawaiian Geographies of Exploration.* Minneapolis: University of Minnesota Press.
Chappell, David A. 1992. "Shipboard Relations between Pacific Island Women and Euroamerican Men, 1767–1887," *Journal of Pacific History* 27, 131–149.
Chappell, David A. 2015. *Double Ghosts: Oceanian Voyages on EuroAmerican Ships.* New York: Routledge.
Charlot, John. 1991. "The Feather Skirt of Nahi'ena'ena: An Innovation in Postcontact Hawaiian Art," *Journal of the Polynesian Society* 100, 119–165.
Charlot, John. 2004. "A Note on the Hawaii Prophecy of Kapihe," *Journal of Pacific History,* 39, 375–77.
Charlot, John. 2010. "Two Hawaiian-Christian Chants," *Anthropos* 105, 29–46.
Chevigny, Hector. 1965. *Russian America: The Great Alaska Venture, 1741–1867.* New York: Ballantine.
Choris, Louis [Ludwig]; Cuvier, Georges; Chamisso, Adelbert von. 2008. *Voyage dans le Pacifique, 1815–1818.* Paris: Chandeigne.
Chun, Malcolm Nāea. 2011. *No Nā Mamo: Traditional and Contemporary Hawaiian Beliefs and Practices.* Honolulu: University of Hawai'i Press/Curriculum Research & Development Group.
Clark, John R. K. 2011. *Hawaiian Surfing: Traditions from the Past.* Honolulu: University of Hawai'i Press.
Coan, Mrs. Titus [Lydia Bingham]. *A Brief Sketch of the Missionary Life of Mrs. Sybil Mosely Bingham.* Read before the Women's Board of the Missions for the Pacific Islands on April 2, 1895, Honolulu. Privately published, 1895.
Colnett, James. 2004. *A Voyage to the North West Side of America: The Journals of James Colnett, 1786–89.* Vancouver: University of British Columbia Press.
Cordy, Ross. 2000. *Exalted Sits the Chief: The Ancient History of Hawai'i Island.* Honolulu: Mutual Publishing.
Cordy, Ross. 2002. *The Rise and Fall of the O'ahu Kingdom.* Honolulu: Mutual Publishing.

Bibliography

Corley, J. Susan. 2008. "The British Press Greets the King of the Sandwich Islands: Kamehameha II in London, 1824," *Hawaiian Journal of History* 42, 69–10.
Corley, J. Susan. 2010. "Kamehameha II's Ill-starred Journey to England Aboard *L'Aigle*, 1823–1824," *Hawaiian Journal of History* 44, 1–35.
Corney, Peter. 1896. *Voyages in the North Pacific* (reprinted from the *Literary Gazette* of 1821). Honolulu: Thomas C. Thrum.
Creed, Victoria. 2008. "Early Western Diminishment of the Hawaiian Women's Rights," Society for Hawaiian Archeology Conference, Hilo, Oct. 17–19, www.waihona.com/articles/diminishment.asp.
Creed, Victoria, and Hanson, Isaaca. February 17, 2008. "Fact or Fiction: A Case Study of a Piracy Charge Against Captain William Buckle of the Whaling Vessel *Daniel IV*," 19th Annual Symposium on 19th Annual Symposium on Maritime Archaeology and History of Hawai'i, University of Hawai'i at Manoa, www.waihona.com/articles/BucklePiracyCharges.asp.
Croft, Lee B. 2017. *Kaumuali'i and the Last of Hawaii's God Kings*. Phoenix: Sphynx Publications.
Cummings, Mrs. A. P. 1842. *The Missionary's Daughter: A Memoir of Lucy Goodale Thurston of the Sandwich Islands*. New York: American Tract Society.
Damon, Ethel M. 1925. "The First Mission Settlement on Kauai," *The Friend* 95, 204–210, 224–235.
Dampier, Robert. 1971. *To the Sandwich Islands on H.M.S. Blonde*. Edited by Pauline King Joerger. Honolulu: University Press of Hawaii.
D'Arcy, Paul. 2003. "Warfare and State Formation in Hawaii," *Journal of Pacific History* 38, 29–52.
D'Arcy, Paul. 2018. *Transforming Hawai'i: Balancing Coercion and Consent in Eighteenth-Century Kānaka Maoli Statecraft*. Action (Canberra): ANU Press.
Daws, Gavan. 1966. "The High Chief Boki," *Journal of the Polynesian Society* 75, 65–83.
Daws, Gavan. 1967. "Honolulu in the Nineteenth Century," *Journal of Pacific History* 2, 77–96.
Daws, Gavan. 1968. *Shoal of Time: A History of the Hawaiian Islands*. Honolulu: University Press of Hawaii.
Daws, Gavan. 2006. *Honolulu, the First Century: The Story of the Town to 1876*. Honolulu: Mutual Publishing.
Day, A. Grove. 1941. "From Manoa to Punahou," *Forty-Ninth Annual Report of the Hawaiian Historical Society*, 5–11.
Day, A. Grove. 1968. *Hawaii and Its People*. New York: Meredith Press, revised edition.
Day, A. Grove. 1968. *Pirates of the Pacific*. New York: Meredith Press.
Day, A. Grove. 1974. *Kamehameha, First King of Hawaii*. Honolulu: Hogarth Press.
Delano, Amasa. 1818. *A Narrative of Voyages and Travels in the Northern and Southern Hemispheres: Comprising Three Voyages Round the World; Together with a Voyage of Survey and Discovery in the Pacific Ocean and Oriental Islands*. Boston: E. G. House, second edition.
Del Piano, Barbara. 2009. "Kalanimoku: Iron Cable of the Hawaiian Kingdom, 1769–1827," *Hawaiian Journal of History* 43, 1–28.
Demos, John. 2014. *The Heathen School: A Story of Hope and Betrayal in the Age of the Early Republic*. New York: Vintage Books.
Desha, Stephen L. 2000. *Kamehameha and His Warrior Kekūhaupi'o*. Translated by Frances N. Frazier. Honolulu: Kamehameha Schools Press, www.ulukau.org/elib/cgi-bin/library?c=elibrary.
Desser, Daphne. 2007. "Fraught Literacy: Competing Desires for Connection and Separation in the Writings of American Missionary Women in Nineteenth-Century Hawai'i," *College English* 69, 443–469.

Bibliography

Dibble, Sheldon. 1839. *History and General View of the Sandwich Islands Mission*. New York: Taylor & Dodd.
Dibble, Sheldon. 1909. *A History of the Sandwich Island*. Honolulu: Thrum.
Dickey, Lyle Alexander. 1901. *Portraits of American Protestant Missionaries to Hawaii*. Honolulu: Hawaiian Mission Children's Society.
Dixon, George. 1789. *A Voyage Round the World*. London: Goulding.
Doyle, Emma Lyons. 1945. *Makua Laina: The Story of Lorenzo Lyons*. Honolulu: Honolulu Star Bulletin.
Duhaut-Cilly, Auguste Bernard. 1999. *Voyage autour du Monde: Îles Sandwich, pendant les Années 1826, 1827, 1828, et 1829*. Vol. 2. Paris: Bertrand, 1835. (A translation by August Frugé and Neal Harlow is available as *A Voyage to California, the Sandwich Islands, and Around the World in the Years 1826–1829*. Berkeley: University of California Press.)
Dwight, Edwin W. 1818. *Memoirs of Henry Obookiah: A Native of Owhyhee, and a Member of the Foreign Mission School*. New Haven: Religious Intelligencer.
Dye, Bob. 1997. "A Memoria of What the People Were: The Sandwich Island Institute and Hawaiian Spectator," *Hawaiian Journal of History* 31, 53–69.
Dye, Bob. 1997. *Merchant Prince of the Sandalwood Mountains: Afong and the Chinese in Hawaii*. Honolulu: University of Hawaii Press.
Dye, Tom. 1994. "Population Trends in Hawai'i Before 1778," *Hawaiian Journal of History* 28, 1–20.
Ehlke, E.; McElhaney, J. K.; Tsutaoka G. 1998. *Oke Ano Ao-ka Wiwo'ole (Profiles in Courage: Three Studies—Medicine and Pharmacy in Hawaii, 1825–1890)*. Honolulu: Hey Jude!, VHS tape available at Wong Audiovisual Center, University of Hawai'i at Manoa.
Ellis, James H. 2002. *Mad Jack Percival Legend of the Old Navy*. Annapolis: Naval Institute Press.
Ellis, William. 1827. *Narrative of a Tour Through Hawaii*. Second Edition. London.
Ellis, William. 1831. *Vindication of the South Seas Mission from the Misrepresentations of Otto Von Kotzebue, Captain in the Russian Navy*. London: Frederick Westley and A. H. Davis.
Ellis, William. 1832. *Polynesian Researches, During a Residence of Eight Years in the Society and Sandwich Islands*. Vol. IV. Second edition. London: Fisher, Son & Jackson.
Emerson, Nathaniel. 1909. *Unwritten Literature of Hawaii: The Sacred Songs of the Hula* (Bureau of American Ethnology Bulletin 38). Washington, D.C.: Smithsonian Institution.
Emory, Kenneth P. 1924 (reprinted in 1969). *Island of Lanai: A Survey of Native Cultures*. Honolulu: Bishop Museum. Bishop Museum Bulletin 12.
Emory, Kenneth P. 1928 (reprinted in 2003). *Archeology of Nihoa and Necker Islands*. Honolulu: Bishop Museum. Bishop Museum Bulletin 53.
Eveleth, Ephraim. 1831. *History of the Sandwich Islands*. Philadelphia: Sunday School Union.
Fillipetti, Sandrine, Ed. 2015. *Journal: Campagne de L'Urainie (1817–1820)*. Paris: Editions du Mercure de France.
Finney, Ben R. 1966. *Surfing, the Sport of Hawaiian Kings*. Rutland, VT: Charles E. Tuttle.
Fornander, Abraham. *An Account of the Polynesian Race, Its Origins and Migrations and the Ancient History of the Hawaiian People to the Times of Kamehameha I*. London: Trubner & Co., 1878, 1880, and 1885 (reprinted, Rutland, VT: Charles Tuttle, 1969).
Fornander, Abraham. 1919–1920. *Hawaiian Antiquities and Folk-Lore*, Edited by Thomas G. Thrum. Honolulu: Bishop Museum Press, Bernice P. Bishop Museum Bulletin 6.
Freycinet, Louis Claude de Saulces de. 1829. *Voyage autour du Monde*. Vol. 2, Part 2, Book IV. Paris: Pillet.
Frierson, Pamela. 1991. *The Burning Island: A Journey Through Myth and History in Volcano Country, Hawai'i*. San Francisco: Sierra Club Books.

Bibliography

Freycinet, Rose de Saulces de Freycinet. 2003. *Woman of Courage: The Journal of Rose de Freycinet on Her Voyage Around the World, 1817–1820.* Translated and edited by Marc Serge Riviere. Canberra: National Library of Australia.

Gapp, Frank W. 1985. "The Kind-Eyed Chief: Forgotten Champion of Hawai'i's Freedom," *Hawaiian Journal of History* 19, 101–121.

Gast, Ross H. 1973. *Don Francisco de Paula Marin: A Biography.* Honolulu: University Press of Hawaii.

Gast, Ross H. 1976. *Contentious Consul: A Biography of John Coffin Jones, First United States Consular Agent at Hawaii.* Los Angeles: Dawson's.

Golovnin, V. M. 1979. *Around the World on Kamchatka, 1817–1819.* Honolulu: Hawaiian Historical Society & University Press of Hawaii.

Gonschor, Lorenz. 2019. *A Power in the World: The Hawaiian Kingdom in Oceania.* Honolulu: University of Hawai'i Press.

Gowen, Herbert H. 1908. *Hawaiian Idylls of Love and Death.* New York: Cochrane Publishing.

Green, Karina Kahananui. 2002. "Colonialism's Daughters: Eighteenth and Nineteenth Century Western Perceptions of Hawaiian Women," in Paul Sickard, Joanne L. Rondella, and Debbie Hippolite Wright, editors, *Pacific Diaspora: Island Peoples in the United States and Across the Pacific,* 221–252. Honolulu: University of Hawai'i.

Greene, Linda Wedel. 1993. *A Cultural History of Three Traditional Hawaiian Sites on the West Coast of Hawai'i Island.* Washington: U.S. Department of the Interior, National Park Service.

Greer, Richard A. 1994. "Grog Sops and Hotels: Bending the Elbow," *Hawaiian Journal of History* 28, 35–67.

Greer, Richard A. 1998. "Along the Old Honolulu Waterfront," *Hawaiian Journal of History* 32, 25–66.

Grigg, Richard W. 2012. *In the Beginning, Archipelago: The Origin and Discovery of the Hawaiian Islands.* Waipahu, HI: Island Heritage Publishing.

Grimshaw, Patricia. 1989. *Paths of Duty: American Missionary Wives in Nineteenth-Century Hawaii.* Honolulu: University of Hawaii Press.

Gulick, Rev. and Mrs. Oramel Hinckley. 1918. *The Pilgrims of Hawaii: Their Own Story of Their Pilgrimage from New England and Life Work in the Sandwich Islands, Now Known as Hawaii.* New York: Fleming H. Revell Company.

Gunson, Neil. 1987. "Sacred Women Chiefs and Female 'Headmen' in Polynesian History," *Journal of Pacific History* 22, 139–172.

Guttman, D. Molentia, and Golden, Ernst. 2011. *African Americans in Hawai'i.* Charleston, SC: Arcadia Publishing.

Hackler, Rhonda E. A. 1969. "The Voice of Commerce," *Hawaiian Journal of History* 3, 42–49.

Hackler, Rhonda E. A. 1986. "Alliance or Cession? Missing Letter from Kamehameha I to King George III of England Casts Light on 1794 Agreement," *Hawaiian Journal of History* 20, 1–12.

Hackler, Rhonda E. A. 2008. "Earnest Persuasion but Not Peremptory Demand: United States Government Policy Toward the Kingdom of Hawai'i, 1820–1863," *Hawaiian Journal of History* 42, 49–67.

Haley, James L. 2014. *Captive Paradise: A History of Hawai'i.* New York: St. Martin's Press.

Halford, Francis. J. 1954. *9 Doctors and God.* Honolulu: University of Hawaii Press.

Handy, E. S. Craighill. 1931. *Cultural Revolution in Hawaii.* Fourth General Session of the Institute of Pacific Relations.

Hays, H. R. 1964. *The Kingdom of Hawaii.* Greenwich, CT: New York Graphic Society Publishers.

Herbert, Don, and Badossi, Fulvio, 1968. *Kilauea: Case History of a Volcano.* New York: Harper & Row.

Bibliography

Herman, Doug. March 25, 2020. "Shutting Down Hawai'i: A Historical Perspective on Epidemics in the Islands," *Smithsonian Magazine*, https://www.smithsonianmag.com/.
Hill, Beth, and Converse, Cathy. 2011. *The Remarkable World of Frances Barkley, 1769–1845*. Victoria, BC: Touch Wood Editions, Second Edition.
Holman, Lucia Ruggles. 1931. *Journal of Lucia Ruggles Holman*. Honolulu: Bernice P. Bishop Museum, Special Publication 17.
Holt, John Dominis. 1985. *The Art of Featherwork in Old Hawai'i*. Honolulu: Topgallant Publishing.
Holt, John Dominis. *Monarchy in Hawaii*. 1995. Second Edition. Honolulu: Ku Pa'a Publishing.
Huetz de Lemps, Christian. 1989. "La France et les Français aux Îles Hawaii au XIXe Siècle," *Revue Française d'histoire d'outre-mer*, 76, 131–141.
Ioannidis, A. G., Blanco-Portillo, J., Sandoval, K. et al. "Native American Gene Flow into Polynesia Predating Easter Island Settlement," *Nature*, July 8, 2020). Summarized by Ewen Callaway, "Ancient Voyage Carried Native Americans' DNA to Remote Pacific islands," *Nature News*, July 8, 2020.
Jackson, Miles M. 2004. *They Followed the Trade Winds: African Americans in Hawai'i* (Social Process in Hawai'i 43). Honolulu: University of Hawai'i Department of Sociology.
James, Van. 1991. *Ancient Sites of O'ahu*. Honolulu: Bishop Museum Press.
James, Van. 1996. *Ancient Sites of Hawai'i*. Honolulu: Mutual Publishing.
James, Van. 2002. *Ancient Sites of Maui, Moloka'i and Lāna'i*. Honolulu: Mutual Publishing.
Jarves, James Jackson. 1843. *History of the Hawaiian Islands*. Boston: Tappan and Dennet.
Joesting, Edward. 1972. *Hawaii: An Uncommon History*. New York: W. W. Norton.
Johnson, Donald D. 1958. "Powers in the Pacific: Tahiti and Hawaii, 1825–1850," *Sixty-Sixth Annual Report of the Hawaiian Historical Society for the Year 1957*, 7–25. Honolulu: Hawaiian Historical Society.
Johnston, Paul. F. 2015. *Shipwrecked in Paradise: Cleopatra's Barge in Hawai'i*. College Station, TX: Texas A & M University Press.
Johnson-Hill, Jack. 1995. "The Missionary-Islander Encounter in Hawaii" *Missiology* 23, 309–350.
Jones, Terry L.; Storey, Alice A.; Matisoo-Smith, Elizabeth A.; Ramirez-Aliago, Josê Ramírez, Editors. 2011. *Polynesians in America: Pre-Columbian Contacts with the New World*. Lanham, MD: Altimira Press.
Judd, Bernice, and Lind, Helen Yonge. 1974. *Voyages to Hawaii Before 1860: A Record Based on Historical Narratives in the Libraries of the Hawaiian Mission Children's Society and the Hawaiian Historical Society*. Honolulu: University Press of Hawaii.
Judd, Gerrit P. 1961. *Hawaii: An Informal History*. New York: Collier Books.
Judd, Laura Fish. 1966. *Honolulu: Sketches of Life in the Hawaiian Islands from 1828 to 1861*. Chicago: Lakeside Press.
Judd, Walter F. 1976. *Kamehameha* (Hawaiian Bicentennial Library 10). Norfolk Island, Australia: Island Heritage.
Judd, Walter. 1999. *Hawai'i Joins the World*. Honolulu: Mutual Publishing.
Ka manao o na alii (Thoughts of the Chiefs). 1827. Utica, NY: W. Williams.
Kaeppler, Adrienne L. 2008. *The Pacific Arts of Polynesia and Micronesia*. Oxford: Oxford University Press.
Kaeppler, Adrienne L. 2013. "Chanting Grief, Dancing Memories: Objectifying Hawaiian Laments," *Humanities Research*, 71–81. Ed. Wild, Stephen, Corn, Aaron and Martin, Ruth Lee. Chicago: University of Chicago.
Kalakaua, His Hawaiian Majesty David, *Legends and Myths of Hawaii*. Edited by R. M. Daggett. New York: Charles L. Webster, 1888; reprinted, Rutland, VT: Charles E. Tuttle, 1972/Honolulu: Mutual Publishing, 1990.

Bibliography

Kam, Ralph Thomas. 2017. *Death Rites and Hawaiian Royalty: Funerary Practices in the Kamehameha and Kalākaua Dynasties, 1819–1953*. Jefferson, NC: McFarland.
Kamakau, Samuel M. 1961. *Ruling Chiefs of Hawaii*. Honolulu: Kamehameha Schools.
Kamakau, Samuel M. 1964. *Ka Po'e Kahiko: The People of Old*. Translated by Mary Kawena Pukui. Edited by Dorothy B. Barrère. Honolulu: Bishop Museum Press. Bernice P. Bishop Museum Special Publication 51.
Kame'eleihiwa, Lilikalā K. 1992. *Native Land and Foreign Desires: A History of Land Tenure Change in Hawai'i from Traditional Times Until the 1848 Māhele, Including an Analysis of Hawaiian ali'i nui and American Calvinists*. Honolulu: Bishop Museum Press.
Kame'eleihiwa, Lilikalā. "Na Wahine Kapu (Divine Hawaiian Women)." Honolulu: Ai Pohaku Press, 1999. (Reprinted in *Women's Rights and Human Rights: International Historical Perspectives*, edited by Patricia Grimshaw, Katie Holmes, and Marilyn Lake. New York: Palgrave, 2001, 71–87, and Honolulu: Short Stack, 2016).
Kanahele, George S. 1986. *Kū Kānaka Stand Tall: A Search for Hawaiian Values*. Honolulu: University of Hawaii Press.
Kanahele, George S. 1995. *Waikīkī, 100 B.C. to 1900 A.D.: An Untold Story*. Honolulu: Queen Emma Foundation/University of Hawaii Press.
Kashay, Jennifer Fish. 1999. "Problems in Paradise: The Peril of Missionary Parenting in Early Nineteenth-Century Hawaii," *Journal of Presbyterian History* 77, 81–94.
Kashay, Jennifer Fish. 2002. "O That My Mouth Might Be Opened: Missionaries, Gender, and Language in Early 19th Century Hawai'i," *Hawaiian Journal of History* 36, 41–58.
Kashay, Jennifer Fish. *Savages, Sinners, and Saints: The Hawaiian Kingdom and the Imperial Contest, 1778–1839*. University of Arizona Ph.D. dissertation, available at repository.arizona.edu/handle/10150/279940.
Kashay, Jennifer Fish. 2008. "Competing Imperialisms and Hawaiian Authority: The Cannonading of Lāhainā in 1827," *Pacific Historical Review* 77, 369–390.
Kashay, Jennifer Fish. 2008. "From Kapus to Christianity," *Western Historical Quarterly* 39, no. 1, 17–39.
Khisamutdinov, Amir A., and Lyovin, Anatole. 2018. *A History of the Orthodox Church in Hawaii: Two Hundred Years on the Road*. London/Washington, D.C.: Academica Press.
Khlebnikov, K. T. 1973. *Baranov, Chief Manager of the Russian Colonies in America* (Materials for the Study of Alaska History 3). Kingston, Ontario: Limestone Press, translated by Colin Bearne and edited by Richard A. Pierce.
Kirch, Patrick Vinton. 2007. *On the Road of the Winds: An Archaeological History of the Pacific Islands before European Contact*. Berkeley: University of California Press.
Kirch, Patrick Vinton. 2011. "When Did the Polynesians Settle Hawai'i?" *Hawaiian Archaeology* 12, 3–26.
Kirch, Patrick Vinton. 2012. *A Shark Going Inland Is My Chief: The Island Civilization of Ancient Hawai'i*. Berkeley: University of California Press.
Kirch, Patrick Vinton. 2018. "The Prehistory of Hawai'i," *Oxford Handbook of Prehistoric Oceania*, 375–395. New York: Oxford University Press.
Kirch, Patrick Vinton, and McCoy, Mark D. 2007. "Reconfiguring the Hawaiian Cultural Sequence: Results of Re-Dating the Halāwa Dune Site (MO-A1-3), Moloka'i Island," *Journal of the Polynesian Society* 116, 385–406.
Kirch, Patrick Vinton, and Sahlins, Marshall. 1992. *Anahulu: The Anthropology of History in the Kingdom of Hawaii, Part I*. Chicago: University of Chicago Press.
Klieger, P. Christian. 2015. *Kamehameha III: He Mo'olelo no ka Mō'ī Lokomaika'i*. San Francisco: Green Arrow Press.
Knowlton, Edgar G., Jr. 1984. "Paul-Émile Botta, Visitor to Hawai'i in 1828," *Hawaiian Journal of History* 18, 13–38.
Kotzebue, Otto von. 1830. *A New Voyage Round the World in the Years 1823–1826*. London: Henry Colburn & Richard Bentley.

Bibliography

Kotzebue, Otto von. 1967. *A Voyage of Discovery, into the South Sea and Bering's Straits.* London: Longman, Hurst, Rees, Orme & Brown, 1821; reprinted, New York: Da Capo Press.

Kuykendall, R. S. 1938. *The Hawaiian Kingdom. Volume 1, 1778–1854: Foundation and Transformation.* Honolulu: University of Hawaii Press, available at http://www.ulukau.org/elib/cgi-bin/library?c=kingdom1.

Kuykendall, Ralph. S., and Day, A. Grove. 1961. *Hawaii: A History.* Englewood, NJ: Prentice-Hall, Second Edition.

La Croix, Sumner. 2019. *Hawaii: Eight Hundred Years of Political and Economic Change.* Chicago: University of Chicago Press.

Langlas, Charles, and Lyon, Jeffrey. 2008. "Davida Malo's Unpublished Account of Keōpūolani," *Hawaiian Journal of History* 42, 27–48.

Laux, Claire. 2011. "Les missionnaires et les autres: les acteurs de la premierère évangélisation de l'Océanie face aux autres Occidentaux," *Histoire et Missionnes Chrétiennes* 20, 25–41.

Ledyard, John. 1963. *John Ledyard's Journal of Captain Cook's Last Voyage.* Edited by James Kenneth Munford. Corvallis: Oregon State University Press.

Lee, Blanche Kaualua L. 2004. *The Unforgettable Spaniard: Hawaii's First Western Farmer.* Second Edition. Pittsburgh: RoseDog Books.

Lemon, Sister Adele Marie, C. S. J. 1956. *Hawaii, Lei of Islands: A History of Catholic Hawaii.* Honolulu: Tongg Publishing.

Levin, Stephanie Seto. 1968. "The Overthrow of the Kapu System in Hawaii," *Journal of the Polynesian Society* 77, 402–430.

Lewis, David. 1994. *We, the Navigators: The Ancient Art of Landfinding in the Pacific.* Second edition. Honolulu: University of Hawaii Press.

Linnekin, J. 1990. *Sacred Queens and Women of Consequence: Rank, Gender and Colonialism in the Hawaiian Islands.* Ann Arbor: University of Michigan Press.

Lisiansky, Captain Urey. [Yuri Fevdorovich Lisyansky].1814. *A Voyage Round the World in the Years 1803, 4, 5 & 6.* London: John Booth.

Long, David F. 1993. *"Mad Jack": The Biography of Captain John Percival, USN, 1779–1862.* Westport, CT: Greenwood Press.

Loomis, Elisha. 1937. *The Journal of E. Loomis.* Edited by William D. Westervelt. Honolulu: University of Hawaii.

Lyon, Jeffrey. 2013. "Malo's Moʻolelo Hawaiʻi: The Lost Translation," *Hawaiian Journal of History* 47, 27–60.

Macrae, James. 1922. *With Lord Byron at the Sandwich Islands in 1825; Being Extracts from the MS Diary of James Macrae.* William F. Wilson, Ed. Honolulu: W. F. Wilson.

Male, G. 1864. *Les Missionnaires Catholiques et les Missionnaires Protestants.* Paris: Jacques Lecoffre.

Malo, Davida. 1903. *Hawaiian Antiquities.* Honolulu: Hawaiian Gazette, translated from the Hawaiian by N. B. Emerson.

Manby, Thomas. June 1929. "Journal of Vancouver's Voyage, 1791–1793," *Honolulu Mercury* 1, 11–23.

Marchand, Étienne. 1800. *Voyage autour du Monde pendant les Années 1790, 1791, et 1792.* Tome I. Paris: Imprimerie de la République.

Marin, Francisco de Paula. 1973. *The Letters and Journals of Francisco de Paula Marin.* Edited by Agnes C. Conrad in Ross H. Gast, *Don Francisco de Paula Marin: A Biography.* Honolulu: University Press of Hawaii.

Mathison, Gilbert Farquhar. 1825. *Narrative of a Visit to Brazil, Chile, and the Sandwich Islands During the Years 1821 and 1822.* London: Charles Knight.

Maude, H. E. 1973. "The Raiatean Chief Auna and the Conversion of Hawaii," *Journal of Pacific History* 8, 188–191.

McCoy, Mark D. 2014. "The Significance of Religious Ritual in Ancient Hawaiʻi," *Journal of Pacific Archaeology* 5, 72–80.

Bibliography

McCoy, Mark D. 2018. "Celebration as a Source of Power in Archaic States: Archaeological and Historical Evidence for the Makahiki Festival in the Hawaiian Islands," *World Archaeology* 50, 242–270.
McCoy, Mark D., and Graves, Michael W. 2010. "The Role of Agricultural Innovation on Pacific Islands: A Case Study from Hawai'i Island," *World Archaeology* 42, 90–107.
McDougall, Walter A. 1992. *Let the Sea Make a Noise: A History of the North Pacific from Magellan to MacArthur.* New York: Basic Books.
McGregor, Davianna Pomaika'i. 2007. *Na Kua'aina: Living Hawaiian Culture.* Honolulu: University of Hawai'i Press.
McGregor, Davianna Pōmaika'i, and MacKenzie, Melody Kapilialoha. 2014. *Mo'olelo Ea O Nā Hawai'i: History of Native Hawaiian Governance in Hawai'i.* Honolulu: Office of Hawaiian Affairs.
McKee, Linda. April, 1971. "'Mad Jack' and the Missionaries," *American Heritage* 22, 30–37, 85–87.
McKenzie, Edith Kawelohea. 1986. *Hawaiian Genealogies: Extracted from Hawaiian Language Newspapers.* Edited by Ishmael W.Stagner II. Laie, HI: Pacific Institute.
Mellen, Kathleen Dickenson. 1949. *The Lonely Warrior: The Life and Times of Kamehameha the Great.* New York: Hastings House.
Mellen, Kathleen Dickenson. 1952. *The Magnificent Matriarch: Kaahumanu, Queen of Hawaii.* New York: Hastings House.
Menzies, Archibald. 1920. *Hawaii Nei 128 Years Ago.* Honolulu: T. H.
Miller, Char. 1988. *Selected Writings of Hiram Bingham (1814–1869), Missionary to the Hawaiian Islands: To Raise the Lord's Banner* (Studies in American Religion). Lewiston, NY: E. Mellen Press.
Miller, Char. July 1989. "Rumors and the Language of Social Change in Early Nineteenth-Century Hawaii," *Pacific Studies* 12, no. 3, 1–28.
Miller, David G. 1988. "Ka'iana, the Once Famous 'Prince of Kaua'i," *Hawaiian Journal of History* 22, 1–19.
Mills, Peter. 1996. "A New View of Kauai as 'The Separate Kingdom' After 1810," *Hawaiian Journal of History* 30, 91–118.
Mills, Peter. 2002. *Hawaii's Russian Adventure: A New Look at Old History.* Honolulu: University of Hawaii Press.
Missionary Letters from the Sandwich Isles Mission to the American Board of Commissioners for Foreign Missions, typescript at the Hawaiian Mission Houses Library, available at hmha.missionhouses.org/collections/show/4.
M'Konochie, Alexander. 1906. "Considerations on the Propriety of Establishing a Colony on One of the Sandwich Islands," Edinburgh: Walker & Greig, 1816; reprinted in *The Annual Report of the Hawaiian Historical Society* 13, 29–43.
Montgomery, James; Tyerman, Daniel; Bennet, George. 1832. *Journal of Voyages and Travels.* Boston: Crocker & Brewster.
Mookini, Esther T. 1998. "Keōpuōlani, Sacred Wife, Queen Mother, 1778–1823," *Hawaiian Journal of History* 32, 1–24.
Moore, Susanna. 2015. *Paradise of the Pacific: Approaching Hawai'i.* New York: Farrar, Straus and Giroux.
Morineau, Auguste de. 1834. *Notice Historique sur les Îles Sandwich, 1778–1833.* Poitiers: Saurin Freres.
Morineau, Auguste de. 1834. "Précis Historique de l'Expédition des Îles Sandwich et des Causes de sa Mauvaise Réussite," *Nouvelles Annales des Voyages et des Sciences Geographiques* 16 (New series, vol. 1), 313–334.
Morison, Samuel Eliot. 1922. "Boston Traders in the Hawaiian Islands, 1789–1823," *Proceedings of the Massachusetts Historical Society* 54, 9–47.
Morris, Nancy J. and Benadetto, Robert. 2019. *Nā Kau: Portraits of Native Hawaiian Pastors at Home and Abroad, 1820–1920.* Honolulu: University of Hawai'i Press.

Bibliography

Morris, Penrose C. 1925. "Kapiolani," *Hawaiian Annual for 1926*. Honolulu: Thomas G. Thrum.
Morris Kapāʻihiahilina, Robert J. 1990. "Aikāne: Accounts of Same-Sex Relationships in the Journals of Captain Cook's Third Voyage (1776–80)," *Journal of Homosexuality* 19, no. 4, 21–54.
Morrison, Robert. 2019. *The Regency Years: During Which Jane Austen Writes, Napoleon Fights, Byron Makes Love, and Britain Becomes Modern*. New York: W. W. Norton.
Mrantz, Maxine. 1975. *Women of Old Hawaii*. Kihei, Maui: Aloha Publishing.
Mrantz, Maxine. 1976. *Hawaii's Whaling Days*. Honolulu: Aloha Publishing.
Muirhead, Desmond. 1962. *Surfing in Hawaii*. Flagstaff, AZ: Northland Press.
Murray, Stephen O. 2000. *Homosexualities*. Chicago: University of Chicago Press.
Newell, Charles Martin. 1895. *Kamehameha, the Conquering King*. New York: G. P. Putnam's Sons.
Nichol, John. 1822. *Life and Adventures of John Nichol, Mariner*. Edited by John Howell. Edinburgh: William Blackwood/London: T. Cadell.
Okihiro, Gary Y. 2001. *Columbia Guide to Asian American History*. New York: Columbia University Press.
Okun, Semen Bentsionovich. *The Russian-American Company*. Cambridge: Harvard University Press, 1951 (Russian Translation Project of the American Council of Learned Societies 9). Translated by Carl Ginsburg, first published in Russian in Moscow in 1939.
Osorio, Jonathan Kay Kamakawiwoʻole. 2002. *Dismembering Lāhui: A History of the Hawaiian Nation to 1887*. Honolulu: University of Hawaiʻi Press.
Owens, Kenneth. 2015. *Empire Maker: Aleksender Baranov and Russian Colonial Expansion into California and Alaska*. Seattle: University of Washington Press.
Partridge, Scott H. 2013. "Two Early Missionaries in Hawaii: Mercy Partridge Whitney and Edward Partridge, Jr," *BYU Studies Quarterly* 52, 136–147.
Patterson, Samuel. 1817. *Narrative of the Adventures and Sufferings of Samuel Patterson Experienced in the Pacific Ocean*. Palmer, MA.
Paulding, Hiram. *Journal of a Cruise of the United States Schooner Dolphin Among the Islands of the Pacific Ocean*. Honolulu: University of Hawaii Press, 1970, with an introduction by A. Grove Day, first published in 1831.
Perbal, Albert (R. P.). 1939. *Les missionnaires français et le nationalisme*. Paris: Librarie de l'Arc.
Perkins, Roland F. 1980. "Kou Haole: The Image of the Chief and Foreigner in the Lahainaluna Moʻolelo Hawaii," *Hawaiian Journal of History* 14, 58–79.
Péron, Pierre François A. 1824. *Mémoires du Capitaine Péron*. Paris: Brissot-Thivars.
Pfeiffer, Regina. 2012. "Christianity Builds a Nest in Hawaii," in Clifford Putney & Paul T. Burlin, editors, *The Role of the American Board in the World: Bicentennial Reflections on the Organization's Missionary Work, 1810–2010*, 269–287. Eugene, OR: Wipf & Stock.
Pierce, Richard A. 1963. "George Anton Schaffer: Russia's Man in Hawaii, 1815–1817," *Pacific Historical Review* 32, 397–406. (Reprinted Kingston, Ontario: Limestone Press, 1976.)
Pierce, Richard A. 1965. *Russia's Hawaiian Adventure, 1815–1817*. Berkeley: University of California Press.
Piercy, LaRue W. 1985. *Hawaii—Truth Stranger Than Fiction: True Tales of Missionary Life and Historic Characters Fictionized in Michener's Hawaii*. Honolulu: Mutual Publishing.
Pietrusewsky, Michael; Douglas, Michele Toomay; Ikehara-Quebral, Rona M.; Goodwin, Conrad Mac. 2016. "The Search for Don Francisco de Paula Marin: Servant, Friend, and Advisor to King Kamehameha, Kingdom of Hawaiʻi," in Christopher M. Stojanowski & William N. Duncan, editors, *Studies in Forensic Biohistory: Anthropological Perspectives*, 67–91. Cambridge: Cambridge University Press.

Bibliography

Portlock, Nathaniel. 1789. *Voyage Round the World*. London: John Stockdale.
Pukui, Mary Kawena. 1995. *Nā Mele Welo (Songs of Our Heritage)*. Edited by Pat Namaka Bacon & Nathan Napoka. Honolulu: Bishop Museum Press.
Pukui, Mary Kawena, and Korn, Alfons L., editors and translators. 1973. *The Echo of Our Song: Chants and Poems of the Hawaiians*. Honolulu: University Press of Hawaii.
Pukui, Mary Kawena, and Varez, Dietrich. 1983. *'Ōlelo No'eau: Hawaiian Proverbs & Poetical Sayings*. Bernice P. Bishop Museum Special Publication 71.
Rainwater, Dorothy T. 1970. "Kaahumanu's Silver Spoons," *Antiques* 97, 728–729.
Ralston, Caroline. 1978. *Grass Huts and Warehouses: Pacific Beach Communities in the Nineteenth Century*. Honolulu: University Press of Hawaii/Canberra: Australian National University Press.
Ralston, Caroline. 1984. "Hawaii, 1778–1854: Some Aspects of *Maka'āinana* Response to Rapid Social Change," *Journal of Pacific History* 19, 21–40.
Ralston, Caroline. 1985. "Early Nineteenth Century Polynesian Millennial Cults and the Case of Hawai'i," *Journal of the Polynesian Society* 94, 307–331.
Restarick, Henry B. 1924. "The First Clergyman Resident in Hawaii," *Thirty-Second Annual Report of the Hawaiian Historical Society*, 54–61. Honolulu: Paradise of the Pacific.
Restarick, Henry Bond. 1924. *Hawaii, 1778–1920, from the Viewpoint of a Bishop*. Honolulu: Paradise of the Pacific.
Reynolds, Stephen. 1938. *The Voyage of the New Hazard to the Northwest Coast, Hawaii and China, 1810–13*. Edited by Judge F. W. Howay. Salem: Peabody Museum.
Reynolds, Stephen. 1989. *Journal of Stephen Reynolds, 1823–1829*. Edited by Pauline N. King. Honolulu: Ku Pa'a Publishing and Salem, MA: Peabody Museum of Salem.
Richards, William. 1825. *Memoir of Keopuolani, Late Queen of the Sandwich Islands*. Boston: Crocker & Brewster.
Rohrer, Judy. 2010. *Haoles in Hawaii*. Honolulu: University of Hawaii Press.
Roquefeuil, Camille de. 1823. *Journal d'un Voyage autour du monde pendant les années 1816, 1817, 1818, et 1819*. Tome II, Paris: Lebel.
Roquefeuil, Camille de. 2000. "Hawai'i in 1819: An Account by Camille de Roquefeuil," *Hawaiian Journal of History* 34, 69–72. Mary Ellen Birkett's first English translation of the sections on Hawai'i from Roquefeuil's *Journal*.
Romaine, Suzanne. 2002. "Signs of Identity, Signs of Discord: Glottal Goofs and the Green Grocer's Glottal in Debates on Hawaiian Orthography," *Journal of Linguistic Anthropology* 12, 189–224.
Rosenthal, Gregory. 2018. *Beyond Hawai'i: Native Labor in the Pacific World*. Oakland: University of California.
Ruggles, Nancy, and Ruggles, Samuel. *Journal from Oct. 23, 1819, to August 4, 1820*. Typescript at the Hawaiian Mission Houses Library, available at hmha.missionhouses.org/files/original/f3e301fde60bddc2a5fc21d61cdc8e89.pdf. Extracts published in *Religious Intelligencer* 5 (April 28, 1821), 770–771, and *Atlantic Monthly* 134 (November 1924).
Sahlins, Marshall David. 1981. *Historical Metaphors and Mythical Realities: Structure in the Early History of the Sandwich Island Kingdom*. Ann Arbor: University of Michigan Press.
Sahlins, Marshall. 1985. *Islands of History*. Chicago: University of Chicago Press.
Sahlins, Marshall. 1989. "Captain Cook at Hawaii," *Journal of the Polynesian Society* 98, 371–423.
Sahlins, Marshall, and Vinton Kirch, Patrick. 1992. *Historical Ethnography* (*Anahulu: The Anthropology of History in the Kingdom of Hawaii*, Vol. 1, Patrick Vinton Kirch & Marshall Sahlins, eds.). Chicago: University of Chicago Press.
Sahlins, Marshall. 1995. *How "Natives" Think: About Captain Cook, for Example*. Chicago: University of Chicago Press.
Sahlins, Marshall. 2000. "Hawai'i in the Early Nineteenth Century: The Kingdom and

Bibliography

the Kingship," *Remembrance of Pacific Pasts: An Invitation to Remake History*, Robert Borofsky, ed. Honolulu: University of Hawai'i Press.

Salazar, H. K. W. 1980. *Kaahumanu Diamond Jubilee: A Brief History*. Honolulu: Kaahumanu Society.

Schaffer, Georg Anton. *The Journal of Dr. Sheffer, Kept by Him During His Stay on Sandwich Islands*. Transcribed by Dmitry Semakin. Translated by Aleksandr Molodin. Available at http://www.fortelizabeth.org/wp-content/uploads/2018/10/The-Journal-of-Dr.-Shefferdraft.pdf.

Schmidt, Robert C., and Strombel, Rose C. "Marriage and Divorce in Hawaii Before 1870," *Hawaiian Historical Review* 2 (January 1966), 267–271.

Schoofs, Robert. 1978. *Pioneers of the Faith: History of the Catholic Mission in Hawaii, 1827–1940*. (Revised by Fay Wrend Midkiff and edited by Louis Boeynaems.) Waikane, HI: Boeynaems.

Schweizer, Niklaus R. 1982. *Hawai'i and the German Speaking Peoples*. Honolulu: Topgalant Publishing.

Scruggs, Marc. 1992. "Anthony Allen, a Prosperous American of African Descent in Early 19th Century Hawai'i," *Hawaiian Journal of History* 26, 55–93.

Seaton, S. Lee. 1974. "The Hawaiian *Kapu* Abolition of 1819," *American Ethnologist* 1, 193–206.

Seiden, Allan. 1992. *Hawai'i, The Royal Legacy*. Honolulu: Mutual Publishing.

Shoemaker, Nancy. 2015. *Native American Whalemen and the World: Indigenous Encounters and the Contingency of Race*. Chapel Hill: University of North Carolina Press.

Silva, Noenoe K. 2000. "The Political Economy of Banning the Hula," *Hawaiian Journal of History* 34, 29–48.

Silverman, Jane. 1987. *Kaahumanu, Molder of Change*. Honolulu: Friends of the Judiciary History Center of Hawaii.

Simpson, Alexander. 1843. *The Sandwich Islands: Progress of Events Since Their Discovery by Captain Cook*. London: Smith, Elder & Co.

Simpson, MacKinnon. 1989. *Whale Song: A Pictorial History of Whaling and Hawai'i*. Honolulu: Beyond Words Publishing Company, second edition.

Sinclair, Marjorie. 1969. "Nahienaena, Hawaiian Princess," *Hawaiian Journal of History* 3, 4–30.

Sinclair, Marjorie. 1971. "The Sacred Wife of Kamehameha I, Keopuolani," *Hawaiian Journal of History* 5, 3–23.

Sinclair, Marjorie. 1976. *Nāhi'ena'ena, Sacred Daughter of Hawaii*. Honolulu: University Press of Hawaii (reprinted by Mutual Publishing in 1995), available from Internet Archives.

Sinclair, Marjorie. 1982. *The Path of the Ocean: Traditional Poetry of Polynesia*. Honolulu: University of Hawaii Press.

Sissons, Jeffrey. 2014. *The Polynesian Iconoclasm: Religious Revolution and the Seasonality of Power*. New York: Berghahn Books.

Smith, Bradford. 1956. *Yankees in Paradise: The New England Impact on Hawaii*. New York: J. B. Lippincott.

Smith, Gene A. 2000. *Thomas ap Catesby Jones: Commodore of Manifest Destiny*. Annapolis: Naval Institute Press.

Smith, Helen Wong. 2016. "The Daniel K. Inouye College of Pharmacy Scripts: Transition from Traditional to Western Medicine in Hawai'i," *Hawai'i Journal of Medicine & Public Health* 75, 87–90, www.ncbi.nlm.nih.gov/pmc/articles/PMC4795336/.

Soehren, Lloyd. January 1966. "The Royal Slide at Keauhou, Kona, Hawaii," *Hawaiian Historical Review* 2, 271–273.

Speakman, Cummins E. Jr. 2014. *Maui: A History*. Honolulu: Mutual Publishing. (Originally published by the Peabody Museum in 1978 as *Mowee: An Informal History of the Hawaiian Island*, updated by Jill Engledow.)

Bibliography

Speakman, Cummins E., Jr., and Hackler, Rhonda E. A. 1989. "Vancouver in Hawai'i," *Hawaiian Journal of History* 23, 31–65.

Spoehr, Anne Harding. 1981. "George Prince Tamoree: Heir Apparent of Kauai and Niihau," *Hawaiian Journal of History* 15, 31–49.

Stark, Suzanne J. 1996. *Female Tars: Women Aboard Ships in the Age of Sail.* Annapolis: Naval Institute Press.

Stauder, Catherine. 1972. "George, Prince of Hawaii," *Hawaiian Journal of History* 6, 28–44.

Stauffer, Robert H. 1983. "The Hawaii–United States Treaty of 1826," *Hawaiian Journal of History* 17, 40–63.

Sterling, Elspeth P., and Summers, Catherine C. 1978. *Sites of Oahu.* Honolulu: Bishop Museum Press.

Stewart, C. S. *Journal of a Residence in the Sandwich Islands During the Years 1823, 1824, and 1825.* Second edition, New York: John. P. Haven, 1828; Third edition, 1830.

Stewart, C. S. 1831. *A Visit to the South Seas in the U.S. Ship Vincennes, During the Years 1829 and 1830.* Vol. 1. New York: John P. Haven (reprinted New York: Praeger, 1970).

Stokes, John F. G. 1932. *The Hawaiian King* (Papers of the Hawaiian Historical Society 19), Honolulu: Hawaiian Historical Society.

Strauss, W. Patrick. 1963. *Americans in Polynesia, 1783–1842.* East Lansing: Michigan State University Press.

Tabrah, Ruth. 1984. *Hawai'i: A History.* New York: W. W. Norton.

Tabrah, Ruth. 1987. *Ni'ihau: The Last Hawaiian Island.* Kailua, Hawaii: Press Pacifica.

Taylor, Albert Pierce. 1926. *Under Hawaiian Skies.* Honolulu: Advertiser Publishing.

Taylor, Albert Pierce. 1928. "Liholiho: A Reassessment of His Character," *Papers of the Hawaiian Historical Society* 15, Honolulu: Bulletin Publishing, 21–39 (reprinted in 1978).

Tengan, Ty P. Kāwika. 2016. "The Mana of Kū: Indigenous Masculinity, Nationhood, Masculinity and Authority in Hawai'i," Matt Tomplinson and Ty P. Kāwika Tengan, editors, *New Mana: Transformations of Classic Concepts in Pacific Languages and Cultures*, 55–75. Canberra: Australian National University Press.

Thiercelin, Louis. 1992. "Waimea, Kaua'i in 1839: An Account by Louis Thiercelin, Whaling Doctor," *Hawaiian Journal of History* 26, 95–121. Christiane Mortelier's translation of excerpts from Thiercelin's *Journal d'un beleiner.*

Thiercelin, Louis. 1995. *Travels in Oceania: Memoirs of a Whaling Ship's Doctor.* Translated by Christiane Mortelier. Dunedin, NZ: University of Otago Press.

Thigpen, Jennifer. 2014. *Island Queens and Mission Wives: How Gender and Empire Remade Hawa'i's Pacific World.* Chapel Hill: University of North Carolina Press.

Thigpen, Jennifer. 2018. "Race, Gender and the Hawaiian Islands Mission," *Oxford Handbook of Religion and Race in American History*, 420–435. New York: Oxford University Press.

Thompson, Christina. 2019. *Sea People: The Puzzle of Polynesia.* New York: HarperCollins.

Thrum, Thomas G. 1910. "First Clergyman in Hawaii," *Hawaiian Almanac and Annual*, 181–182. Honolulu: Thrum.

Thurston, Lucy. 1882. *The Life and Times of Mrs. Lucy G. Thurston, Wife of Rev. Asa Thurston, Pioneer Missionary to the Sandwich Islands, Gathered from Letters and Journals extending Over a Period of More Than Fifty Years.* Ann Arbor, Michigan: S. C. Andrews, Second Edition. (Reprinted, Honolulu: The Friend, 1934.)

Titcomb, Margaret. 1948. "Kava in Hawaii," *Journal of the Polynesian Society* 57, 105–171.

Tracy, Joseph. 1842. *History of the American Board of Commissioners for Foreign Missions.* Second Edition. New York: M. W. Dodd.

Tregaskis, Richard. 1973. *The Warrior King: Hawaii's Kamehameha the Great.* New York: Macmillan.

Bibliography

Trevelyan, G. M. 1966. *British History in the 19th Century and After, 1782–1919*. New York: Harper & Row.
Turnbull, John. 1805. *A Voyage Round the World in the Years 1800, 1801, 1802, 1803, and 1804*. Vol. 2. London: Richard Phillips.
Tyerman, Daniel. 1841. *Voyages and Travels Round the World by the Rev. Daniel Tyerman and George Bennet, Esq*. London: Snow, second edition.
Vancouver, George. 1984. *A Voyage of Discovery to the North Pacific Ocean and Round the World, 1791–1795*. Edited by W. F. Lamb. London: Hakluyt Society.
Van Dyke, Jon. M. 2008. *Who Owns the Crown Lands of Hawai'i?* Honolulu: University of Hawai'i Press.
Villiers, Alan. 1967. *Captain James Cook*. New York: Charles Scribner's Sons.
Vowell, Sarah. 2011. *Unfamiliar Fishes*. New York: Riverhead Books.
Wagner, John P. 1973. "Sandalwood Bonanza," Clayton R. Barrow, Jr., Editor. *America Spreads Her Sails: U.S. Seapower in the 19th Century*. Annapolis: Naval Institute Press.
Wagner, Sandra E. 1985. "Mission and Motivation: The Theology of Early American Mission in Hawaii," *Hawaiian Journal of History* 19, 62–70.
Wallace, Lee. 2003. *Sexual Encounters: Pacific Texts, Modern Sexualities*. Ithica, NY: Cornell University Press.
Warne, Douglas. 2002. "George Prince Kaumuali'i, the Forgotten Prince," *Hawaiian Journal of History* 36, 59–71.
Warne, Douglas. 2008. *Humehume of Kaua'i: A Boy's Journey to America, an Ali'i's Return Home*. Honolulu: Kamehameha Publishing.
Warshaw, Nathaniel Bright. 2010. *The History of Surfing*. San Francisco: Chronicle Books.
Webb, Nancy, and Webb, Jean. 1963. *The Hawaiian Islands: From Monarchy to Democracy*. New York: Viking.
Westervelt, W. D. 1916. *Hawaiian Legends of Volcanoes*. Boston: G. H. Ellis.
Westervelt, W. D. 1922. "Kamehameha's Method of Government," *Annual Report of the Hawaiian Historical Society* 30, 24–38.
Westervelt, W. D. 1923. *Hawaiian Historical Legends*. New York: Fleming H. Revell; reprinted, Rutland, VT: Charles. E. Tuttle, 1977.
Westervelt, W. D. 1923. "The Passing of Kamehameha I," *Annual Report of the Hawaiian Historical Society* 31, 29–36.
Whitman, John B. 1979. *An Account of the Sandwich Islands: The Hawaiian Journal of John B. Whitman, 1813–15*. Edited by John Dominis Holt. Honolulu: Topgallant Publishing and Salem, MA: Peabody Museum.
Whitney, Mercy. *Journal, 1821–1827*. Ms. at Hawaiian Mission Houses Library, available at hmha.missionhouses.org/items/show/102.
Williams, Glyndwr. 2007. *The Death of Captain Cook: A Hero Made and Unmade*. London: Profile Books.
Williams, Julie Stewart, and Tune, Junelyn Ching. 2001. *Kamehameha II: Liholiho and the Impact of Change*. Honolulu: Kamehameha Schools.
Williston, Samuel. *William Richards*. Cambridge, MA. Privately published, 1938.
Wiltgen, Ralph M. 2010. *The Founding of the Roman Catholic Church in Oceania, 1825–1850* (Princeton Theological Monograph 143). Eugene, OR: Pickwick Publications.
Winne, Jane Lathrop. 1928. *Kuakini and Hulihee: The Story of the Kailua Palace*. Honolulu: Daughters of Hawaii.
Withington, Antoinette. 1937. *Hawaiian Tapestry*. New York: Harper and Brothers.
Withington, Antoinette. 1953. *The Golden Cloak*. Honolulu: Hawaiiana Press.
Woods, Thomas A., editor. 2018. *Kōkua Aku, Kōkua Mai: Chiefs, Missionaries, and Five Transformations of the Hawaiian Kingdom*. Honolulu: Hawaiian Mission Children's Society.
Wyban, Carol Araki. 1992. *Tide and Currents: Fishponds of Hawai'i*. Honolulu: University of Hawai'i Press.

Bibliography

Wyndette, Olive. 1968. *Islands of Destiny: A History of Hawaii*. Rutland, VT: Charles E. Tuttle.

Young, Chester Raymond. 1967. "American Missionary Influence on the Union of Church and State in Hawaii During the Regency of Kaahumanu," *Journal of Church and State* 9, 165–179.

Young, Kanalu G. Terry. 2012. *Rethinking the Native Hawaiian Past*. New York: Routledge.

Yzendoorn, Reginald. 1927. *History of the Catholic Mission in the Hawaiian Islands*. Honolulu: Honolulu Star-Bulletin.

Zambucka, Kristen. 1977. *The High Chiefess Ruth Keelikolani*. Honolulu: Mana Publishing.

Zug, James. 2005. *American Traveler: The Life and Adventures of John Ledyard, the Man Who Dreamed of Walking the World*. New York: Basic Books.

Zwiep, Mary. 1990. "Sending the Children Home: A Dilemma for Early Missionaries," *Hawaiian Journal of History* 24, 39–68.

Zwiep, Mary. 1991. *Pilgrim Path: The First Company of Women Missionaries to Hawaii*. Madison: University of Wisconsin Press.

Index

Adams, John Quincy 136, 162
'Ahahui Ka'ahumanu 176
aikāne 23, 31, 84, 107, 112, 158, 179, 214
alcohol consumption 27, 48, 52, 59, 94, 100, 102–104, 118, 122, 133, 139, 141, 146, 168–169
Alexander I of Russia 40, 47–48, 52–55
Allen, Anthony 3, 103, 112, 133, 216
Amelika *see* United States
American Board of Commissioners for Foreign Missions 73–77, 80–84, 94, 99, 109, 117, 132, 140, 147, 167, 169
Anderson, Peter 37, 38
Andrews, Lorrin 172
Anglicans *see* Church of England
Anson, George, Lord Byron 4, 124–128, 213
Arago, Jacques 67, 78, 203
Argonaut see Colnett, James
Armand, Abraham 5, 147, 185
Astor, John Jacob 49
Australia 37, 46

Bachelot, Alexis 5, 147, 149–154, 164–165, 173, 200, 200*n*57
Balaena 99
Barkley, Frances 26, 28, 210
Beachcombers 52, 95, 100, 113, 143, 204
Beaver 45
Beretania *see* Britain
Big Island (aka Hawai'i) 7, 24, 33–38, 62, 69–72, 106, 140, 172, 174–176; *see also* Hilo; Kailua; Kealakekua; Kilauea; Kona; Mauna Kea; Mauna Loa
Binamu *see* Bingham, Hiram
Binamuwahine *see* Bingham, Sybil
Bingham, Hiram 78, 81–86, 88, 93–95, 97, 106–107, 112, 115–117, 122, 130–132, 134–135, 137–139, 141, 143, 151–153, 158, 160, 166–168, 170–172
Bingham, Sybil 76, 79–81, 88–89, 92, 94–95, 97, 102–103, 105, 117, 128, 145, 171
Black, William 88, 205
Blatchley, Abraham 139–140

Bloxam, Andrew 147, 205, 209
Boit, John 38, 87, 205
Boki 77–78, 102, 106, 111, 115–116, 123–126, 129, 132–133, 137–138, 140, 143–144, 146–147, 150–151, 154, 156–160, 163–164, 207
Botta, Paul-Émile 158–159, 199, 205, 211
Britain 20, 23–25, 31, 37, 48, 82, 86, 116, 126, 132–135, 140, 156, 168; *see also* England; London; Scotland
Buckle, William 4, 134–136, 155–156, 196*n*9, 207
Byron *see* Anson, George

Calvinism 73–76, 86, 113, 168
Calvinists 84, 86, 91–92, 98, 102–106, 109, 126–130, 135–136, 146, 148, 151–163–165
Canning, George 124
Chamberlain, Daniel 76, 80–81, 84, 98
Chamberlain, Jerusha 76, 80–81, 84, 98
Chamberlain, Levi 110, 130, 144, 163–164, 178, 206
Chamisso, Adelbert von 58, 84, 206
Chappell, David 129, 206
Charles X 149, 164–165
Charlton, Richard 4, 124, 133–134, 143, 157–158, 160–161, 165
China 25, 34, 40, 48–49, 55, 57, 73, 137
Choris, Ludwig 54–61, 206
church and state 82, 133, 149, 153–157, 163–168, 219; *see also* freedom of worship
Church of England 50, 81, 85, 91, 115, 125–126, 147–148, 153, 198*n*2
Clark, Ephraim 164
Clerke, Charles 23, 27
Colnett, James 26, 206
Cook, James 17–28, 87, 147, 177, 186*n*37, 187*n*49, 204, 212, 215–217
Columbia Rediviva 25, 27, 87
Council of Chiefs 37, 41, 59, 65, 115, 120, 124, 133, 165

221

Index

Daniel IV 4, 134–136, 207
Davis, Isaac 37–38
Davis, William 127
Discovery 16, 18, 22,-23, 28, 45
Dixon, George 25, 208
Dolphin 136–140
Duhaut-Cilly, Auguste Bernard 58, 208

Ellis, William 95, 99, 104–106, 109, 111–116, 120, 130, 133, 191*n*22, 208
England 28, 38, 57, 62, 74, 104, 115–116, 123–124, 126, 132, 135
epidemics 27–28, 40, 42, 45, 50–52, 60, 97, 119, 126, 129, 144–145, 210; *see also* sexually-transmitted infections
Equator 99

Foreign Mission School 74–77, 98, 109, 196*n*3, 208
France 25–26, 67; *see also* French mission
freedom of worship 74, 151, 154, 156–157, 164
French mission 147–166, 199*n*54
Freycinet, Louis de 67, 147, 149, 190*n*31, 193*n*9, 204, 206, 208
Freycinet, Rose de 67, 147, 149, 190*n*31, 193*n*9, 204, 206, 208
fur traders 25–27, 43, 47, 49, 59, 61–52

George III of Great Britain 37, 269, 209
George IV of Great Britain 115, 124–126, *177*
Globe 100
Gustavus III 26

Ha'aheo o Hawai'i 95–96, 193*n*15, 210
Hale o Keawe 169
Hāna 12, 18, 174
Hanna, James 25–26
heiaus 14, 22, 24, 34–35, 46–47, 50, 52–55, 58–60, 62, 64, 68, 70–72, 86–87, 105–106, 113, 141, 152, 174, 176, 178, 190*n*9
Hewahewa 69–70, 77, 87, 105
Hilo 34, 40, 90, 109, 124–126, 167
Hoapili 3, 33, 112, 115, 141, 155, 168
Holman, Lucia 5, 80–81, 84, 86, 88–89, 93–94, 193*n*8, 210
Holman, Thomas 5, 80–81, 84, 86, 88–89, 93–94, 193*n*8, 210
holokū 79
Honoli'i, John 76–77, 191*ch*5*n*10
Honolulu 46, 52–54, 56–57, 99–100, 102–103, 105–106, 117, 120, 133, 136–141; *see also* French mission; Manoa; Waikīkī
Hopu, Thomas 76–78, 191*ch*5*n*10

Howell, John 50, 198*n*2
hula 14, 35, 41, 84, 87, 94, 104–106, 111, 146, 163, 168, 173, 177, 180, 204, 208, 21; *see also* Laka
Hull, Isaac 137
Humehume 27, 77–78, 85, 113, 119–122, 128, 218

Imperial Eagle see Barkley, Frances
incest 31–32, 120–121, 195*n*39

Jackson, Andrew 161–162
John Palmer 155, 170
Jones, John Coffin, Jr. 55, 83, 95, 97–98, 100, 103–104, 124, 133–134, 148, 150, 154, 157, 160, 163, 192*n*32, 209
Jones, Thomas ap Catesby 141–144, 197*n*37, 205, 216

Ka'ahumanu 57
Kahakuha'akoi Wahinepio 134–135
Kaho'olawe 7, 13, 24
Kahului 174
Ka'iana 31, 34, 157, 188*n*28, 213
Kailua (Kailua-Kona) 26, 61–62, 65–70, 82–84, 111–112, 160, 176
Kalākua 3, 31, 33, 78–79, 89, 94, 113
Kalanimōkū 13, 33, 46–47, 54, 56, 62, 67, 71, 78, 83, 94–95, 112, 116, 118–123, 126, 131, 134, 139, 143–144, 146, 1560, 154, 207
Kalani'ōpu'u 3, 19–20, 23–24, 30–31, 157, 177
Kamehameha I (the Great) 1, 2, 12–15, 18–20, 24, 27, 29–67, 69, 81, 96, 103, 111, 172, 174, 176–178, 187*n*57, 188*n*17, 188*n*20, 188*n*28, 188*n*30, 190*n*31, 192*n*32, 194*n*47, 198*n*2, 204, 207, 209, 210, 217, 218
Kamehameha II *see* Liholiho
Kamehameha III *see* Kauikeaouli
Kamehameha, Prince David 145
kanikau 40, 171–172
Kanui, William 77, 91*ch*5*n*10
kapu meetings 118
kapus 12, 14–15, 17, 22, 42, 45–56, 48–52, 58–62; abolition of kapus 66–72
Kaua'i 7–8, 13, 16–17, 26–27, 39–40, 43–44, 47, 54, 66, 70, 76, 84–85, 92, 94–96, 107, 118–122, 131, 147–148, 176, 183, 217, 218; *see also* Waimea
Kauikeaouli (Kamehameha III) 45, 48, 118, 120–121, 124, 127–129, 133–134, 137–138, 143–147, 150, 153–154, 158–160, 163, 167–168, 170–173, 177, 195*n*21
Kaumuali'i 13, 27, 40, 44, 47, 54–56, 70,

222

Index

77, 84–85, 92–93, 95–96, 98, 107–108, 119–120, 178, 184, 207
Kealakekua 18–24
Keali'iahonui 122–123, 128, 131
Ke'eaumoku 'Opio 41, 46, 64, 98, 117
Ke'eaumoku Pāpa'iahiahi 12, 24–25, 40
Kekuaokalani 66–72
Keli'imaika'i (Kalanimalokuloku) 39, 51
Kilauea 8, 209
Kina'u 4, 105, 145, 152, 159–160, 168, 172–173, 176–177, 192n38, 192n45
King George 25
Kona 33, 36, 45, 62, 65, 69–70, 83, 88, 90, 174–176; *see also* Kailua; Kealakekua
Kotzebue, Otto von 5, 55, 122–123, 130, 147–148, 206, 208, 211, 212
Krusenstern (Kruzenshtern), Ivan Fyodorovich 26, 55
Kū (Kūkailimoku) 14, 34–35, 66, 71, 177, 217
Kuakini 4, 13, 53, 61, 67, 93, 98, 112, 156, 160, 166, 168–169, 172, 218

Lāhainā 37, 99–100, 109, 111–113, 115, 120, 122, 133–135, 155, 167–169, 174, 211
Lahainaluna High School 128, 167, 200n2
Laka 14, 87, 106
Lāna'i 7, 13, 24, 35, 141, 160, 178, 210
Law of the Splintered Paddle 39
Ledyard, John 22, 31, 212, 219
Liholiho (Kamehameha II) 2, 41, 47, 60, 61–62, 64–72, 78, 80, 82–84, 87, 89–92, 94–97, 99, 102–107, 109, 113–114, 118–120, 122, 133–144, 147, 172–173, 178–177, 217, 218; voyage to London 115–116, 13–126
Liliha 4, 115, 123, 146, 157, 159, 163, 167–169
Lisyansky (Lisianski), Yuri Fyodorovich 26, 40, 212
literacy 91–93, 97, 106, 108, 118–119, 121–123, 144, 151
London 123–124, 149, 156
London Missionary Society 85, 95, 104–106, 109, 116
Loomis, Elisha 4, 78, 86, 98, 103, 116–117, 120–122, 124, 134, 212
Loomis, Maria 4, 78, 86, 98, 103, 116–117, 120–122, 124, 134, 212
Lord Byron *see* Anson, George
Louis Philippe, King of France 164–165, 199n54

Macrae, James 127–128, 213
Makahiki 16, 18, 20, 22–23, 30, 69–71, 141

Manby, Thomas 49, 289, 213
Marchand, Étienne 26, 213
Margaret 46
Marín, Don Francisco de Paula 5, 64–66, 102, 150, 156, 160, 209, 213, 214
marriage 29–32, 35, 39, 77, 80–81, 96, 98, 106, 113, 120, 128, 138, 144–145, 151, 158, 160, 170, 187n10, 188n26, 216
Maui 7, 11–13, 18, 36, 29, 31–39, 44, 88, 106, 112–113, 120, 122, 141, 158, 160, 167, 169, 169, 174–175, 210, 216; *see also* Hana; Kahului; Lāhainā; Wailuku
Mauna Kea 7, 76
Mauna Loa 7–8, 76, 122
medicine 13, 27–28, 42, 46, 50, 53, 86, 93–4, 97, 126–127, 170, 193n6, 208, 209, 216
Moloka'i 7, 13, 29, 35, 38, 47, 106, 140, 160, 210–211
Monroe, James 162
Morineau, Auguste de 147, 149–150, 155, 213
Morse, Samuel 81
Mother Hubbard (dress) 79

Nadezhda 26
Nahi'ena'ena 4, 120, 124, 127, 144–145, 158, 150, 163, 195n38, 216
Nāmāhāna 'i Kaleleokalani 3, 11–12
Nāmāhāna Pi'ia 3, 31, 116, 122, 126, 147, 160
Neva 26, 40, 47
Nihoa 7, 108
Ni'ihau 7, 9, 11–13, 17, 27–28, 39, 44, 66, 94, 96, 119, 217
Nu'uanu 38, 104, 172, 176–177

O'ahu 7, 13, 26, 28–29, 39–40, 42–45, 53–54, 66, 86, 100, 106, 112, 116, 121, 141, 146, 163, 168–169, 176–178, 190n9, 199n53, 206, 210, 217; *see also* Honolulu; Nu'uanu; Waikīkī
'Opukaha'ia 73–75, 86, 169, 208

Paulding, Hiram 137–140, 214
Peacock 141–143
Percival, John 5, 136–143, 197n30, 208, 212
Péron, Pierre François 88, 214
La Pérouse, Jean François de Galaup, Comte de (Count) 25
Perseverance 42
Pōmare II of Tahiti 52, 61, 71, 76
Pōmare III of Tahiti 95, 98
port regulations 57, 111, 127, 134–140, 243; *see also* prostitution
Portlock, Nathaniel 25–26, 29–30, 50, 215

223

Index

Prince of Wales 28
Princesa Real see Quimper, Manuel

Queen Charlotte 25
Quimper, Manuel 25–26, 28, 204

Raccoon **52**, 88, 205
Resolution 16, 18–19, 22–23, 28, 45
Reynolds, Stephen 111, 140, 144–145, 157–158, 215
Richards, Clarissa 85, 110–112, 114, 117, 10–121, 124, 134–135, 155–156, 215, 218
Richards, William 85, 110–112, 114, 117, 10–121, 124, 134–135, 155–156, 215, 218
Rives, Jean-Baptiste (John) 5, 84, 115, 149–150, 153, 203
Roquefeuil, Camille de 62, 215
Ruggles, Nancy 4, 79, 84–85, 95, 126, 133, 148, 210, 215
Ruggles, Samuel 4, 79, 84–85, 95, 126, 133, 148, 210, 215
Rurik 55, 206
Russia 25–26, 40, 47–48, 52–56, 85, 97, 178, 204, 205, 206, 208, 211, 213, 214
Russian Orthodox 97, 147–148

Samwell, David 20, 30–31, 73
Sandalwood ('iliahi) 43, 49, 54, 57, 59, 66, 81, 97–98, 103, 107, 136, 144, 163, 218
schools 42, 82, 85, 89, 92–93, 97–98, `02, 107, 109, 116–119, 122, 128, 140–141, 158–159, 163, 166–167, 176, 207
Scotland 119
sexually transmitted infections 27–28, 50, 144–145
Short, Patrick 5, 147, 150, 200n57
Simpson, Alexander 158, 216
Solide see Marchand, Étienne
Spain 25–26, 52
Stewart, Charles 110–113, 117, 120, 122, 124, 148, 162–163, 217
Stewart, Harriet 110–113, 117, 120, 122, 124, 148, 162–163, 217

Stockton, Betsey 109–110, 128, 167, 196n58
surfing 11, 30, 89, 97, 105, 119, 122, 193n21, 206, 208, 214, 218

Tahitians 2, 5, 9, 24, 27, 52, 61–62, 95, 100, 105, 112–113, 187n49, 204, 210, 213; see also Pōmare II; Pōmare III
temperance movement 102–103, 168–169, 205
Thurston, Asa 4, 79–81, 86, 90, 94, 102–103, 207, 217
Thurston, Lucy 4, 79–81, 86, 90, 94, 102–103, 207, 217
Tonquin 49
Tupaia 2, 24, 187n49

Union 38, 205
Unitarians 103–104, 135–136, 248, 157, 162, 198n4
United States of America 25, 27, 35, 37–38, 45, 48–49, 73–75, 85–87, 91, 95, 99, 106, 119, 124, 129, 133, 135–137, 140–141, 143, 154, 157, 161–162, 196n3, 203, 206, 209, 217
Uranie 67, 203–204

Vancouver, George 4, 23–24, 35–37, 41, 43, 48–49, 156, 213, 217, 218
Vascilieff, Michael 97

Waikīkī 43, 53, 102, 105, 113, 158
Wailuku 174–175
Waimea (Kaua'i) 16–17, 54–56, 107, 121, 131, 178, 217
Waverly 165
Wellington 140
Whaling 27, 99–102, 134, 139, 143, 155–157, 169, 205, 207, 214, 216, 217
Whitney, Mercy 4, 79–80, 84–85, 02, 94, 96, 130, 134, 145, 214, 218
Whitney, Samuel 4, 79–80, 84–85, 02, 94, 96, 130, 134, 145, 214, 218

Young, John 4, 27, 37–38, 50, 53, 56, 81, 84, 205

www.ingramcontent.com/pod-product-compliance
Ingram Content Group UK Ltd.
Pitfield, Milton Keynes, MK11 3LW, UK
UKHW041950140426
5217IPUK00014B/726